THE ISRAELITES

An introduction

Antony Kamm

London and New York

First published 1999
by Routledge
11 New Fetter Lane, London, EC4P 4EE

Simultaneously published in the USA and Canada
by Routledge
29 West 35th Street, New York, NY 10001

Routledge is an imprint of the Taylor & Francis Group

© 1999 Antony Kamm

Line drawings © 1999 Jennifer Campbell

Typeset in Garamond by
J&L Composition Ltd, Filey, North Yorkshire
Printed and bound in Great Britain by
TJ International Ltd, Padstow, Cornwall

British Library Cataloguing in Publication Data
A catalogue record for this book is available from the British Library

Library of Congress Cataloging in Publication Data
Kamm, Antony.
The Israelites : an introduction/Antony Kamm.
Includes bibliographical references and index.
1. Jews–History–To 135 A.D.   2. Bible.   O.T.–History of Biblical
events.   I. Title.
DS121.K23   1999
933–dc21   98–53884

ISBN 0-415-18095-3 (hbk)
ISBN 0-415-18096-1 (pbk)

THE ISRAELITES

Antony Kamm draws on Biblical, archaeological, historical, and critical sources to present a straightforward, objective and largely chronological account of the culture which produced the Old Testament and from which Christianity derives, from its origins to the destruction of Jerusalem by the Romans in 135 CE.

This succinct study traces the history of the Israelites against the turbulent background of the times, and describes their society, religion and ultimate dispersal through the ancient world. The text is complemented by charts, maps, photographs and line drawings.

The Israelites is an accessible, user-friendly guide which will be indispensable to students and general readers.

Antony Kamm read Classics and English at the University of Oxford. He is a former lecturer in publishing studies at the University of Stirling. He is the author of *The Romans: An Introduction, Second edition* (Routledge 1999).

Also by Antony Kamm:

THE ROMANS: AN INTRODUCTION

'Kamm writes with sensitivity, intelligence and vitality. He tells a good story and is remarkably un-stuffy. . . . He allows the Romans to speak for themselves whenever possible and his familiarity with English literature prompts a number of happy comparisons. . . . The gusto of the writing and the sweep of the narrative will enthuse all but the most dour reader.'
Journal of the Association of Classical Teachers

'A valuable work of introduction and reference that anybody would be happy to possess.'
Classics Ireland

'In easily digestible chapters, Kamm outlines the major aspects of Roman history and society, encompassing politics, culture, technological developments and social mores. Well chosen extracts from Roman and Greek writers make for colourful and enjoyable reading. . . . All in all, this is a sound introduction to the Roman world and a handy quick-reference book.'
The Jewish Chronicle

'As well as selecting and summarizing, Kamm has found space for considerable incidental detail which adds much to the book's appeal. This is no dry epitome reduced to bare bones, for he presents numerous quotations from an interestingly wide range of ancient authors and repeatedly includes the *particular* individual, story, or details, which convey the flavour in a way which the mere accumulation of facts and generalizations would not.'
The Classical Review

'C'est une introduction réussie destinée aux étudiants de lettres classiques autant qu'un guide appréciable pour ceux d'autres disciplines où une compréhension de l'histoire romaine est souhaitée. Le lecteur en général y trouvera aussi son compte.'
Les Études Classiques

CONTENTS

FIGURES

CHARTS

MAPS

PREFACE

This is an account of the inhabitants of the kingdoms of Israel and Judah, from their origins to the obliteration of Jerusalem in 135 CE, when Jews, who were now dispersed throughout the Roman empire and in the regions to the east, ceased to be able to regard the city as a tangible focus of their religious and political affiliations. The more inclusive terms BCE (Before the Common Era) and CE (Common Era) are used to denote the historical periods which in other contexts are indicated by BC and AD. I have employed the historic present tense when paraphrasing extracts from the Biblical narrative. The locations of peoples and places mentioned in the text and captions are shown on one or more of the maps, and can be found by means of the index.

Except where stated otherwise, Biblical quotations are from *Tanakh: The Holy Scriptures* (1985), published by the Jewish Publication Society, Philadelphia, USA, also referred to as the Jewish Bible. Other Biblical quotations are from the *Authorised Version* (AV), and from *The New English Bible* (1970), published jointly by Oxford University Press and Cambridge University Press (NEB). The quotation from the Koran on page 58 is from the Penguin translation (4th edn, 1974) by N. J. Dawood.

I have where appropriate followed the Jewish Bible for names of places and people. Alternative systems of transliteration that may be identified are due to the variety of sources which have been used for other terms. The coins illustrated are from the Hunterian Museum of Glasgow University coin collection, whose curator, Dr J. D. Bateson, has given me considerable help. For his good-humoured comments and sound advice, I am much indebted to my editor, Richard Stoneman, who suggested that I should write this book. I am also grateful to Coco Stevenson, his assistant editor, for her practical support; to Fintan Power for his organisational skills as production editor; to David Saunders for his unerring instinct as a copy-editor, and for his calming advice; to David Williams, who made sense of, and added artistry to, my roughs of the maps; and to Tamar Wang, who read the proofs, for her methodical mind and her scholarship.

A. K.

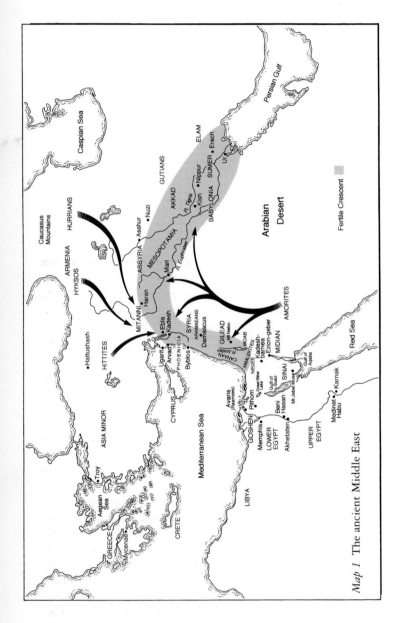

Map 1 The ancient Middle East

See also map of Canaan on page 24.

1

THE ORIGINS OF THE ISRAELITES

It is with the patriarch Abraham, in about 1800 BCE, that the story of the Israelites properly begins, though it is at the time of Moses and the Exodus from Egypt that they first emerge as a people with an identity.

Abraham was descended from Shem, one of the sons of Noah (Gen. 11:10ff.). Shem's descendants, known as Semites, correspond to the ethnic and linguistic groups of the Mesopotamian Fertile Crescent and its immediate surroundings – the term Semite today embraces peoples of the Middle East and northern Africa who originally spoke the related languages of Aramaic, Akkadian, Arabic, and Ethiopian, as well as Hebrew.

When Abraham, following the instructions of his God, set out from Haran, on the northern edge of the Fertile Crescent, with his wife Sarah and his extended family, to journey on foot to the land of Canaan, the Middle Bronze Age was under way.

At that time northern Britain was occupied by the 'Food Vessel' culture: the people of the brilliant Wessex culture in the south were traders and builders, and were responsible for restructuring the religious monuments of Stonehenge into the form in which they appear today. On the island of Crete in the Mediterranean Sea, the Minoan civilisation was already in its middle phase.

There had been dynastic rulers in Egypt for over a thousand years. The Great Pyramids and the Sphinx were already six hundred years old. Egyptian astronomers had worked out a solar calendar of 365 days. There was a literature of Egyptian prose and verse, recorded in hieroglyphics. Egyptian doctors had a surgical textbook comprising forty-eight case studies, which may have been written down as early as 3000 BCE.

The Egyptians probably got the idea of writing from the Sumerians, with whom there is evidence of a lively cultural exchange. The Sumerians are the earliest recorded inhabitants of the eastern wing of the Fertile Crescent. Between 2850 and 2360 BCE they controlled an empire of about a dozen independent city-states, each ruled by a king. The most notable of these were Ur, Erech, and Kish, though in each case the city itself would be in modern terms no larger than a substantial village, perhaps three-quarters of a square mile in extent.

The religious beliefs of the Sumerians, which can be traced back to the fourth millennium BCE, embraced a pantheon with an elaborate structure, mythology, and philosophy. Their writing (cuneiform) was inscribed on tablets of clay with a stylus in horizontal lines reading from left to right. A very early clay tablet, discovered at Nippur, records a mythical deluge which has close affinities with the Biblical Flood. There are further parallels with the flood narrative in the Akkadian epic of the legendary king of Erech, Gilgamesh, which dates from the beginning of the second millennium BCE. The earliest written version of the Gilgamesh epic that we have was inscribed between 1750 and 1400 BCE. It could well have been transmitted to Canaan in this or in oral form by ancestors of the Israelites.

In about 2300 BCE, the Akkadians, under their dynamic ruler Sargon, defeated the Sumerians and created their own empire, which lasted until 2180 BCE, when it was destroyed by waves of Gutians from the mountains of the north-east. Though Akkadian survived into the first millennium BCE as the language of international diplomacy and trade, the Sumerian civilisation emerged from these invasions in better shape, with Ur briefly becoming a considerable power in its own right – the famous ziggurat of Ur was built during this period. In about 1950 BCE Ur too fell, to an Elamite invasion. Though centres of wealth and culture continued to exist, with commercial links between them, it was an age of consistent turmoil and uncertainty, of hostile incursions, and of huge movements of nomadic and semi-nomadic peoples throughout the whole region of what is now Asia Minor, the Caucasus, and the Middle East. In such circumstances there is nothing unusual about the mere fact of Abraham's journey from Haran to Canaan, or even an earlier migration (Gen. 11:31), in the company of his father, from Ur to Haran.

The 800-mile trek between Ur and Haran took travellers for most of the way through fertile or pastoral country alongside the river Euphrates. There was an alternative route in regular use, along the river Tigris. The two cities were linked through trade, and also through religious observance: both were centres of the cult of Nanna, the Mesopotamian moon god. Nanna was the son of Enlil, lord of the air, who had forced his attentions on a young goddess called Ninlil while she was bathing in a canal.

Trade routes connecting all parts of the Fertile Crescent had been established at least as early as the beginning of the third millennium BCE by the city-state of Ebla in Syria, through whose territory the first stage of Abraham's journey would take him. The archaeological site of Ebla was discovered in 1964. Its royal archive of fifteen thousand tablets inscribed in cuneiform revealed evidence of diplomatic and economic relations with eighty kingdoms. The most notable of these was Asshur, which subsequently gave its name to Assyria. The Eblaites employed the Sumerian system of writing, but their language proved to be a hitherto unknown Semitic form. It was superseded in about 2000 BCE when a new, Akkadian-speaking, Amorite dynasty succeeded the ancient one in Ebla.

AMORITES AND ARAMAEANS

In all the historical comings and goings, the Amorites are the people most frequently referred to. Their name, written in cuneiform as *Amurru*, means 'Westerners', a reference to their settlements in north-western Mesopotamia and northern Syria, to which they had migrated from their original homelands in the Arabian Desert. They were not so much a racial entity as a collection of peoples speaking a variety of Semitic dialects. When Ur finally fell, Amorites poured into the area, appropriated most of the ruling positions, and adopted the Akkadian/Sumerian cultures that they found. They also overflowed into Canaan, and it is not improbable that Abraham's mission coincided with one of these incursions.

The Biblical Aramaeans were descended from Aram, who, like his great-uncle Abraham, was a descendant of Shem (Gen. 10:22). Abraham's son Isaac married his cousin Rebekah, daughter of Bethuel 'the Aramean' (Gen. 25:20). Isaac's son Jacob married Leah and Rachel, daughters of Laban 'the Aramean' (Gen. 31:20, 24), Rebekah's brother (Gen. 24:28). An enigmatic passage in Deuteronomy (26:5) refers to a patriarch as a 'fugitive [NEB 'wandering' or 'homeless'] Aramean'.

A Biblical Aramaean pedigree for the Israelites is thus inescapable, but the historical Aramaeans do not appear on the scene until about 1100 BCE, as a collection of tribes in northern Syria who ultimately established a state centred on Damascus. Two explanations have been offered for the Aramaean ancestry of the Israelites. The first is that the patriarchal Aramaeans were Amorites of 'proto-Aramaean stock'. The second is that the use of the name is a conscious anachronism

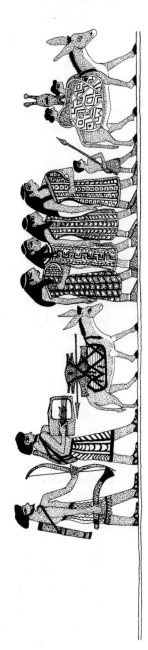

introduced into the Biblical account at the end of the second millennium BCE, at a time when the patriarchal homeland of Haran was in a region occupied by the Aramaeans. In the same way we use terms such as Middle East or Syria to describe regions or areas in the ancient world. A similar argument has been used to explain 'Ur of the Chaldeans' as Abraham's birthplace (Gen. 11:28; 15:7) – the historical Chaldeans, who appear to have had Aramaean affiliations, occupied the southern part of Babylonia in the eleventh century BCE.

NOMADS

Abraham and his kin were semi-nomads, to whom Haran was the homeland to which one returned to find a wife. So Abraham in due course despatched his aide Eliezer from Canaan to seek a suitable partner for his son Isaac (Gen. 24). Isaac's son Jacob, after deceiving his twin brother Esau, was sent back to Haran to be out of the way, and urged to seek a wife there rather than marry a Canaanite (Gen. 28:1).

The way of life of these nomads can be reconstructed from contemporary texts such as those in Akkadian found at the Amorite centre of Mari. They bred sheep, usually of the white, fat-tailed variety, black goats, and small cattle, and used donkeys to carry their baggage and tents, and food and water. The animals fed off the land, and needed to be moved on when supplies were exhausted. Stops were sometimes long enough for crops to be sown and harvested, and even for small

Figure 1 (opposite) Detail of a wall painting, in colour, from the tomb of Khnumhotpe, overseer of the eastern desert region of Egypt, at Beni Hasan. Dated to approximately 1890 BCE, that is about or just before the time of Abraham, it shows a group of Semitic nomads from Canaan, eight men, four women, and three children, being presented by two Egyptian attendants, one of whom holds up a document with their details. The leader of the group is bending over a gazelle; the next man holds the horn of an ibex. The warriors are armed variously with bows, spears, curved swords, and (the man at the rear) an axe of the duckbill type of the Middle Bronze Age. The man one from the rear carries a lyre, and has a skin water bottle on his back. The two curiously shaped objects on the donkeys' backs have been identified as goatskin bellows, such as were used by metal-workers. The men wear embroidered kilts or tunics which are predominantly red. The longer tunics of the women are patterned in red, blue, and yellow. The two leading men are barefoot. The rest of the men wear sandals, but the women and the boy have skin boots. The various signs and symbols are Egyptian hieroglyphs, each representing a word or a sound value.

village settlements to be established. There was a hierarchical structure, based on the family: extended families or clans were grouped into
tribes, supervised by a tribal confederacy.

There is a glimpse of a nomadic band on the move in the Egyptian
semi-autobiographical narrative known as *The Tale of Sinuhe*, which
can be dated almost precisely within the few years after 1960 BCE.
Fearful of a court plot to kill him, Sinuhe escapes on foot towards
Canaan. On the way,

> I collapsed from thirst, utterly dried out. My throat was on
> fire with the taste of death. Then a glimmer of hope! I heard
> the lowing of cattle. Some nomads came in sight. Their leader
> had been in Egypt and recognised me. He gave me water, and
> boiled some milk for me, and then took me to his clan. They
> were very kind to me.

Travel writing is a comparatively modern literary genre. Vast distances were covered in the ancient world without anyone bothering to
describe what it was like to be the traveller. While the journey from
Haran to Canaan was shorter by some 200 miles than the one from Ur
to Haran, the conditions would have been very different, involving
desert and mountain terrain. Much of the rest of the going would have
been across rugged ground, covered with boulders and sparse scrub.
The 'wild beasts' referred to in Exodus 23:11 and elsewhere in the
Bible are likely to have included the Palestinian lion, the Syrian brown
bear, wolves, hyenas, jackals, scorpions, and several species of snake, of
which today at least thirty-five are extant in the region. 'The ambus-
cade of bandits who murder on the road to Shechem' (Hosea 6:9) must
have been a perpetual hazard and a continual fear for travellers.

Travel conditions are unlikely to have deteriorated between the age
of the patriarchs and 1481 CE, when Meshullam of Volterra, an Italian
rabbi, travelled to Palestine and back in fulfilment of a vow. He wrote
in Hebrew an account of his journey. The caravan which he was due to
accompany from Gaza to Jerusalem, along a route which at some point
must have been crossed by Abraham, was delayed by a bandit scare
until it could muster a strength of at least 4,000 men.

> From Gaza to Jerusalem is all desert. Every man must carry
> on his horse or donkey a sack of biscuits and one of straw and
> fodder, as well as water skins, for there is only salt water on
> the way. You must also take a supply of lemons. Lemon juice
> is the only remedy for insect bites. These reddish insects are
> the size of two flies. Lemon juice prevents the bite getting

infected. I was never in my life in such pain as I was one night. You have to travel slowly. For one thing, there is so much dust and sand that horses can sink up to their knees. Also the dust rises and gets into your mouth, so that you can die of thirst. If you survive all this and your horse does not die on the way, there are other hazards. Lying in wait along the trail are men hidden up to their neck in the sand. They put a stone in front of them so that they can observe but cannot themselves be observed. When they see a likely caravan coming, they dig themselves out and call the rest of the band, who are mounted on horses as swift as leopards and have bamboo lances tipped with iron.

THE HEBREWS

The God to whom Abraham responded in Haran was a completely new, and revolutionary, God, whose initial revelation was, 'Go forth from your native land and from your father's house to the land that I will show you. I will make of you a great nation . . .' (Gen. 12:1ff.). To those of the Jewish faith, or of similar thinking, divine–human communication is possible and has occurred. Others may prefer to believe that Abraham, understanding, through some form of religious experience, that he had been called by God, journeyed to Canaan to find a new home and establish there the worship of the true God; in the same way and with the same purpose, the Pilgrim Fathers sailed across the Atlantic to New England in 1620 CE.

Once in Canaan, Abraham's clan moves by stages, as is the manner of nomads, from Shechem to a spot between Bethel and Ai (to stop near a town was common practice), and then to the Negeb. They see out a period of drought and famine in Canaan by going to Egypt (as was usual in difficult times), and then return to the Negeb.

After going on to Mamre, the normally peaceable Abraham is nettled into taking violent action. He leads 318 of his followers against some bandit kings, kidnappers of Abraham's nephew Lot, who has opted out of the nomadic lifestyle to settle in the area of Sodom and Gomorrah. At this point (Gen. 14:13) Abraham is referred to as a 'Hebrew'. From a strictly Old and New Testament standpoint, the Hebrews became known as Israelites, and then as Jews. The historical Hebrews, however, constituted a social stratum of stateless nomads known to the Akkadians as *Habiru* and the Egyptians as *'Apiru*, who were found all over western Asia at the time of the patriarchs and for several hundred years afterwards. In times of difficulty they might hire themselves out as mercenaries, or even as slaves. It could be said that the Israelites who eventually emerged out of Egypt under the leadership of Moses were all also 'Hebrews', but that not all the Hebrews who began the epic journey were Israelites.

At some point the fortunes of the Hebrews were affected by the activities of the Hyksos, a name from the Egyptian which means 'rulers of foreign lands'. A portmanteau people of Semitic and Indo-European origins, the Hyksos employed their secret weapons, the war-chariot, bronze protective armour, and composite bows which had a greater range than those of their enemies, to such purpose that in about 1720 BCE they successfully invaded Egypt, and for the next 170 years dominated the northern part of the land itself, establishing a capital and a ruling house at Avaris. The invasion was mounted from Canaan, which the Hyksos occupied during the eighteenth and seventeenth centuries BCE. At other times between about 2000 and 1250 BCE Canaan was controlled by Egypt.

GOD'S COVENANT

The promise that God subsequently makes to Abraham as chief of his clan is as crucial to the subsequent history of the land of the Israelites as it is to that of the Israelites themselves. 'To your offspring I assign this land, from the river of Egypt to the great river, the river Euphrates' (Gen. 15:18); the inhabitants of the land, among them the Canaanites, Amorites, Hittites, and Jebusites, go with the territory. The bond is sealed in a ritual manner (Gen. 15:9ff.), involving cutting sacrificial animals in two and passing between the halves, which recurs in Jeremiah 34:18–19.

The undertaking is repeated, on the first of many occasions, in Genesis 17, where Abraham is further promised unlimited offspring – the twin blessings of land and descendants were prized above all by those who depended on pasture for their livelihood. As a sign on the part of the human participants in the Covenant, every male is to be circumcised. This ritual, widely practised then and now, especially in desert regions, is to be performed on the eighth day after birth. Circumcision is the symbol of participation in the Covenant that God made with Abraham. While traditionally it continues to be maintained among Jews, it is not, except for converts to Judaism, obligatory, as it is for Muslims. To be Jewish, it is generally speaking enough for a child to be born of a Jewish mother.

The Hittites appear in Genesis 15 and elsewhere in the Bible as inhabitants of Canaan. From them Abraham purchased the burial site (Gen. 23:3ff.), in which were also interred his nearest and dearest, including his grandson Jacob. Esau, Jacob's elder twin, had two Hittite wives (Gen. 26:34). The historical Hittites, however, were an Indo-European people who in about 2000 BCE pushed into Asia Minor, where they found, and assimilated into their ways, the Hattian civilisation. While maintaining as a base their capital city of Hattushash, the Hittites participated aggressively in the subsequent regional movements of peoples, and their empire, for a brief period between about 1590 and 1525 BCE, incorporated Babylon.

The Jebusites, also listed as inhabitants of the Promised Land, were probably of Hurrian stock, as also were the Hivites (Exod. 3:8). The Hurrians, a non-Semitic people originating in the Caucasian mountain regions of Armenia, appear in written records which date from about 2150 BCE. From these and later evidence, it would appear that by 1600 BCE they were settled as immigrants throughout the region, and they established a short-lived kingdom of Mitanni in northern Mesopotamia. So many of them found their way into Canaan, that the Egyptians referred to it as Hurru (land of the Hurrians).

THE CHILDREN OF ISRAEL

Whether or not Abraham, who is regarded as the father of the Jewish people, his son Isaac, and Isaac's son Jacob, actually survived their Biblical spans of years (Gen. 25:7; 35:28; 47:28 respectively), the historical period during which they lived was one of continued unrest and voluntary and involuntary tribal and racial movement.

Isaac is a shadowy, symbolic figure when his Biblical record is compared with the determination, fortitude, and resourcefulness displayed by his father and by his son. Jacob, in the course of his bid to be reconciled with his brother Esau, has a profound spiritual experience at Jabbok ford (Gen. 32:23ff.). One outcome of it is that he assumes the name Israel, 'champion of El'. El, one of the names under which the clan god of Abraham was worshipped, was a common term among the Canaanites and others to indicate the chief god of a pantheon, and appears also as a frequent element in personal names in the Eblaite texts.

The Bible describes how in due course, having lost, and found, his son Joseph, who has become in the meantime viceroy of Egypt, Jacob and the rest of his family settle in Egypt, in the fertile area of Goshen, in the delta of the Nile. The account (Gen. 37:18–28) of how Joseph's jealous brothers, instead of killing him at Dothan, sell him off for twenty pieces of silver to a party of Ishmaelite (that is, Arab) traders with camels carrying resinous gum and incense from Gilead to Egypt, contains such authentic detail that if, as some have argued, the whole story of Joseph in Egypt is a novella, then it was certainly written with historical insight. For the western trade route through Canaan from northern Gilead to Egypt did go by way of Dothan, and during the first half of the second millennium BCE the average price of a slave *was* twenty pieces (or shekels) of silver. And if the authenticity of these points is accepted, then the several references in Genesis to camels, which were once thought to be anachronisms, may also be taken as evidence that the domestication of the camel had taken place, probably in southern Arabia, during the age of the patriarchs.

Just before his death, Jacob addresses his twelve sons in order: Reuben, Simeon, Levi, Judah, Zebulun, Issachar, Dan, Gad, Asher, Naphtali, Joseph, and Benjamin (Gen. 49:1–27). These are to be the progenitors of the original twelve eponymous tribes of the Israelites. Then, as his dying wish, he asks to be interred in the family burial plot in Canaan (Gen. 49:29ff.). His embalmed body, accompanied by all the family except the youngest children, and by members of the Egyptian court and administration, with an escort of Egyptian chariots and cavalry, is taken back to Canaan (Gen. 50:7–10).

Seventy 'children of Israel' (AV) originally accompanied their father to Egypt (Exod. 1:5), where they prospered and multiplied, a group within a class of immigrants described as Hebrews. According to the Biblical narrative there comes a time when there is a new ruler in Egypt 'who did not know Joseph' (Exod. 1:8). The Israelites, as they are now called, are subjected to a collective outburst of anti-Semitism on the part of the authorities whose parallels echo menacingly throughout history.

> [The new ruler] said to his people: 'Look, the Israelite people are much too numerous for us. Let us deal shrewdly with them, so that they may not increase; otherwise in the event of war they may join our enemies in fighting against us and rise from the ground.' So they set taskmasters over them to oppress them with forced labor; and they built garrison cities for Pharaoh: Pithom and Raamses. But the more they were oppressed, the more they increased and spread out, so that the Egyptians came to dread the Israelites.
>
> (Exodus 1:9–12)

The Children of Israel

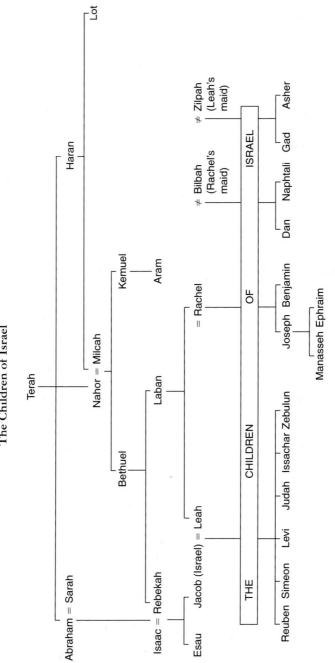

The next part of the campaign is horrific! All Hebrew male infants are henceforth to be drowned at birth (Exod. 1:22). The way in which the baby son of an Israelite couple cheats death mirrors the Sumerian legend of the third millennium BCE describing the birth of the Akkadian ruler Sargon, inscribed in cuneiform on a tablet of the first millennium BCE:

> My mother was a high priestess [or temple prostitute]. I did not know my father. She bore me in secret, and put me in a basket of rushes, sealing the lid with pitch. Then she put the basket into the river, which did not wash over me. The basket floated downstream to Akki, the drawer of water . . .

The Israelite infant is found and brought up by a daughter of Pharaoh (Exod. 2:5–10), who names him Moses. He will grow up to lead the Israelites out of Egypt and back to the land which God had promised Abraham. In the course of this heroic journey, he emerges also as lawgiver, prophet, and religious leader.

While several archaeological sites in north-eastern Egypt have been nominated as the actual Pithom and Raamses, it is generally agreed that two cities with these names were rebuilt during the administrations of Seti I (c. 1305–c. 1290 BCE) and Rameses II (c. 1290–c. 1224 BCE), and that Raamses was the former Hyksos capital of Avaris. Egyptian sources confirm that Hebrew slaves were used in state building works during the thirteenth century BCE. Even without the somewhat tenuous archaeological evidence of Israelite conquests in Canaan towards the end of the thirteenth century BCE, this would suggest that it was Seti I 'who did not know Joseph' and who originally oppressed the immigrant Hebrew community, and that Rameses II was the pharaoh of the Exodus, which thus began in about 1280 BCE. These conclusions would appear to be supported by the evidence of the stone slab erected by Merneptah, thirteenth son and successor of Rameses II, in about 1219 BCE. Celebrating his victories in Syria and Canaan, it refers specifically to 'Israel', a people located, but possibly not yet finally settled, in Canaan. This is the first recorded reference to the Israelites outside the Bible.

Biblical chronologies refer variously to a period which equates to 430 years for the sojourn in Egypt. This takes us back from the conjectured date of the Exodus to about 1710 BCE, when the Hyksos had just taken over in northern Egypt. As foreigners in the land, they would have been more likely than the ruling Egyptians to show favour to Hebrew immigrants who were, like themselves, of Semitic stock.

According to this alternative theory, the ruler 'who did not know Joseph' was Ahmose I, who in about 1552 BCE expelled the Hyksos from Egypt.

MOSES: THE MAKING OF A HERO

We know nothing about Moses outside the Bible, and the Biblical narrative is a glorification of the true God of the Israelites rather than of the extraordinary human personality who was the means through which the will of God was exercised, and who patiently brought the Israelites to respect and worship God as a way of life. Moses was the founder of the Jewish faith, as Jesus and Muhammad were the founders of the two other world religions, Christianity and Islam, both of which have origins in Judaism.

Exodus 6:16–20 states that Moses was a great-grandson of the Levi who emigrated to Egypt with Jacob, and was the son of Amram, whose father was Kohath, son of Levi. Since this would reduce the sojourn in Egypt to a matter only of three generations, it has been concluded that the names probably do not refer to a succession of fathers and sons, but that Moses' family name was Amram, of the clan of Kohath, which belonged to the tribe of Levi.

The story of the birth and childhood of Moses (Exod. 2:1–10), even discounting the parallels with the earlier Sargon story, is the stuff rather of folklore than of biography, with the added element of irony. The princess who finds him in the reeds, unwittingly returns him to his natural mother for nursing, and then adopts him and brings him up for leadership, is the daughter of the ruler responsible for ordering the deaths of all Hebrew male babies. Yet the name Moses (Hebrew, Mosheh), which is from an Egyptian word *mose* meaning 'to be born of', *does* have royal connections in that it occurs in the names of pharaohs such as Thutmosis and Rameses, or even on its own as a shortened form of the name of a ruler.

That Moses is aware of his Israelite heritage is clear when he strikes and kills an Egyptian overseer who is maltreating a Hebrew slave (Exod. 2:11ff.). He recognises his ambivalent position as an honorary Egyptian nobleman, when two scrapping Hebrews refuse to accept his authority. Frightened also for his skin when Pharaoh learns of the killing, he takes refuge in the desert of the Negeb.

In the course of his forty years (a Biblical numerical symbol for a generation) in self-imposed exile, he marries and has a family (Exod. 2:16–22). There is a new ruler in Egypt now, but still the Israelites suffer (Exod. 2:23–25). In a poetic scene of stunning effect and dramatic dialogue (Exod. 3–4), the God of Abraham, of Isaac, and of Jacob materialises as the caring God of all the Israelites, whose rescue from Egypt and resettlement in the land promised to Abraham has now devolved on a reluctant Moses.

In the course of the exchange, Moses asks (Exod. 3:13), 'When I come to the Israelites and say to them "The God of your fathers has sent me to you," and they ask me, "What is His name?" what shall I say to them?' The enigmatic answer has been variously translated, or sometimes not translated at all, but is taken to mean 'I am who I am' or 'I shall be who I shall be'. Then, in verse 15, appears for the first time the name YHWH – at the time that the Bible was first written down, and until the early years of the first century CE, the Hebrew written language had no vowels, but it is believed, from comparing the Hebrew texts with Greek texts, that the name was spoken as Yahweh. Yahweh is derived from the verb which means 'to be', and can be translated 'He who is' or 'He who causes to be'. From it comes the term Yahwism, to describe the religion of the patriarchs and of the ancient Israelites.

From about 500 BCE the name Yahweh was considered so sacred that it was not to be spoken aloud. When the Bible was read out, the word *Adonai*, meaning '(My) Lord', was substituted for it. As a reminder to the reader, indicators representing vowels from *Adonai* were combined with the consonants Y H W H; in Christian circles this monogram later came wrongly to be perpetuated as Jehovah.

Moses now expresses further reservations about his mission. Even after God has demonstrated a couple of morale-boosting conjuring tricks (Exod. 4:1–8), he still makes excuses, this time that he lacks confidence as a speaker. He even asks God to appoint someone else in his place (Exod. 4:13). So it is that his elder brother Aaron addresses the Israelites about God's purpose, demonstrates God's powers to them and to Pharaoh, and initiates the earlier catastrophes that now afflict the Egyptian people, though it is Moses through whom God indicates his will and to whom his instructions are given direct.

The plagues of Egypt – rivers of blood (putrid water and dead fish), frogs, lice (or mosquitoes), insects (or flies), cattle disease, boils, hail, locusts, darkness, child mortality – have been interpreted in various ways. A succession of natural disasters, each being the cause of the one that follows, has been used to explain the first six. Hail, locusts, and darkness caused by sandstorms are intermittent occupational hazards in that region. There is nothing abnormal either about a sudden incidence of a plague afflicting the children of the Egyptians but not of the

Israelites, who lived apart in the Goshen area, or of the plague itself, in the form, it has been speculated, of a release of mycotoxins into the air from contaminated granaries. The writer may have chosen to particularise the deaths of the eldest child in each case as poetic retribution for the killing of the newly born Hebrew males.

In the Israelite tradition, however, these events are signs or wonders, indicative of God's power to intervene in the affairs of nature and of human beings. In this case, too, God's express intention to stiffen Pharaoh's heart (Exod. 4:21) and the way in which Pharaoh is forced finally to submit to God's purpose in spite of having by the exercise of free will stiffened his own heart (Exod. 8:15; 9:34), emphasise the significance in Israelite history of the liberation from slavery.

The first of the annual spring celebrations decreed by God (Exod. 12:2–27) marks also the night when the Egyptian first-born children died and Pharaoh finally cracked. Its observances may contrast rather starkly with the modern Jewish festival of Passover, with its family rituals and general jollification, but both commemorate the same event. Sacrifice as a means of human–divine mediation was widely practised throughout the ancient world. In this case the blood of the family paschal lamb is not to be poured out over the ground, nor is the animal then to be cut up into pieces, some of them to be burnt as the offering and the remainder stewed for human consumption. The blood of the slaughtered lamb is to be retained in a bowl and splashed on to the doorposts and lintel of every Israelite home as a sign to Yahweh to 'pass over' that house in his terrible journey of retribution. The animal is then to be roasted whole, entrails and all, and eaten the same night with bitter herbs and unleavened bread (that is, baked from dough that has not been given time to rise). Those who participate in the meal are to wolf it down, dressed and shod as though prepared for imminent departure on the road.

THE EXODUS

Outside the Bible, there is no evidence of any hurried emigration, though it might hardly be expected that Egyptian sources would record an event of such potential embarrassment as the mass defection of a considerable slave population. Quite how many started out is open to question. The Biblical (Exod. 12:37) 600,000 men (that is, of military age), together with the older men, and the women and children, would have constituted a vast army of footsloggers which has been estimated at between two and three million, plus their livestock and herds. Such an exodus at one time would have proved an even greater logistical nightmare than the one Moses traditionally had to contend with, were it not that we already know from a reference (Exod. 1:15–22) to a period only a generation earlier, that the whole Hebrew community was served by just two midwives. For those looking for a more realistic figure, then, it may be found by restricting the company to the genuine descendants of the original seventy children of Israel, plus the 'mixed multitude' (Exod. 12:38) of other Hebrews which accompanied them: a total which has been estimated at six or seven thousand in all.

On the march, the Israelites are joined by other groups, including members of the Midianite clan of Jethro, Moses' father-in-law (Num. 10:29–32). Jethro himself at one point comes out to meet Moses in the Sinai desert, bringing with him Moses' wife, Zipporah, and their two sons. He gives his son-in-law some sound advice about the delegation of authority: 'The thing you are doing is not right; you will surely wear yourself out, and these people as well. For the task is too heavy for you; you cannot do it alone' (Exod. 18:17–18).

Various routes for the journey have been suggested and mapped, and natural explanations have been proposed for some of the phenomena that occur on the way, including occasions when Moses strikes running water from the rock (Exod. 17:6; Num. 20:11). The Biblical narrative itself offers a rationale for the most spectacular of them all. Pharaoh, not for the first time, has a change of mind if not also of heart. He sets out after them with all his chariots, his main task force spearheaded by a crack battalion, each chariot of which, unusually, carries a third man to back up the normal crew of archer and armed driver (Exod. 14:7). The fugitive Hebrews, caught between their pursuers and a neck of marshy deep known as the Sea of Reeds, are enabled to cross when 'the Lord drove back the sea with a strong east wind all that night, and turned the sea into dry ground' (Exod. 14:21). The pursuing army is engulfed when the tide returns. The exultant chant of Miriam, elder sister of Moses, as she leads the Israelite women in a dance, is one of the oldest pieces of poetry in the Bible, and is possibly from an eyewitness account: 'Sing to the Lord, for He has triumphed gloriously; / Horse and driver He has hurled into the sea' (Exod. 15:21).

The Sea of Reeds is assumed to have been east of Raamses, and the crossing to have taken place near present-day El Qantara on the Suez Canal, or farther upstream, just to the north or south of the Great Bitter Lake, which may then have been connected to the Gulf of Suez. Whether the freak of nature which caused the tidal wave is regarded as coincidental or providential matters as little as the sources of the ten plagues: to the Israelites, the crossing of the Sea of Reeds and the destruction of the Egyptian army is a crucial event in their early history. It symbolises not only their emergence as a people but also the supreme revelation of God's power as the deliverer of his people. It is regularly recalled, not just at the festival of Passover, but at all times of general uncertainty: 'Your way was through the sea, / Your path, through the mighty waters; / Your tracks could not be seen. / You led Your people like a flock / in the care of Moses and Aaron' (Psalm 77:20–21).

THE WILDERNESS YEARS

Whether the Biblical forty years from the start of the journey to the death of Moses in sight of its goal is a round figure or represents, as it does elsewhere, a generation, there was enough incident and drama on the way to fill a lifetime. It was not just the conditions, the unwieldy nature of the slowly moving concourse whose members had long forgotten their nomadic origins, the necessity of making two vast detours, dangers, warfare, tantrums, and incidences of recidivism and plague, that delayed the entry of the Israelites into the Promised Land; it was also that on the way Moses had to train them to be worthy of the land which God had promised them and of the privilege of being his chosen people.

Nowhere are Moses' powers of leadership, and his patience, better illustrated than in his reactions to the continual griping of his charges. The complaints begin only a few days after their miraculous rescue from death at the hands of the Egyptian hordes by the Sea of Reeds. The water at the stopping-place is, they claim, undrinkable; Moses duly purifies it for them (Exod. 15:23–25). Only a few weeks later, freedom has lost its appeal if it has to be enjoyed under desert conditions: better to die in comfort and comparative luxury in Egypt than starve in the wilderness, cry the Israelites (Exod. 16:2–3). Soon, however, there is both fowl to eat, as providentially a flock of migrating quail flop down to earth for a rest period (Exod. 16:13), and also bread or sweetish porridge, made from manna (Exod. 16:14–16), a sap from the tamarisk tree. Order is restored, but only until the next water shortage (Exod. 17:2–7)!

Later, instead of being uplifted by Moses' revelations of God's Covenant at Sinai, and by God's continued presence on the march, the Israelites seem more concerned with their stomachs than with their deliverance. 'If only we had meat to eat! We remember the fish that we used to eat free in Egypt, the cucumbers, the melons, the leeks, the onions, and the garlic. Now our gullets are shriveled. There is nothing at all! Nothing but this manna to look to!' (Num. 11:4–6).

Then the complaints become personal. Aaron and Miriam, the elder siblings of Moses, start a whispering campaign against him (Num. 12:1–2). They are jealous of the fact that God speaks only through Moses. They also do not like the fact that Moses originally made a mixed marriage with a non-Israelite, or has subsequently acquired a further, non-Israelite, wife. Finally, even when the Israelites are within sight of the Promised Land, there are repeated criticisms of the leadership itself of Moses and Aaron (Num. 14:2–5; 16:3, 12–14; 20:2–13), and a further outcry about the food (Num. 21:5).

THE COVENANT AT SINAI

The first five books of the Bible, Genesis, Exodus, Leviticus, Numbers, and Deuteronomy, are known as the Pentateuch (from the Greek term meaning 'five scrolls'). In Jewish tradition, they are the Torah, which means 'law', both written and oral, and the teaching of it. The Torah is central to the religion of the Israelites. Genesis is in effect an introduction to the four succeeding books, of which Exodus tells the story of Moses up to and including the momentous affirmation of the Covenant, and Leviticus is chiefly an exposition of various laws and observances. Numbers takes up the story of the Israelites from the second year of the Exodus. Deuteronomy comprises a review of events since the Covenant, a restatement of the legislation and ethical principles inherent in it, and an account of Moses' final acts and speeches and of his death.

The Torah is also known as the Five Books of Moses, reflecting a belief that he was their author. Scholars have detected at least four main sources. Two of these seem to date from the period 1000–800 BCE. A third is represented by the book of Deuteronomy, which is generally held to derive from the 'scroll of the Teaching' (2 Kings 22:8ff.) found while the Temple was being refurbished in the eighteenth year of the reign of Josiah (c. 622 BCE); it may have been deliberately compiled for the purpose of being 'discovered' as the climax to Josiah's campaign of reforms. A fourth source, which includes much of the law relating to priests, has been identified as being contemporary with the period of the enforced exile of the Israelites in Babylonia at the beginning of the sixth century BCE or to date from shortly afterwards.

Arguably the most influential event in the history of the Israelites occurred about three months into the journey. The Wilderness of Sin has been successfully negotiated. A band of troublesome Amalekites, who claim a monopoly of the watering-holes in the desert, have been sent packing by Joshua, Moses' military commander, with a hand-picked force (Exod. 17:8–16). The Israelites are now camped some-where in the Sinai desert, below a mountain called Sinai or Horeb. The actual site of the grandest of the visions of Moses cannot be deter-mined. It has been inferred, from references to fire, smoke, and other violent manifestations of nature in the Biblical account, that the most likely location would be in northern Arabia, east of the Gulf of Aqaba, where traces of volcanic activity have been found, but these references may simply be poetic licence. A more likely candidate is Jebel Musa (Arabic, Mount of Moses), 2,244 metres high and of forbidding aspect, near the southern tip of the Sinai peninsula.

God's preliminary message from the mountain confirms the unique relationship between him and the Israelites, reaffirms the promise to Abraham, and establishes that his Covenant is binding also on succeed-ing generations: 'Now then, if you will obey Me faithfully and keep My covenant, you shall be My treasured possession among all the peoples. Indeed, all the earth is Mine, but you shall be to Me a kingdom of priests and a holy nation' (Exod. 19:5–6).

Allowing for two separate traditions as to the sequence of events, when Moses, carrying the stone tablets inscribed by God with the Ten Commandments, returns down the mountainside after the forty days and nights which he has spent in contemplation and in communion with God (Exod. 32:15–16), he finds that the Israelites, having given up waiting for him, have reverted to the old, pagan ways of worship. This is the first occasion on which the Israelites renege on their pact with God: it is not by any means the last.

In Exodus 34, the actual tablets which become the permanent repository of the commandments are a second set, carved by Moses at God's instructions to replace the pair that Moses has shattered in anger at the backsliding of the Israelites, and re-inscribed by God (34:1) or lettered by Moses at God's dictation (34:27).

The Ten Commandments (Exod. 20:3–17) represent the core of the pact. The first four express people's duty to God, the other six their social duty to each other. These ten basic rules of everyday conduct are held in the greatest respect today by Christians as much as by Jews, even if some branches of Christianity differ between each other as to the way they are to be numbered. The total corpus of Mosaic law presented in the Torah constitutes, generally speaking, a combination of absolute, or apodictic, law (you shall . . . , you shall not . . .) and conditional, or case, law (if you do this, then the consequence will be . . .). The absolute laws of the Torah state how you should behave if you want to be appreciated by God, and by your fellows. They cover a wide range of social, and anti-social, practices, and include the celebrated 'Thou shalt love thy neighbour as thyself' (AV Lev. 19:18). The conditional laws have their counterparts in modern legal systems. They also have similarities with Mesopotamian law codes of the second millennium BCE, especially that of the notable ruler of Babylon, Hammurabi (1728–1686 BCE), which itself was based on even earlier Sumerian and Akkadian legal traditions. While this does not necessarily confirm Mesopotamian antecedents for the Israelites, it does at least indicate a Mesopotamian influence in Canaan which was reflected when the Mosaic code was finalised.

The detailed and elaborate instructions in Exodus 25–27 and 35–37 for constructing the Ark of the Covenant and the Tabernacle, also referred to as the Tent of Meeting, are believed to derive from an amalgamation of two traditions. The writers identified with the period of the Babylonian exile were reflecting their own tradition of the Temple in Jerusalem as the central, permanent shrine of Divine worship, housing among other things the Ark, which was never removed – it would have been difficult to do so, for the one described in Exodus would have weighed about 10 tons. Into this account they subsumed the earlier tradition associated with the time of Moses. The Mosaic Ark was a portable chest containing the tablets of the Ten Commandments, surmounted by a gold device, guarded by two cherubim, in which or on which God's invisible presence was enthroned.

The Ark now accompanies the Israelites along the way. It recurs as a significant feature of the crossing of the river Jordan and the destruction of Jericho (Josh. 6:3–6). It is toted to Mount Ebal to be the centrepiece of Joshua's religious presentation (Josh. 8:30–35). It is taken out of the sanctuary at Shiloh to boost Israelite morale in their campaign against the Philistines (1 Sam. 4).

Whether the original Tent of Meeting housed the Ark is not clear. It is carried around with the Israelites as a temporary structure which Moses erects outside the main camp. God arrives in a 'pillar of cloud', which he leaves at the entrance to the tent before going inside to commune with Moses (Exod. 33:7–11). Even when the desert wanderings of the Israelites are over and the tent becomes a more permanent structure, God's dwelling place is still a portable tabernacle (2 Sam. 7:6). There is also a significant passage in the prophetic writings: 'When you gaze upon Zion, our city of assembly, / Your eyes shall behold

Jerusalem / As a secure homestead, / A tent not to be transported, / Whose pegs shall never be pulled up, / And none of whose ropes shall break' (Isa. 33:20). Ark and tent are thus essential features of the desert religion of the Israelites.

The priests responsible for carrying the Ark to Joshua's concourse at Mount Ebal are Levites, no longer one of the Twelve Tribes of the Israelites, but a separate priestly class. This status seems to have been bestowed on them at some point during the journey to the Promised Land. To make up the number to twelve, a figure which had mystical significance in the ancient world, two tribes, Manasseh and Ephraim, after Joseph's sons, replaced the tribe of Joseph.

THE PROMISED LAND

The real miracle was that during the remaining years of the desert trek Moses persuaded a simple and in some respects barbarous people, whose ancestors had been semi-nomads and who themselves had all their lives been slaves, to accept, in a polytheistic age, that there was only one God, and that his message and his laws must be carried with them to their new homeland. There was something special about these proto-Israelites which ensured the continual survival of remnants of them even in the face of backsliding and destruction. Up to this time, blood or kinship was the only criterion for the recognition of a community or social group. The Israelites were a community united by faith in a single God; moreover it was a faith which, as the Ten Commandments demonstrate, is to be expressed also in the life of the community. And the community itself was a party to God's pact.

The backsliding, however, began almost immediately. After moving on to Kadesh-barnea, near the border of Canaan, the Israelites encamp while Moses assesses the tactical situation. On God's prompting, he selects one man from each of the twelve tribes to infiltrate into Canaan and spy out the land, giving them a detailed briefing (Num. 13:17–20). After forty days the scouts return. Their findings are unanimous, but their advice is inconclusive. In spite of the advantages of the land itself, tangible evidence of whose produce they have, as good spies, brought back with them, the verdict of the majority of them is that the inhabitants of the land are too powerful, and individually too gigantic, to be overcome.

There is the usual outcry! Joshua and Caleb, the minority in the scouting party, are all for going in and taking Canaan by storm, whatever the opposition. The general reaction of the Israelites themselves is to moan: 'If only we had died in the land of Egypt . . . or if only we might die in this wilderness! Why is the Lord taking us to that land to fall by the sword? Our wives and children will be carried off. . . . Let us head back for Egypt' (Num. 14:1–4). They even threaten to submit their leaders to a barrage of stones (Num. 14:10). God intervenes. He is so angry at the people's attitude that Moses has to calm him down (Num. 14:17–19). Even so, the Israelites are sentenced to wander in the wilderness for the full forty years, and all the scouts except Joshua and Caleb are struck down with plague (Num. 14:26–38).

The people now display their contrariness. They arm and attempt to force their way through the Negeb and into Canaan by the most direct route. Moses remains in the camp with the Ark, having warned them: 'Why do you transgress the Lord's command? This will not succeed. Do not go up, lest you be routed by your enemies, for the Lord is not in your midst. For the Amalekites and the Canaanites will be there to face you, and you will fall by the sword' (Num. 14:41–43). Predictably, the Israelites, more used to marching than to fighting, are thrown into disarray by the Amalekites of the plain and the Canaanites of the hills (Num. 14:44–45).

There is nothing for it but to try again from the east. This involves a vast detour, and further hazards, calling for diplomacy on the part of Moses in dealing not only with his refractory charges but also with unfriendly rulers through whose territory it is necessary to pass. When Sihon, an Amorite king, refuses the Israelites permission even to travel along the ancient main road linking the Gulf of Aqaba and Damascus, and backs up his decision with a show of force, Moses turns military commander and the Israelites achieve a surprising victory (Num. 21:21–25): there is some suggestion that the Israelite numbers were boosted by Hebrew fugitives from Sihon's rule. Not only that, but, with God's help, they go on to defeat Og, ruler of Bashan (Num. 21:35), he of the king-sized (13ft × 6ft) iron bedstead (Deut. 3:11).

The Israelites, having occupied a deep strip of territory on the east bank of the river Jordan, encamp on the plains of Moab, beside the Dead Sea (Num. 22:1). This is the situation still, after the extraordinary episode of Balaam and his talking ass (Num. 22:21–35). Its humorous elements are a dramatic counterpoint to the main theme of the story, the power of God to nullify the traditional efficacy of the spoken blessing or curse. Balaam is hired by the king of Moab to pronounce a curse on the Israelites. Instead he blesses them:

How can I damn whom God has not damned,
How doom when the Lord has not doomed?
As I see them from the mountain tops,
Gaze on them from the heights,
There is a people that dwells apart,
Not reckoned among the nations,
Who can count the dust of Jacob,
Number the dust-cloud of Israel?

(Numbers 23:8–10)

Balaam is also reflecting the opinion prevailing in the ancient world that the Israelites were not so much a nation as a people with a religious identity: 'For you are a people consecrated to the Lord your God: of all the peoples on earth the Lord your God chose you to be His treasured people' (Deut. 7:6).

As the Israelites prepare to enter Canaan from the east, there is a hitch. The tribes of Reuben and Gad, seeing that the land on the east bank of the river Jordan is particularly suitable for cattle farming, ask to settle where they are. Moses reluctantly agrees that they and half the tribe of Manasseh should do this, provided that they still participate in the military campaign against Canaan as 'shock-troops' (Num. 32:32).

Moses is now anticipating his own death. Deuteronomy incorporates his farewell speech to the people, largely a recapitulation of the Israelite epic to date and of the precepts of God. Then, Joshua having been nominated as his successor (Deut. 31:23), Moses climbs to the summit of Mount Nebo (also known as Pisgah). Just before he dies, he is shown the territory which is God's promise to the Israelites: 'Gilead as far as Dan; all Naphtali; the land of Ephraim and Manasseh; the whole land of Judah as far as the Western Sea; the Negeb; and the Plain – the Valley of Jericho, the city of palm trees – as far as Zoar' (Deut. 34:1–3).

This is less than the original Covenant with Abraham proposed, and barely includes the lands which the Israelites had recently conquered and within which they were at present settled. It still, however, had to be acquired.

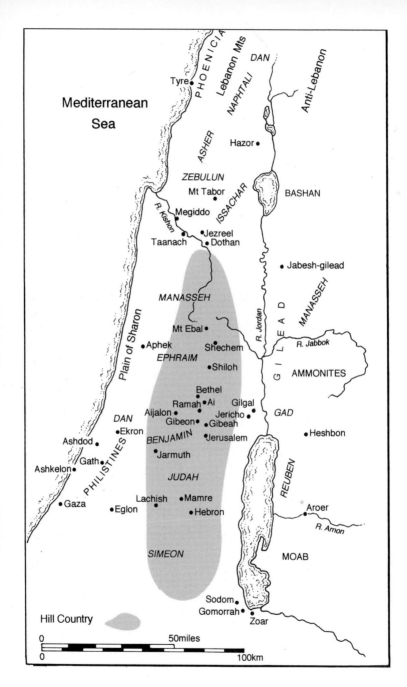

Map 2 The Land of Canaan

24

2

THE LAND OF THE ISRAELITES

The Biblical personage called Canaan was the son of Ham, second son of Noah (Gen. 10:6). Numbers 34:2–12 represents the most detailed description of the extent of the Biblical land of Canaan, effectively incorporating at its northern end the two facing mountain ranges of Lebanon and Anti-Lebanon. The land is to be apportioned between nine and a half tribes, Reuben, Gad, and half the tribe of Manasseh having already 'received their portions across the Jordan, opposite Jericho, on the east, the orient side' (Num. 34:15). Canaanite influence, however, extended beyond the northern boundary and along the western coastline of Syria, taking in the cities of Sidon (also the name of Canaan's eldest son) and Tyre, and the significant archaeological site of the seaport of Ugarit. This narrow strip of Syrian/Lebanese territory was later recognised as the land and ancient civilisation of the Phoenicians.

THE CANAANITES

Canaan in the Late Bronze Age had no political identity; its city-states, each with its own king operating from within his city's fortifications, were under Egyptian administration. Economically and culturally, however, as well as geographically, Canaan was a significant centre of the Aegean and Middle-Eastern region, besides offering a convenient north–south highway for invaders, traders, and migrants.

Canaanite society was feudal. A wealthy ruling class, possibly recruited from those of non-Semitic origins, dominated the Semitic population, who were the agricultural workers and pastoralists of the plains, and the forced labour for the building of fortifications and aristocratic mansions. The heavily wooded mountainous regions were sparsely populated. Landless, often lawless, Habiru roamed the areas which were not controlled by any city-state, their numbers frequently augmented by disaffected peasants, runaway slaves, and mercenaries who were being badly paid or not paid at all.

Canaan supplied timber, textiles and dyes, oil, wine, spices, and honey for export: imports were mainly metals, precious stones, and manufactured goods such as pottery. Workshops produced copper tools, bronze armour, chariots, jewellery and plate, and quality ceramic ware.

Canaanite religious beliefs and practices were based on an elaborate mythology which had elements in common with that of other societies in the ancient world, and, as befitted an agricultural society, reflected the annual cycle of birth, life, and death. These were not just inimical to the Mosaic faith of the incomers, as Biblical references (for example 2 Kings 17:7–18) make clear, but also incompatible with it. The Israelites did not worship nature, nor did they indulge in sympathetic magic, such as was practised by Canaanite congregants who publicly had sexual intercourse with male as well as female temple prostitutes as a means of stimulating the fertility of nature. The sanctuaries, or 'high places', that the Canaanites built to their various gods, and what went on in them, were as intrinsic to their agricultural existence as the tractor and other mechanical aids are to ours: with the difference that their lives as well as their livelihoods depended on the regular cycle of nature. Baal worshippers sought to *control* their gods: to worship Yahweh was to *serve* him.

Titular head of the Canaanite pantheon, as in other Semitic theogonies, was El. The most significant executive deity, however, was Baal, god of rain and storm, and also of the fertility which depends on water. Baal is sometimes interchangeable with Hadad, which may be an alternative name used on occasions when his real appellation was too holy to be invoked (as was that of the God of the Israelites), or else represents the name under which that deity was worshipped in more easterly areas of the region. The antithesis to Baal, and his deadly antagonist, was Mot, god of drought and therefore of death. One of the ritual sacrifices at a festival towards the end of winter which celebrated the pruning of the vines, and thus the excision of the withered branches which Mot represents, was to boil a kid in its mother's milk: this practice was specifically forbidden to the Israelites (Exod. 23:19) and became a permanent prohibition of the Jewish dietary laws.

Three goddesses, Asherah, Astarte (Biblical Ashtaroth), and Anat, collectively represented sex and fertility, while also being deities of battle. Asherah, wife of El, mother of gods, was worshipped in the form of a carved wooden post or pillar: this cult object (wrongly translated in AV as 'grove') became a major irritation to Israelite prophets and religious leaders, as is illustrated in Judges 6:25–31 and elsewhere: 'The Israelites . . . set up pillars and sacred posts for themselves on every lofty hill . . . and they worshiped fetishes [AV, NEB 'idols'] concerning which the Lord had said to them, "You must not do this thing"' (2 Kings 17:10–12). Fetishes in the form of naked figurines representing either Asherah or Baal's wife Astarte, about 15 centimetres high and mass produced from moulds, have been found. Images of Astarte/Ashtaroth are several times cited in the Bible (for example 1 Sam. 7:3) as being worshipped by backsliding Israelites.

Anat, sister of Baal or possibly his daughter, was young, virginal, desirable, and especially violent, being described in a Phoenician epic poem as 'wading in blood up to her thighs'. It was she who annually rescued Baal from the attentions of his enemy Mot, whom she then cleaved with a sickle, beat with a flail, burned in the fire, and ground between millstones, scattering the bits over the fields.

That we know some of the original mythology of the Canaanite pantheon is due to the discovery at Ugarit (now Ras Sharma) in 1929 of a series of texts of the first half of the fourteenth century BCE, written on clay tablets in cuneiform in an alphabetical script. That the alphabet was most likely to have been a Canaanite invention is not in dispute. Its brilliance lay in the recognition that human speech consists of a relatively small number of different sounds, each of which can be represented by a distinctive symbol.

There were thirty characters in the Ugaritic alphabet, twenty-seven consonants and three vowel sounds. The original alphabet on which it was based, known as Proto-Sinaitic, comprised just the twenty-seven consonants. It is likely to have been invented in inauspicious circumstances, by a Canaanite prisoner of the Egyptians doing forced labour in the turquoise mines in Sinai in about 1530 BCE. This user-friendly alphabetical system comprised simple images: for ease of memory the first letter of the pictured word represented the chosen phonetic unit. It was taken up in the Canaanite homeland in a form which is called 'Proto-Canaanite'. From this developed the Ugaritic alphabet, and its Canaanite and Aramaic counterparts.

From the Canaanite system derived the Early Hebrew alphabet, the original script of the Hebrew Bible. This was gradually replaced after the fifth century BCE by a descendant of the Aramaic alphabet, known as Square Hebrew, now the printing type of modern Hebrew.

The two languages of Hebrew and Aramaic, which have a common Semitic ancestry, developed side by side. After the Babylonian exile in the sixth century BCE, Aramaic, the international language of diplomacy

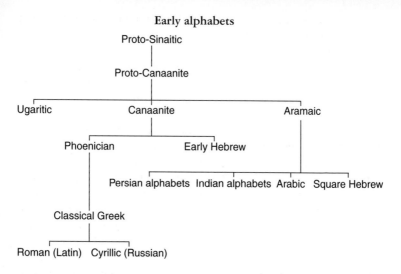

and commerce, became the spoken language of the Jews, by whom Hebrew had now become regarded as a classical and literary medium. Aramaic is also the language of certain verses in the Hebrew Bible, and of the original version of Josephus' *The Jewish War*, written between 70 and 75 CE.

The Phoenician branch of the Canaanite alphabet, in much the same way as the Phoenicians themselves, came to have profound influence on the ancient Mediterranean world, and is a direct ancestor of the alphabet used for the English, Romance, Scandinavian, German, and other European languages, and also, in another form, Russian.

THE PHOENICIANS

The name Phoenicians for the people of the northern Canaanite strip of coastline was coined by the ancient Greeks, who used it to describe those Canaanites with whom they were most familiar. The Old Testament and other early records generally make no such distinction, or refer to them as inhabitants of individual cities, Ugarit, Arvad, Byblos, Sidon, Tyre, each of which had its own ruler.

The historical Phoenicians were Canaanites culturally, and probably also racially – both peoples were most likely of Amorite descent. They had common religious beliefs, deities, and practices, with particular local applications. Astarte was especially worshipped at Byblos, where annually the death of the vegetation god whom the Greeks called Adonis was commemorated in her sanctuary. It was the custom on this occasion for believers to shave their heads; women who were unwilling to do so were required instead to prostitute themselves to strangers, and hand over their earnings to the goddess. The Baal whose worship, with that of Asherah, Jezebel, daughter of the king of the island city of Tyre, brought to the kingdom of Israel in the ninth century BCE on her political marriage to Ahab was Baal-Melqart, the official god of Tyre.

Another Canaanite deity with specific Phoenician connections was the corn god Dagan, who as Dagon was appropriated by the Philistines and worshipped at Ashdod (1 Sam. 5) and Gaza (Judg. 16:23). He turns up also in Mesopotamia, where, in an eighteenth-century BCE letter found at Mari, his priest demands that human sacrifice be made to the spirit of the king's father. That human, and specifically child, sacrifice was a feature of the Canaanite/Phoenician religion is amply attested by Biblical references (for example, 2 Kings 16:3 and 23:10). The Phoenicians exported the practice to their colonies along the north African coast. In the sanctuary of the goddess Tanit (equivalent to Astarte) at Carthage, the city which produced Hannibal and flourished in the fourth and third centuries BCE until destroyed by Rome, have been found thousands of urns in which are the cremated remains of small children.

The cities of the Phoenicians flourished at the beginning of the second millennium BCE. They were comparatively small (the raised mound on which Ugarit stood measured about 1,000 by 500 metres, with a tiny harbour a mile away in the bay of Minet el-Beida), were probably unhealthy, and were always in danger of attack from aggressive neighbours. Perhaps it was as a reaction to their circumstances that by the middle of the third millennium the Phoenicians had become formidable seafarers and shipbuilders. The Palermo Stone, a slab of black diorite unearthed in Byblos, records the despatch to Egypt in about 2600 BCE of forty ships carrying local cedar wood. The wood was for the construction of three ships, each 52 metres long, the remains of one of which are believed to be those discovered in 1954. For shorter journeys, the timber was floated along the coastline on rafts, as it was in the tenth century BCE for Solomon's temple complex, which also depended on Phoenician craftsmen for its design and construction.

While the modern alphabet is the Phoenicians' most significant legacy to western civilisation, to the ancient world it was the range of dyes known as Tyrian purple, extracted from two species of sea snail found along the coast. It was with this that the decorative stripe on the togas of Roman senators, and also of boys of the upper classes in Rome, was coloured.

Figure 2 Ivory plaque, 25 cm long, of between 1350 and 1150 BCE, from the palace treasury of the Canaanite city of Megiddo. From its shape and from the position of the holes, it may have been intended to be attached to the sheath of a short sword or dagger. A Canaanite king sits on a throne whose supports are two cherubim, or sphinxes, such as guarded the seat of God on the Mosaic Ark, and the Ark itself in Solomon's Temple in Jerusalem. Behind him refreshments are being prepared. A female attendant serves him with a drink from a bowl, while another plays for him on a nine-stringed harp. A warrior, armed with shield and short spear or javelin, heralds the appearance of two naked (and circumcised) prisoners-of-war. They are shackled to the pair of horses that draw their captor's war chariot, which is equipped with arrow quivers and a spear, and is followed by a soldier with a curved sword. The ambience of the scene is reflected in the Biblical descriptions of Solomon's court.

THE AMARNA PERIOD AND AFTER

Events in Egypt during the fifteenth to thirteenth centuries BCE, while the Israelites were in bondage there, had a crucial bearing on the situation in Canaan and on the subsequent Israelite occupation of it. The way between Egypt and Mesopotamia lay through Canaan, which had further strategic significance as a buffer between Egypt and potentially hostile peoples from Asia Minor, the Caucasus, and Mesopotamia itself. Because of the nature of the broken terrain, central government of Canaan, whether administered from within or without, would have been difficult to maintain even were it not for the fact that each city-state was independent of the rest.

The Egyptians did not finally push the dreaded Hyksos beyond the river Orontes and Phoenician territory until about 1450 BCE, in the time of Thutmosis III, who had on his first campaign in 1479 defeated a confederacy of Canaanite rulers at Megiddo. The new boundary of Egyptian influence was now threatened by the Hurrian kingdom of Mitanni. Hostilities were finally terminated by an ongoing marriage treaty whereby each ruler of Mitanni gave a daughter in marriage to the pharaoh of Egypt. This also strengthened both kingdoms against potential aggression from the Hittites in Asia Minor.

This was the situation at the beginning of the Amarna period, so called because for a time the Egyptian royal capital was at Akhetaten (modern Tell el-Amarna) in southern Egypt, where the extraordinary cache was found of more than 350 foreign office documents, in the form of clay tablets inscribed in cuneiform, dating from the first half of the fourteenth century BCE. They are written in Akkadian, the diplomatic language of the time, but with Canaanite accretions, and comprise letters which offer a graphic perspective on the prevailing political climate in Canaan. None of them appears to have been answered.

These letters, and Ugaritic and Hittite texts of the times, reveal not only an overall administration that is near breakdown and an indigenous peasant population ripe for revolution, but also serious harassment and occupation of territory by organised groups of Habiru/Hebrew incomers.

The situation in Egypt itself deteriorated under Pharaoh Amenophis IV (c. 1353–c. 1335 BCE), who, as a principal plank of a series of wide-ranging reforms intended to bring the mass of the people nearer to god and to social equality, pronounced that the sole god was Aten, the Sun. He changed his own name to Akhenaten (Splendour, or possibly Effective Spirit, of Aten), and set up a new court at Akhetaten (Horizon of Aten). While his successor, the Tutenkhamen whose tomb provided modern archaeology with one of its richest and most romantic discoveries, reversed the edicts, and removed the court to the old royal palace at Memphis, Akhenaten's preoccupation with domestic matters had serious repercussions on the international front.

Problems with the Hittites reached such a pass that on the death of Tutenkhamen his widow wrote to the Hittite king offering to marry one of his sons. That the marriage never took place was due to the young man being assassinated en route by disaffected Egyptians: that war was averted may have been due to an outbreak of plague among the Hittite people, who also had to keep an eye out for the Assyrians taking the opportunity of making a strike against them from the east.

The Eighteenth Dynasty in Egypt closed with the death in about 1306 BCE of Haremhab, a military man who exercised his energies finally to restore the ancient worship and in reorganising the civil service. The Amarna period, which is sometimes taken also to include the long reign of Akhenaten's father, Amenophis III (c. 1391–c. 1353 BCE), lasted about fifty years. Briefly, it generated a new, more realistic art form, whose finest manifestations are, ironically, on Haremhab's tomb. With the beginning of the Nineteenth Dynasty, and the accession of Seti I, we are in the putative lifetime of Moses himself.

Meanwhile the Hittites, helped by the Hebrew uprisings in Canaan and by the unsettling effect on the Egyptian administration of alliances against it on the part of Canaanite kings, had extended their power into Canaan itself. The crisis finally came to a head in about 1285 BCE when Rameses II, the pharaoh of Exodus, and his army were ambushed and set upon by a considerable force under the Hittite king, Muwattalis (c. 1306–c. 1282 BCE), near Kadesh on the river Orontes. Each side claimed victory, but both were so severely mauled, and their influence so much dented, that in about 1270 BCE they agreed to a peace treaty, copies of which, engraved on silver in Egyptian and Hittite versions, have been recovered in Egypt and Turkey respectively.

At the same time other powers, large and small, were taking advantage of the situation. The movement of the 'Sea Peoples' from the area round the Aegean Sea, which had begun at the beginning of the Amarna period, gathered force. It finally swept away the Hittites and poured through Canaan, where one of its elements, the Philistines, finally settled on the south-west coast, and ultimately gave their name to the land of Palestine. The surge continued right up to the borders of Egypt, where Merneptah (c. 1224–c. 1211 BCE), the successor of Rameses II, and his forces, having already almost succumbed to an invasion of Libyan peoples from the west, managed only at great cost to stave off being engulfed.

Merneptah was also forced to act in Canaan against continued disruption by subject city-states and also against the Hebrews. These were the circumstances which prompted his victory inscription recording his victory over 'Israel', as well as over the Sea Peoples and Libyans. Whether these Israelites had come with the Mosaic migration from Egypt, or were a group called Israel who had settled among the Hebrews in Canaan earlier, cannot categorically be established. Certainly the tentative timescale attached to the Biblical account of an Israelite armed incursion into Canaan is consistent with these Israelites being there as a result of it; while the confused situation in Canaan itself, reflected in the Amarna letters, which had not had any opportunity to be resolved, provided circumstances in which an invasion by a comparatively small and inexperienced fighting force could succeed.

THE ISRAELITE OCCUPATION

According to the book of Joshua, forty years after the controversy over the spies' mission into Canaan, and Moses now being dead, Joshua assumes supreme command of the military invasion of Canaan: that tribal jealousies and individual traditions are set aside on this occasion is implied in Joshua 1:10–18. Within five years (Josh. 14:7, 10), he conquers the land by means of three lightning, death-dealing strikes, spearheaded by the men of the two and a half tribes which have already settled on the east bank of the Jordan – the other tribesmen follow behind with their families and possessions, their primary task being to occupy, and then defend if necessary, the conquered territory.

The campaign opens with a providential landslide, of a kind recorded subsequently in 1267 CE and 1927 CE, which blocks the Jordan and allows the Israelites to cross into Canaan on dry land. The walls of Jericho crumble at the blast of trumpets, and there is wholesale slaughter (Josh. 6:20–21). The same fate is meted out to Ai, whose forces are inveigled into leaving their city unguarded (Josh. 8:14–25). It is after this victory that Joshua, having made a temporary detour to the north, builds an altar on Mount Ebal, overlooking Shechem, and reads aloud to the assembled Israelites the teaching of Moses (Josh. 8:30–35).

Central to the second phase is the curious episode of the Canaanite coalition. On his way south, Joshua is deceived into making an irrevocable peace treaty with what turn out to be the inhabitants of Gibeon and three other cities in the area (Josh. 9:3–21). Five Amorite kings, of the city-states of Jerusalem, Hebron, Jarmuth, Lachish, and Eglon, band together to take reprisals against the Gibeonites, who demand Joshua's protection (Josh. 10:5–7). The running battle which ensues is remarkable also for being the only occasion on which 'the Lord acted on words spoken by a man' (Josh. 10:14). The words, from a lost collection of Israelite heroic songs, are the famous 'Stand still, O sun, at Gibeon, / O moon, in the Valley of Aijalon' (Josh. 10:12).

The five kings escape the slaughter, only to suffer a peculiarly nasty fate. When Joshua hears that they have hidden in a cave near the Israelite camp, he has the entrance blocked up with boulders, and puts a guard outside, until he is ready. Then, having humiliated the kings in front of his whole army, he has them killed and impaled on stakes (Josh. 10:16–26).

Having now secured the south of the country, Joshua turns his attentions against a northern coalition, which he finally sees off with a resounding victory at Hazor, whose city he burns, and whose king and all inhabitants he puts to the sword (Josh. 11:1–11). 'Thus Joshua conquered the whole country, just as the Lord had promised Moses; and Joshua assigned it to Israel to share according to their tribal divisions. And the land had rest from war' (Josh. 11:23). But not quite. Certain territories, mainly to the south-west, east, and north still remain 'to be taken possession of'. It is God's purpose himself to 'dispossess' them for the Israelites, among whom they are to be apportioned in advance (Josh. 13:1–7).

The archaeological evidence to support this version of the Israelite campaign of conquest is at best inconclusive. Certain Canaanite towns, including Hazor, *were* destroyed towards the end of the thirteenth century BCE, Hazor in a manner consistent with the book of Joshua, and also with Deuteronomy 7:5: 'You shall tear down their altars, smash their pillars, cut down their sacred posts, and consign their images to the fire.' Jericho is a problem in that its walls were destroyed and the city burned much earlier, in what is suggested to have been about 1550 BCE, probably by the Egyptians, though the earthquake theory, which has been used to support the Biblical account, still has its adherents. Military historians, however, have explained this aspect of the campaign in tactical terms, in which the walls of Jericho are merely symbolic of city defences lulled into a sense of false security by repeated manoeuvres which only finally become the means of attack, a strategy which has been employed many times since, and recently against the state of Israel itself by Syria and Egypt before the war in October 1973. There are difficulties too with what is thought to have been Ai, which was destroyed at about the same time as Jericho and not occupied again until the twelfth century BCE. In this case it has been argued that it may not have been Ai that the chronicler intended, but nearby Bethel, which suffered a tremendous fire during the latter half of the thirteenth century BCE.

Orgies of bloodletting were commonplace in the ancient world, except where one of the objects of the exercise was to obtain slaves. The Israelites were waging a holy war in the name of their God against those whose religious practices they had been taught to abominate. They did not need slaves, in which capacity they already had the fickle Gibeonites to serve as 'hewers of wood and drawers of water' (Josh. 9:21). As agriculturalists they needed the land, which at that time could not support an unlimited population – the whole territory nominally to be occupied by the Israelite tribes was less than 300 kilometres long and 100 wide, and much of that was mountains. Thus, the argument goes, in terms of the traditions of their times, wholesale slaughter was justified. With regard to booty, a standard method of paying armies in the ancient world, all removable objects were instead dedicated to God; the Israelites were banned absolutely from benefiting personally from anything that had been 'proscribed for the Lord' (see Josh. 6:17–19, 24; and 7).

The historian of the book of Joshua was primarily concerned with showing how God's promise was gloriously fulfilled through the agency of the legendary figure of Joshua. That much of the indigenous population still survived is acknowledged in the farewell address put into the mouth of Joshua which comprises chapter 23 of his story:

> 'The Lord has driven out great, powerful nations on your account. . . . Should you turn away and attach yourselves to the remnant of those nations – to those that are left among you – and intermarry with them, you joining them and they joining you, know for certain that the Lord your God will not continue to drive these nations out before you.'
>
> (Joshua 23:9–13)

It is when one considers the Joshua account in terms of the subsequent decentralised campaign in Judges 1, and in particular the admission that the tribe of Judah 'took possession of the hill country; but they were not able to dispossess the inhabitants of the plain, for they had iron chariots' (Judg. 1:19), that a different picture emerges. This has been taken historically to be from an earlier tradition and to be more authentic. There were hostile invasions, by individual tribes or groups of tribes, over a considerable number of years, and subsequently military expeditions from the hills on to the plains: only when these had resulted in a substantial occupation of Canaan, could the momentous gathering of the tribes described in Joshua 24 occur, and a unified Israelite community begin to emerge.

But was there an Israelite conquest of Canaan at all? Protagonists of an alternative theory suggest that the original incursions were peaceful migrations into the hill country by groups of nomadic or semi-nomadic peoples in search of pasture for their animals. They became farmers. At some point in the eleventh century BCE bands of them began to move down into the fertile land of the plains, where they clashed with the folk from the Canaanite city strongholds.

A further theory is that the Exodus from Egypt of a community of former slaves, bound together by their relationship with their God, was the spark that set off a peasants' revolt, initially in the Amorite kingdoms of Transjordan, which spread westwards through Canaan. This, it is claimed, is consistent with the volatile situation illustrated in some of the Amarna letters. In the turmoil, many of the Canaanite rulers were overthrown, and in their place emerged the Israelite confederacy of tribes.

It is generally accepted that the initial settlement was only in the hill country. The final occupation was more likely to have been evolutionary than revolutionary, and to have involved elements of conquest from within and from outside Canaan, peaceful infiltration, and internal rebellion, as well as intermarriage or simply fraternisation between peoples of the same (Semitic) stock, and wholesale defection to the Israelite cause of groups and clans of dwellers in Canaan.

THE TRIBAL LEAGUE

The book of Joshua ends with the great convocation of Israelites that Joshua calls at Shechem (Josh. 24). This strategically placed, circular fortress city was an ancient Canaanite religious centre with Israelite connections: it is where God appeared to Abraham, and where Abraham (Gen. 12:7) and later Jacob (Gen. 33:20) built altars, and where the bones of Joseph, which the Israelites brought from Egypt, were now interred in the plot of land which Jacob had purchased (Josh. 24:32). Substantial remains at ground level on the 4.5-hectare site have been discovered of the original Canaanite temple, built in about 1650 BCE. Shechem had also been a hotbed of Hebrew activity since the Amarna period.

According to the Biblical account, Joshua, before all the tribes and 'Israel's elders and commanders, magistrates and officers', solemnly recounts, in God's name, the outline of the history of the Israelites, from Abraham, Isaac, and Jacob, to the events of the Exodus and the occupation of Canaan. The people are then given a stark choice: to 'revere the Lord and serve Him with undivided loyalty' or 'If you are loath to serve the Lord, choose this day which ones you are going to serve – the gods that your forefathers served beyond the Euphrates, or those of the Amorites in whose land you are settled' (Josh. 24:14–15).

The assembled company unanimously give him their support. Joshua, however, presses on:

> 'You will not be able to serve the Lord, for He is a holy God. He is a jealous God; He will not forgive your transgressions and your sins. If you forsake the Lord and serve alien gods, he will turn and deal harshly with you and make an end of you, after having been gracious to you.' But the people replied to Joshua, 'No, we will serve the Lord.'
>
> (Joshua 24:19–21)

After eliciting further affirmative responses, Joshua 'made a covenant for the people and he made a fixed rule for them' (Josh. 24:25).

The Israelites, once pastoral nomads and for years wanderers in some form in the desert, now settled into an agricultural existence within a culture whose worship of nature had been for centuries a logical expression of its needs and hopes. The formality of the ceremony at Shechem, however, is seen not just as a necessary reaffirmation of the central principle of Israelite society, but as a means of mass conversion of other groups who had joined their ranks: some of these, such as the Kenizites and the Kenites, may have entered Canaan from the south at an earlier stage.

The Israelites had no central administration. They were a confederacy or sacral league of twelve autonomous tribes united by their belief in their one, invisible God, and in his laws. Each of the twelve took a monthly turn at looking after the central shrine at Shiloh, where the Ark of the Covenant was kept. Here, and probably at other centres too, the three annual festivals were held: the feast of unleavened bread, the feast of weeks, and the feast of the ingathering, today observed respectively as Pesach, Shavuot, and Sukkot. All three had their origins in agricultural rites which were performed in pre-Israelite times, now adapted to celebrate God's mighty works. In particular the agricultural feast of unleavened bread, celebrating the first harvesting of the barley crop, seems to have been combined with the pastoral celebration of the lambing season, and then reinterpreted to refer to the last of the plagues of Egypt and to the hasty escape of the Israelites from slavery.

TRIBAL LEADERS

The book of Judges is a series of splendid old tales which largely defy being put into any chronological framework. Collectively, though, they illustrate the lessons inherent in the account of the gathering at Shechem and the problems of decentralised and ad hoc government.

The Covenant with God needs to be reaffirmed by each generation. Without this, there is an inexorable cycle of events such as is presaged in Judges 2:10 to 3:4. Israelites succumb to the temptations of the worship of local gods; God is angry and delivers them into the hands of enemies; the people complain bitterly; God relents and provides them with a leader whose military skills win the day for them; after the leader's death, the pattern repeats itself.

The Hebrew word which has been translated as 'judge' has a rather different meaning to that of the legal functionary. The Jewish Bible (1985) does not use the appellation 'judge' at all as a translation, preferring 'chieftain', with 'lead' for the verbal use of the form. The office of tribal chieftain in the book of Judges is non-hereditary, the functionary being chosen by God and invested with divine-inspired charisma. The chieftain is a war leader and also arbitrates in cases of dispute: the Israelites come to Deborah 'for decisions' (Judg. 4:5). While the Bible refers generally to 'Israelites' as the victims of oppression, chieftains call only on those tribes who will serve under their command. Tribal jealousies are rife, and can develop into tribal war (Judg. 12:1–6). That there is no formal appeal mechanism against the actions of a lawless tribe and no sanctions except communal violence is illustrated by the consequences of the gang rape and murder of a Levite's concubine by a bunch of bisexual Benjaminite louts (Judg. 19–21). Not for nothing does the chronicler end his account, 'In those days there was no king in Israel; everyone did as he pleased' (Judg. 21:25).

In spite of its confused chronology, the book of Judges does in other respects too illuminate events of the period, and in particular highlights the areas from which dangers to the Israelite confederacy emanated. Archaeological evidence from Megiddo *has* been used, however, to date to about 1125 BCE the extinction by Deborah and her military commander Barak of the main threat from within Canaan. Deborah is one of a line of Biblical heroines, among them Sarah, Miriam, Esther, and Judith, who played a decisive role in Israelite and Jewish history. She has her post-Biblical counterparts, too, in Salome Alexandra, ruler of Judaea 76–67 BCE, and in the African warrior queens, Dahiyah Kahina (*fl.* 690 CE) of Maghreb and Judith of Ethiopia (tenth century CE). Deborah's problem was 'the inhabitants of the plain' and their 'iron chariots' (Judg. 1:19), which were exerting a stranglehold on the Jezreel Valley, overlooked by the Canaanite fortresses of Megiddo and Taanach. The valley was not only a crucial trade route between Egypt and Mesopotamia, but it effectively cut the Israelite domains at that point into two. Periodically Canaanite chariot patrols would surge out and take the offensive against settlements of the Israelites.

There are two versions of the battle in which Deborah and Barak defeated Sisera, commander of the Canaanite forces in the region: one in prose (Judg. 4:6–16) and one in verse (Judg. 5). The latter, known as the Song of Deborah, is a subjective as well as stirring account, possibly by someone contemporary with the events it describes, and is regarded as one of the earliest examples of poetry in Hebrew. While both the Biblical chronicler and the poet give the victory to God, military historians have awarded credits to Deborah. The use of what they see as diversionary tactics by a second force of Israelites enabled Deborah and Barak and the men of Naphtali and Zebulun to charge down from the foothills of Mount Tabor on Sisera's forces at precisely the moment when the Canaanite chariots were bogged down in marshy ground made treacherous by a providential storm, which caused the river Kishon to overflow. The *coup de grâce* for Sisera was delivered by another female militant, Jael, whose husband, Heber the Kenite, may have been a double agent. Jael gives Sisera refuge. When he is asleep, exhausted from the battle and his ignominious flight from the disaster, she hammers a tent peg right through his temple and into the ground (Judg. 4:17–22).

Other chieftains were called to deal with oppressors from outside the immediate environs of Canaan. Bands of wandering Amalekites and Midianites came from the south in search of temporary pasture-lands to occupy in times of drought. The harder the drought, the longer they stayed. 'For they would come up with their livestock and their tents, swarming as thick as locusts; they and their camels were innumerable' (Judg. 6:5). The southern tribes of the Israelites, Judah and Simeon, had no answer to these mounted incursions, and melted away into hideouts in the mountains, leaving their lands and newly sown fields to the invaders. (Subsequently the members of the tribe of Simeon seem to have been subsumed within the tribe of Judah or to have been dispersed among the northern Israelites.)

The central tribes too seemed bent on evasive tactics, until a combined force of Amalekites, Midianites, and other desert raiders swept through Gilead, across the river Jordan, and into the Jezreel Valley. God's choice of leader seems an unlikely one, the youngest son of a family whose clan is the 'humblest in Manasseh' (Judg. 6:15), but Gideon makes an impressive start by destroying his own father's Baal-worship objects and setting up an altar to Yahweh in their place, and then mustering the tribes of Manasseh, Asher, Zebulun, and Naphtali (Judg. 6:23–35). The actual victory, though, is achieved by a commando force of just three hundred, who attack at night (Judg. 7:1–22).

According to the Bible, it would seem that Gideon is now offered a hereditary kingship over all the Israelites, which he refuses in no uncertain terms: 'The Lord alone shall rule over you' (Judg. 8:23). Opinions are divided as to the significance, or even relevance, in a pan-Israelite context, of the establishment of Abimelech, Gideon's son by a concubine, as a Canaanite-style king of the city-state of Shechem (Judg. 9). Be that as it may, after three years the citizens throw him out, and the revolt spreads through the state. Abimelech returns with an army and destroys Shechem, only to die himself after a woman drops a millstone on his head from the roof of a tower during an attack on another town. Certainly Shechem *was* demolished in about 1100 BCE, and this is taken to have been done by Abimelech.

The Moabites to the south-east are undone by Ehud. It would appear that they had overrun the Reubenite territory to the east of the Dead Sea and crossed the Jordan into Canaan. Ehud is left-handed, which enables him to get into the presence of the Moabite king without the guards spotting that he has a double-edged stabbing sword under his cloak on his right-hand side. The king is messily assassinated. The fords back over the Jordan are seized by Ehud's forces and ten thousand Moabites are systematically slaughtered (Judg. 3:15–30).

Jephthah, the son of a prostitute, lives in the family home of his father in Gilead until his half-brothers drive him out. He reacts by becoming a bandit chief (Judg. 11:1–3). He is called back to command the Israelite offensive against the Ammonites, who inhabit the desert regions to the east of Gilead. The campaign opens with a diplomatic exchange between Jephthah and the Ammonite king, in which the latter claims that he is only occupying lands which the Israelites took from his people on their way into Canaan. Jephthah's reply has been echoed many times since in similar circumstances: 'While Israel has been inhabiting Heshbon and its dependencies, and Aroer and its dependencies, and all the towns along the Arnon for three hundred years, why have you not tried to recover them all this time?' (Judg. 11:26). When the Ammonite king does not answer, Jephthah goes to war.

The accretion to the story of Jephthah (Judg. 11:30–40), whereby in return for victory he pledges himself to sacrifice 'whatever comes out of the door of my house to meet me' (Judg. 11:31), which turns out to be his daughter and only child, is taken as confirmation that though the practice was forbidden, child sacrifice was still an issue. It also has a ritualistic significance in that in order to prepare herself for death, the daughter and her companions 'went and bewailed her maidenhood upon the hills' for two months (Judg. 11:38). This has been seen to represent the need for a young woman to adjust herself, with the support of her childhood friends, to her forthcoming marriage and to the abrupt change of circumstances and family which this involves. The ritual came to be publicly observed at an annual four-day festival for nubile young women in memory of Jephthah's daughter, which is referred to in Judges 11:39–40.

The Philistines on the south-west coast of Canaan are in Judges a subject primarily of folklore. They are opposed by Shamgar, who slays six hundred of them personally with an oxgoad (Judg. 3:31). Samson goes one better: his score is a thousand, with the jawbone of an ass (Judg. 15:16). Samson is not a leader of men. He is a loner, with a penchant for practical jokes of a destructive kind and an ultimately fatal weakness for Philistine women. Yet it is the Philistines who now, having forced Samson's tribe of Dan to leave their traditional territory and seek new lands in the north, are the major threat to the Israelite tribal confederacy.

THE PHILISTINES

Today a 'Philistine' is someone who is impervious or opposed to culture. The poet–critic Matthew Arnold (1822–88), in *Essays in Criticism* (1865), suggested that its usage in English originally referred to 'a strong, dogged, unenlightened opponent of the chosen people, of the children of the light' ('Essay on Heinrich Heine'). The judgement of history and archaeology is that the latter definition is nearer the truth, without reflecting the full story.

Referred to in the Bible pejoratively as 'uncircumcised' (Judg. 14:3 and elsewhere), which marks them out as non-Semitic strangers to the region, the Philistines were, according to Egyptian sources, one of several groups of Sea People whose incursions came to a climax in about

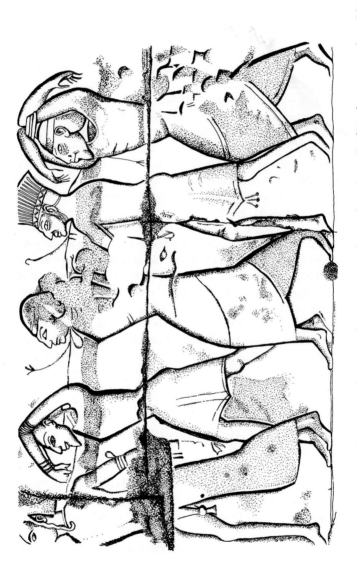

Figure 3 Prisoners of Rameses III, after the land battle in about 1187 BCE, depicted on the wall of his fortress-temple at Medinet Habu: a Libyan, a Syrian, a Hittite, a Philistine, and another Syrian.

1200 BCE. In their distinctive plumed headgear and tasselled tunics, they disembarked on the Syrian coast, and, according to an Egyptian fresco, took their families and belongings into battle with them in two-wheeled ox-carts. They attacked by land, and also by sea, along the coast of Canaan and Egypt, but were repulsed and finally defeated in the eighth year of the reign of Pharaoh Rameses III (c. 1194–c. 1163 BCE), who let the Philistines settle on Canaanite land in return for supervising Egyptian interests there.

The Philistines originally came from the island of Crete, where the general upheavals in the eastern Mediterranean began in about 1400 BCE with the final destruction, by earthquake, volcanic eruption, or invasion, of the magnificent Minoan civilisation. Survivors settled in Cyprus, where they were joined after about 1250 BCE by refugees from the Trojan wars, and by Mycenaeans from the Greek mainland fleeing from the mass invasions of Dorians from the north which finally put an end to their civilisation in about 1200 BCE. The cumulative effect brought the Philistines to the lands of the Levant — Syria, Canaan, Egypt, and Libya. And where many of them ended up, in precisely the area of Canaan which the Bible designates as Philistine territory, there have been considerable finds of decorated pottery, influenced by Mycenaean designs, which dates from this time. Israelite pottery is clumsy in comparison.

The Philistines established themselves in five districts, centred on Ashdod, Ashkelon, Gaza, Gath, and Ekron, of which the first three have been identified. Each district had its own ruler, called a *seren* (plural: *serenim*), under whom was a level of *sarim*, translated as 'commanders' or 'officers'. The people comprised original incomers and their descendants, and native-born Canaanites, whose religious beliefs and practices the Philistines adopted. Their armed forces, which were initially employed in Canaan as Egyptian mercenaries, used chariots (with a driver and two spearmen) and cavalry as well as infantry, who wore upper body armour and usually carried an iron long-sword as well as a spear and round shield. A mobile unit of professional soldiers was available to be despatched to any garrison which was in trouble; the garrisons themselves were augmented by local auxiliaries.

The Philistines' seamanship enabled them in the twelfth and eleventh centuries BCE to rival the sea-coast cities of Phoenicia as traders. Through their military skills and strategies they were able to dominate the southern plains of Canaan and to look to expand their territories into the foothills and mountains, the strongholds of the Israelites. There was no need for the Philistines to divest themselves of Egyptian control. It began to lapse of its own accord after the death of

Rameses III, apparently as a result of a harem plot, when he had ruled for thirty-two years.

At some point in the development from bronze to iron in about 1200 BCE, the Philistines had acquired the necessary knowledge to obtain iron from its ore by heating it, and to forge the metal into formidable instruments of war as well as agricultural implements. Though they did not invent the process, they jealously guarded the copyright from their neighbours. So much so that, according to the Biblical account,

> No smith was to be found in all the land of Israel, for the Philistines were afraid that the Hebrews would make swords or spears. So all the Israelites had to go down to the Philistines to have their plowshares, their mattocks, axes and colters sharpened. The charge for sharpening was a *pim* [two-thirds of a shekel] for plowshares, mattocks, three-pronged forks, and axes, and for setting the goads.
>
> (1 Samuel 13:19–21)

Thus even when the Israelites were concerned just with domestic pursuits, the Philistines still exercised a hold over their daily lives. In battle, the Philistines appeared invincible against the Israelite voluntary tribal levies. The crisis came to a head in about 1050 BCE. According to the Bible, the Israelites, having marched out against the Philistine base camp near Aphek in the ideal chariot terrain of the Plain of Sharon, are routed in a first encounter. They then have the Ark of the Covenant fetched from its sanctuary at Shiloh so that God 'will be present among us and will deliver us from the hands of our enemies' (1 Sam. 4:3). It is carried by two priests whose outrageous behaviour has scandalised the people and shamed their father, the High Priest Eli

Figure 4 (opposite) Sculptured marble panel (57 cm × 35 cm) in the Louvre, emanating from Ashkelon. The central figure, who wears a row of enormous pearls round her neck and her waist, and whose fingers are thrust into the waistband of her narrow skirt, has been identified as Astarte, whose temple at Ashkelon Herodotus in the fifth century BCE described as the oldest dedicated to her anywhere in the ancient world. The grouping suggests a tripartite divinity such as the Babylonian/Assyrian moon trio of Sin, Shamash, and Ishtar. If, as has also been surmised, the panel dates from the Graeco-Roman period, when Ashkelon was an independent, Hellenistic city state with a Jewish community, it illustrates how the worship of pre-Israelite gods was entrenched in the region.

(1 Sam. 2:12–22). Initially the Ark puts fear into the hearts of the Philistines, who then, nettled rather than rattled, inflict a crashing defeat on the Israelites, capture the Ark itself, and kill its attendants (1 Sam. 4:6–11).

How the Ark is eventually restored by the hand of God is the subject of 1 Samuel 5–6. It gives the Philistines nothing but trouble, including outbreaks of vandalism in their holy temple, infestations of mice, and horrendous attacks of piles which afflict 'young and old' and cause 'great panic' (1 Sam. 5:9). After seven months of this, the Philistines voluntarily return the Ark to the nearest point on the border of Israelite territory, together with compensation of five gold mice and five gold haemorrhoids (1 Sam. 6) – symbols of the carriers and the symptoms of the plague.

That Jeremiah 7:12, 'Just go to My place at Shiloh, where I had established My name formerly, and see what I did to it because of the wickedness of My people Israel', refers to the destruction of the sanctuary itself by the Philistines would seem to be confirmed by archaeological evidence and by the fact that Shiloh plays no further part in Israelite history. The Philistines also established garrisons in significant centres, even in the Benjaminite foundation of Gibeah and the strategic Canaanite town of Megiddo.

The Philistines had all the military and moral advantages: the Israelites only had their faith in their God, and even that was at a low ebb. That the Philistines never conquered the whole land was initially due to the vision of one man.

SAMUEL: LEADER AND KING-MAKER

For this period, and until the death of Solomon and the end of the united kingdom of the Israelites in 925 BCE, we have the vividly written texts of I and 2 Samuel and 1 Kings 1–11, which are accepted as largely contemporary accounts.

Samuel means 'asked of God'; his mother prays at Shiloh for his birth and in return dedicates him to the service of God. He is brought up at Shiloh by Eli, the High Priest. While still quite young, he hears the voice of God one night in the sanctuary. When this and further intimations of God's intentions are realised, Samuel is recognised as a prophet (1 Sam. 1–3).

It is presumed that after the Aphek disaster and the destruction of Shiloh, Samuel returned to his home town of Ramah. When he emerges once more into the Biblical account it is as a middle-aged, fully-fledged religious leader, circuit judge, military supremo, and politician. He was not a traditional kind of 'judge' whose leadership was largely temporal and charismatic, but a new form of leader whose spiritual and prophetic guidance embraced political as well as religious issues. The biggest political issue of the time was the inadequacy of the tribal league to present a united front; only by the appointment of a single head of government who would also command the armed forces could the Philistine threat be averted for good.

It is indicative of Samuel's agonising over a step which, if it led to the establishment of a monarchy, would be inimical to Israelite tradition as well as to his own personal status, that there are two conflicting versions in the Bible of how the enigma was eventually resolved. The first, pro-monarchist, account (1 Sam. 9:1 to 10:16; and also 11) is regarded as the earlier. Saul, 'an excellent young man; no one among the Israelites was handsomer than he; he was a head taller than any of the people' (1 Sam. 9:2), has been selected by God to be Samuel's choice of ruler. He comes into the presence of the prophet seeking advice as to the whereabouts of some lost asses, and ends up being secretly anointed king of Israel. He is publicly acclaimed king after mobilising the entire Israelite forces to relieve Jabesh-gilead, whose citizens had been ordered by Ammonite hordes to surrender on particularly humiliating and painful terms, and achieving a stunning victory. 'Samuel said to the people, "Come, let us go to Gilgal and there inaugurate the monarchy." So all the people went to Gilgal, and there at Gilgal they declared Saul king before the Lord. They offered sacrifices of well-being there before the Lord; and Saul and all the men of Israel held a great celebration there' (1 Sam. 11:14–15).

The alternative account (1 Sam. 10:17–27; and also 12) is more pro-democratic. Samuel bows to popular pressure and selects a king for them by lot at a meeting of all the tribes. It turns out to be Saul. 'And all the people acclaimed him, shouting, "Long live the king!" Samuel expounded to the people the rules of monarchy, and recorded them in a document which he deposited before the Lord' (1 Sam. 10:24–25). Chapter 12 constitutes the text of Samuel's address to the Israelites, upholding the supreme authority of God:

> 'Far be it from me to sin against the Lord and refrain from praying for you; and I will continue to instruct you in the practice of what is good and right. Above all you must revere the Lord and serve Him faithfully with all your heart; and consider how grandly He has dealt with you. For if you

persist in your wrongdoing, both you and your king shall be
swept away.'

(1 Samuel 12:23–25)

The establishment of a monarchy was a response to a political situation. Ultimately, however, it was their distinctive religion which
enabled the Israelites to survive.

Map 3 Israel and Judah

3

KINGS AND PROPHECIES

The establishment of the monarchy took place towards the end of the eleventh century BCE. The Israelites now had a king and they had permanent settlements, which in terms of the ancient world at that time qualified them to be a nation. Thus God's promise to Abraham, 'I will make of you a great nation' (Gen. 12:2; see also 18:18), was now on its way to being fulfilled; it was to be further realised by Saul's successor David, who extended the boundaries of his rule to incorporate a small empire. Just as in the 'Augustan Age' of Rome and the 'Elizabethan Age' of Elizabeth I in England the political and cultural achievements of the times inspired a national literature of classic quality and dimensions, so it was with the period of the early monarchy of the Israelites. It is generally accepted that the Israelite national epic in prose which comprises one strand of the Pentateuch was compiled from oral tradition in about 950 BCE by a writer known to us as the 'Yahwist' (J), because of a preference for the use of 'Yahweh' to refer to God – the contribution of the 'Elohist' (E), who generally uses the designation 'Elohim', was written down about a century later. That a Hebrew alphabetical script existed at the time of David's son Solomon is attested by the discovery at Gezer of a tablet of soft limestone in the form of a calendar, inscribed, possibly as a tutorial exercise, with some lines illustrating activities during the farming year and dating from this period.

It was fundamental to the tradition of the Israelites that they were God's chosen people: to the Yahwist, it was natural to describe this in terms also of nationhood, at a time when the Israelites were establishing themselves as prominent in a world in which there were already several other nations, and when their faith was particularly vulnerable to erosion by outside influences. The Elohist picks up the allusion: 'Now then, if you will obey Me faithfully and keep My covenant, you shall be My treasured possession among all the peoples. Indeed, all the earth is Mine, but you shall be to Me a kingdom of priests and a holy nation' (Exod. 19:5–6). This is interpreted to imply not that the Israelites are expected to lead a consecrated, self-contained religious existence, but that they have a mission beyond national boundaries. This mission is recalled, three hundred years later, by the poet of the later books of Isaiah, writing from exile in Babylon, when successive monarchal blunders and failings had reduced the Israelites' fortunes to an all-time nadir:

> For He has said:
> 'It is too little that you should be My servant
> In that I raise up the tribes of Jacob
> And restore the survivors of Israel:
> I will make you a light of nations,
> That My salvation may reach the ends of the earth.'

> (Isaiah 49:6)

SAUL: KING OF THE ISRAELITES

While because of, or perhaps in spite of, the intervention of Samuel, the first Israelite monarchy combined elements of Israelite and counter-Israelite tradition, the status quo was as far as possible maintained. There was no attempt to establish a feudal system such as operated in the city-states of the Canaanites and Philistines. The tribes maintained their identity and organisation. Saul was acclaimed as war leader because of his charisma, in the same way as were the tribal chieftains of the book of Judges. His headquarters at Gibeah was, archaeology reveals, not so much a palace as a rustic fortress. He had no elaborate court, and his harem appeared to comprise just one wife, Ahinoam (1 Sam. 14:50), and one concubine (2 Sam. 3:7), by whom he had two sons (2 Sam. 21:8).

There were no precedents to guide Saul in his civil and administrative duties at a time when industry, agriculture, and economy, as well as warfare, were being revolutionised by the Iron Age, though, from 1 Samuel 14:47–48 and 52, it would appear that he was constantly at war, and from other references that he had little time for anything else but his personal problems. Saul's senior officer was his first cousin Abner (1 Sam. 14:50–51) – he strengthened his army by taking on to a permanent staff any soldier who particularly impressed him (1 Sam. 14:52). In the face of continual trouble from the Philistines and other powers, he was expected to exhibit charismatic quality on the battlefield again and again, and against considerable odds: when he embarked on his campaign to dislodge the Philistines from the fortified base they had established at the strategic position of Michmash, only he and his son Jonathan of all his troops carried iron weapons (1 Sam. 13:22). And he still had to contend with the thundering of Samuel, even after the old man's death.

At first Saul treated Samuel with the greatest respect, in his capacity as the most prominent seer-priest in the land. There are two stories of their falling out. In 1 Samuel 13:8–14, with the Philistines mustering for war, Saul waits for Samuel to come and make the necessary sacrifice, which Samuel has said he will do in a week's time. When, after seven days, there is still no Samuel, and his men begin to drift away, Saul performs the sacrifice himself. In 1 Samuel 15, Samuel instructs Saul to annihilate the Amalekites and destroy all their possessions according to the rules of holy war. When Saul spares Agag, the Amalekite king, and the Israelite troops appropriate for themselves the best of the sheep and oxen, which Saul ingenuously suggests they intend to sacrifice to God, Samuel blows his top. He brushes away Saul's apologies, and personally hacks Agag to death. The breach is absolute: 'Samuel never saw Saul again to the day of his death' (1 Sam. 15:35).

Now Samuel schemed to replace Saul with the young hero David, eighth son of Jesse, from Bethlehem. It was all too much for Saul. The manifestations of his madness, persecution mania, contradictory behaviour, irrational anger, and violent changes of mood between ecstasy and dark despondency, are consistent with the symptoms of what is today recognised as manic depression.

1 Samuel 28 records that when, after Samuel's death, the Philistines menace once again, and Saul is unable to obtain any divine guidance through the normal channels, he secretly seeks the help of a medium at En-dor, though he has himself banned the activities of such people. Reluctantly she conjures up for him the ghost of Samuel, who is as uncompromising from beyond the grave as he was in life. A shocked Saul, who has not eaten for twenty-four hours, is counselled by the woman and his staff to eat a meal which she prepares for him. Then he goes out to meet his fate.

Saul's end is told in 1 Samuel 29–31. David, who has distanced himself from Saul's insane jealousy and hired himself out as a Philistine mercenary, is conveniently sidelined, so that he does not have to fight against his own people. The Israelites' defeat at Mount Gilboa is devastating, and complete. Saul, severely wounded by several arrows, commits suicide on the battlefield. His three sons, including Jonathan, beloved by David, are killed alongside him. The bodies of all four are carried off by the Philistines and impaled on the city wall of Beth-shan, from which they are taken down for burial by the loyal citizens of Jabesh-gilead, who have marched through the night to perform their self-appointed task.

The study of Saul in 1 Samuel is a rounded portrait of a tragic hero. While it is accepted that the events of his reign are historical, there is some confusion as to when they occurred. The Saul who is acclaimed by the people as the king–deliverer of the Israelites is a young man. 1 Samuel 13:1 is unclear about his precise age, but some scholars accept the Hebrew text reading that he reigned for 'two years', arguing that the actual events described do not require any longer time span. Relations between Saul and David, however, suggest a longer period, to allow for the fact that Saul has four sons, of whom at least three are capable of bearing arms (1 Sam. 14:49 and 31:2), and two daughters of marriageable age (1 Sam. 18:17–20), and for Michal, the younger of these, to be married to David and then given by her father to another man after David has acquired two more wives (1 Sam. 25:39–44). Whether he reigned for two years or twenty years, Saul's death in about 1005 BCE left the Israelites effectively at the mercy of the Philistines. It also opened the way for the rise to political power of one of the most talented and romantic figures of the ancient world – the subject of numerous works of art, including paintings by Caravaggio, Pesellino, Raphael, Rembrandt, Rubens and Konrad Witz, sculptures by Donatello, Michelangelo, and Verrocchio, and modern novels by Joseph Heller, Stefan Heym, Dan Jacobson, and Allan Massie.

THE HOUSE OF DAVID

A man like David was bound to attract legends such as those which present him in youth as a giant-killer and a soother of the king's distemper. Though there is nothing inherently impossible about his single-handed destruction of Goliath (1 Sam. 17:12–58), there are dis-crepancies within the story and with the earlier account of David's first playing for Saul (1 Sam. 16:14–23) to suggest that they emanate from a variety of sources. His claims to succeed Saul, however, were impec-cable by the standards of the times. He was divinely designated, he was a member of the royal house through his first marriage, and he had amply demonstrated not only gallantry in battle, but also political cunning. After Saul's behaviour forces him to go over to the Philistine side, he uses his private army of four hundred debtors, dissidents, and desperados to attack enemies of the Israelites (leaving no one alive, in case they should reveal the truth), while maintaining to his Philistine master that he has actually raided the Israelites (1 Sam. 27:8–12). With an eye to the future, he also sends some of the spoil from his raids to the elders of his own tribe of Judah and to other personal supporters of his cause (1 Sam. 30:26–31).

So it was that at Hebron, chief town of the Judaeans, after the deaths of Saul and his sons, 'The men of Judah came and there they anointed David king over the House of Judah' (2 Sam. 2:4). Since the Philistines' victory at Mount Gilboa had effectively given them control of the Israelite settlements in Canaan, this is regarded as having been sanctioned by them. Unfortunately for the Davidists, there was another contender, Ishbosheth (also known as Ishbaal), Saul's fourth son, who was not at the battle at Gilboa. Sponsored by Abner, his cousin and Saul's former army commander, Ishbosheth assumed regal responsibilities from Mahanaim, a position well out of the firing line which was the chief stronghold of the Gadites east of the river Jordan.

The first showdown between the rival sides took place at the pool of Gibeon. The 'pool' itself, excavated in 1956/57, is a cylindrical shaft, cut into the limestone, 37 feet across and 35 feet deep; a spiral staircase with solid balustrade, gouged out of the inside wall, winds down to the mouth of a tunnel which curves to a depth of a further 45 feet and opens into a chamber filled by water from a spring.

The encounter is described in 2 Samuel 2:12–32. The two groups, one on each side of the pool, glare at each other. Then Abner, in charge of Ishbosheth's men, proposes to Joab, David's commander, that they settle the issue with a gladiatorial contest between twelve young Benjaminites, for Ishbosheth and twelve men of Judah. After a drawn encounter in which all twenty-four die simultaneously, general fighting breaks out, with David's men gaining the upper hand.

The final solution to the dispute (2 Sam. 3:6 to 4:12) is a messy one, even by the standards of the times. Abner, by appropriating Saul's concubine for himself, is seen by Ishbosheth to have designs also on Saul's throne. Abner now offers to deliver the rest of Saul's kingdom to David, who readily accepts it on condition that he also gets back Michal, his first wife, thus further strengthening his entitlement to the whole of the kingdom. She is detached from her weeping husband and rejoins David's expanding harem. Abner, who to save himself has reluctantly killed Joab's brother after the affair at the pool of Gibeon, is murdered by Joab in the resulting blood feud. Ishbosheth is assassinated while sleeping by two of his own company commanders, who cut off his head and present it to David. David appears displeased, and has them executed and mutilated, but he is now, at the age of 37 (2 Sam. 5:4–5), undisputed king of all the Israelites, in which capacity he is, as has become customary, publicly accepted and anointed by the elders of the people.

The Philistines, clearly alarmed at this turn of events, make an armed incursion along the Valley of Rephaim, most probably with the intention of cutting the new kingdom in half, but are routed by David and the troops he had garrisoned at Adullam. It says much about the inflexibility of the Philistine character that they try the identical tactics again. This time David ambushes them in the valley from the wooded slopes, takes them in the rear, and pursues them 'from Gibeon all the way to Gezer' (1 Chron. 14:16).

David's subsequent capture of Jerusalem and its establishment as his capital was a political as well as a military masterstroke. Originally occupied by a Hurrian dynasty, it had been since before the Israelite infiltrations into Canaan a stronghold of the Jebusites, who had successfully and apparently with considerable ease resisted all attempts to destroy the city's independence. There are two brief accounts of its fall (2 Sam. 5:6–9 and 1 Chron. 11:4–7), from which it would appear that the crucial attack on the Jebusite stronghold of Zion, led by Joab, was through the rock tunnel under the eastern wall from the Spring Gihon, Jerusalem's main water supply, and then up a 150-foot perpendicular shaft. The Jebusites are taken by surprise, and David affirms his victory by calling the town 'City of David', and consolidates its position by making it the administrative and religious centre of his kingdom.

It is a measure of the piecemeal nature of the Israelite settlement of Canaan that Jerusalem had remained in local hands for so long. Situated on the rocky spine which carried the main north–south route holding the territory together, it had effectively caused the separation of the occupying tribes into a northern and a southern group. To the west, the plains were held by the Philistines. Precipitous cliffs flanked the Dead Sea to the east, while hostile peoples still controlled the lands on the other side of the river Jordan. By settling his capital between the two groups of tribes on land which had never belonged to either, and ensuring free passage between them, David had a kingdom which was now demonstrably as well as theoretically united.

He also raised a professional army of part-time conscripts from the tribes and mercenaries, commanded by career officers. The tribal levies, mobilised at times which did not coincide with the harvest season, were often specialist fighters. In 1 Chronicles 12 there are references to the ambidextrousness of the Benjaminites with bow and sling, the speed over mountainous terrain of the Gadite infantrymen, the intelligence-gathering of the Issacharites, and the versatility of the Zebulunites in using whatever weapons the situation demanded. With troops such as these he finally removed the threat of the Philistines, forcing them out of the plains, back to their coastal region, and into the position of having to pay tribute to him. He defeated the Amalekites right to the borders of Egypt in the south. He subjugated the Moabites, the Edomites, and the Ammonites, thus removing the threat to the Israelite settlers to the east of the river Jordan and also securing a hold on the vital trade route between the Gulf of Aqaba and Arabia, along which passed the riches of the Orient. He extended his empire into Syria, far beyond Dan, with campaigns against Aramaean states and by making Damascus an Israelite garrison city. He concluded a peace treaty with the Phoenician king of Tyre, Hiram (970–935 BCE), who supplied the timber and craftsmen to build David's palace at Jerusalem (2 Sam. 5:11), and he established trade links with the Euphrates region. The surviving Canaanite city-states were made to accept his kingship, which replaced that of their existing rulers, but retained their culture and religious practices. For the time being, the name Israel now denoted a considerable area as well as a significant power.

According to 2 Samuel 5:5, David ruled over all the Israelites for thirty-three years. During this time he established an administrative machinery which, for want of any suitable precedent, seems to have been based on Egyptian practice. He was a constitutional rather than an absolute monarch, who reigned under the auspices of God, and was sensitive to public opinion and to the advice of counsellors such as the prophets Nathan and Gad. Justice was still administered by local judges, but anyone had the right to appeal directly to the king, as the ultimate authority. In 2 Samuel 20:23–26 a number of royal officials are named. These include the commander of the tribal levies (and also commander-in-chief during battle), the commander of the 'Cherethites and the Pelethites' (the king's personal household troops) and probably also of the other mercenaries who fought alongside the tribal levies, the king's herald (that is, his official spokesman), the secretary of state, and the officer in charge of 'forced labor'.

The unfortunate Ammonites, after their defeat, were set to work by David 'with saws, iron threshing boards, and iron axes, or assigned . . . to brickmaking' (2 Sam. 12:31). That forced labour, with its unhappy echoes of slavery in Egypt, was a feature of life at this time for Israelites as well, is suggested by the amount of building and repair work which has been found on the eastern slope of David's Jerusalem, involving the use of enormous, rough-cut stones.

It was probably because of its implications for forced labour, or military service, or taxation, or for all three, that the census of all Israelites, David's most ambitious civil measure, met with such public resentment (2 Sam. 24). Less controversial was his organisation of temple musicians and singers (and also doorkeepers) into guilds (1 Chron. 25). That David was a poet and musician is entrenched in Biblical and non-Biblical tradition: 'With his whole heart he sang hymns of praise, / to show his love for his Maker. / He appointed musicians to stand before the altar / and sing sweet music to the harp' (Ecclesiasticus, also known as 'Wisdom of Ben Sirach', NEB 47:8–9); 'On David We bestowed Our favours. We said: Mountains, and you birds, echo his songs of praise' (Koran 34). That he wrote the elegy for Saul and Jonathan (2 Sam. 1:19–27) and some of the Biblical psalms is incontestable.

Significantly, because it indicates David's intention to link state with faith, and with the old order, his inner council of royal officials included two chief priests. They were Zadok, and Abiathar, who was of the ancient line of Eli, High Priest at the sanctuary at Shiloh, and was the only survivor of Saul's insane massacre of the priestly family for helping David when he was on the run (1 Sam. 21–22). David also retrieved the Ark of the Covenant from the 'house of Abinadab on the hill' (1 Sam. 7:1) in Kiriath-jearim, where it had been kept ever since its return by the Philistines several generations earlier, and had it brought in triumph to his city of Jerusalem, where, after discussion with Nathan, it was installed not in a permanent building but in a portable tabernacle, as was the Israelite tradition. As part of the celebrations, David, dressed, it would appear, only in the most vestigial of priestly garments, 'whirled with all his might before the Lord' (2 Sam. 6:14). His royal consort Michal was duly affronted, and when he returned home raged at him for making an exhibition of himself in front of slavegirls.

> David answered her: 'It was before the Lord who chose me instead of your father and all his family and appointed me ruler over the Lord's people Israel! I will dance before the Lord and dishonor myself even more, and be low in my own esteem; but among the slavegirls that you speak of I will be honored.' So to her dying day Michal daughter of Saul had no children.
>
> (2 Samuel 6:21–23)

Whether David took umbrage at her remarks and declined to sleep with her again, or whether Michal was unable to have children (they had had none up to that time), there is ample evidence of David's potency in other directions. While he was in Hebron, he had six sons, each by a different wife (2 Sam. 3:2–5), of whom Amnon, the eldest, Absalom, the third, and Adonijah, the fourth, were to play leading parts in the machinations of the succession. He had a further eleven sons when he ruled in Jerusalem, not including sons of concubines (1 Chron. 3:5–9). The Bible names only one daughter, Tamar, sister of Absalom. She, too, was caught up in the terrible cycle of events recorded in 2 Samuel 9–20 and 1 Kings 1–2 which is known as the Court History or Succession Narrative.

Central to the narrative is the affair (2 Sam. 11) between David and Bathsheba, a respectable married woman whom he sees having a bath while he is taking the air on the palace roof. Her husband, Uriah the Hittite, is away with the army, serving as a mercenary at the siege of the Ammonite town of Rabbah. David sends for her and seduces her. She becomes pregnant.

While David's subsequent behaviour is even more disgraceful, his actions are not so much those of a despotic ruler as of a ruthless politician: fearful for his reputation, prepared to resort even to murder when his attempt at subterfuge fails, and willing to accept public humiliation when he is found out.

Uriah is brought back, ostensibly for consultation about the military situation, and encouraged to go and sleep with his wife. This he will not do, even after David gets him drunk, because the rules of holy war forbid sexual intercourse during active service. Uriah is returned to duty, unwittingly carrying his own death warrant, a personal order to Joab to get him killed in battle.

What was intended to be the perfect crime, instead brings on the House of David the ultimate curse. Bathsheba is at least now free to become another of David's wives. Their infant son falls desperately ill, and dies when he is only a week old. David's reaction puzzles his courtiers, who ask him why, now the child is dead, he has abandoned his state of mourning. He replies, 'Now that he is dead, why should I fast? Can I bring him back again? I shall go to him, but he will never come back to me' (2 Sam. 12:23). For the first time in the narrative David speaks as a human being, rather than as a scheming politician: the mask has cracked.

Then 'David consoled his wife Bathsheba; he went to her and lay with her. She bore a son and she named him Solomon' (2 Sam. 12:24). The jockeying for the succession now began. There was no precedent to act as a guide; it was simply assumed generally that the heir to the throne of David would be one of his legitimate sons.

The chain of paternal disasters continues in 2 Samuel 13–20, which records also the first bid for the throne. When Amnon, the eldest son, rapes his half-sister Tamar and throws her out into the street, neither David nor her brother Absalom appear to be very keen to do anything about it. Absalom even tells Tamar to pull herself together. He is simply biding his time. Two years later he strikes. Amnon is assassinated and Absalom prudently disappears. It is three years before he returns to Jerusalem, and a further two before he is reconciled with his father. Having first made himself popular with the people, he is now ready to try for the throne itself, which he does with the support of Ahithophel, one of David's most trusted advisers. Absalom proclaims himself king in Hebron, and then, with an army of supporters, marches on Jerusalem. David, surprisingly, panics, and takes flight with his personal guard and other loyal troops, and all his household except ten concubines. Absalom arrives, and on Ahithophel's advice has sexual intercourse with his father's concubines publicly, in a tent specially erected on the palace roof, in order to affirm his right to his father's throne.

The rebellion is put down. Ahithophel, whose military advice has been ignored, hangs himself. Absalom, caught by the hair in the branches of a tree, is ignominiously slaughtered by Joab. This, however, is only the end of the beginning. Further revolts break out, fuelled by political differences between north and south. These too are extinguished by force.

The House of David had now lost its two principal heirs to the throne, and David his two favourite, and, reading between the lines, only favoured sons. He now deals quite ruthlessly with survivors of the line of Saul, which still has its supporters. Once again, the slippery Gibeonites are at the heart of the action. It would appear that at some point 'Saul had tried to wipe them out in his zeal for the people of Israel and Judah' (2 Sam. 21:2). Now, in expiation of the blood guilt, they demand the deaths of seven of Saul's male issue. David spares Mephibosheth, Jonathan's crippled son, but hands over to the Gibeonites Saul's two sons by his concubine, and the five sons of Saul's daughter Merab. 'They impaled them on the mountain before the Lord; all seven of them perished at the same time' (2 Sam. 21:9).

What was at stake for the Israelites themselves was more than just the choice of a temporal ruler. To some the person of the king was a divine manifestation of the cult to which in traditional pagan style they subscribed. Others recognised that a covenant between God and the House of David had been superimposed upon the Mosaic Covenant, guaranteed for generations (2 Sam. 7:11–16 and Psalm 89:4–5). Others maintained the older tradition that the king was as answerable as they were to the strictures of God. Others simply rejected the notion of a dynastic succession altogether.

David was now an old man, so devoid of domestic comforts that his courtiers supplied him with an attractive young virgin simply to warm him up in bed (1 Kings 1:1–4). At the end a pathetic figure, whose human errors had been largely responsible for the personal tragedies which dogged his life, he dithered about the succession, as other potentates have done since. Inevitably, the court was divided. David's eldest surviving son Adonijah, supported by Joab and Abiathar, establishes his entitlement by proclaiming himself king. Nathan rushes to Bathsheba, and urges her to remind the king that he has already promised her that Solomon should succeed. David is persuaded that this is the case. Galvanised by circumstances into making a decision, he has Solomon officially anointed king by Zadok. Solomon is merciful to his half-brother: 'If he behaves worthily, not a hair of his head shall fall to the ground; but if he is caught in any offense, he shall die' (1 Kings 1:52).

David died in about 965 BCE. Especially in the light of subsequent national disasters, later chroniclers and commentators portray David as a great king who presided over a golden age. So much so that a hope was built into Israelite belief that a Messiah, of the line of David, would come and reunite the scattered tribes of Israel and restore Jerusalem to its proper status. 'Messiah' (Hebrew *mashiach*) means 'anointed', and in the Old Testament is applied to someone consecrated in this fashion for a high office such as king, priest, or prophet, or even a non-Israelite such as Cyrus, king of Persia, for whom God has decreed a special function (Isa. 45:1). While there are references in the prophetic books to an ideal human leader who will take in hand the redemption, that is the physical salvation by God, of the Jewish people, the use of the term Messiah for such a person is post-Biblical. The Greek term is *christos* (in English, Christ); in Christian theology redemption refers to the act of Jesus in redeeming mankind from sin by his death.

THE WISDOM OF SOLOMON

The Hebrew word *hochmah* is usually translated as 'wisdom', but especially in the Bible it also means 'skill'. While tradition has attributed human wisdom in abundance to Solomon, it was primarily by political awareness that he furthered his own interests and those of his realm, if not also those of all his people. First, however, it was necessary to secure his position.

The wily Adonijah enlists the help of Bathsheba to intercede with her son for Abishag the Shunammite, David's final but still virginal bedmate, to be given to Adonijah as his wife (1 Kings 2:13–22). Solomon, interpreting this quite rightly as a pitch also for David's throne, has him executed. He then deals summarily with other supporters of Adonijah and Saul.

Now, if the Biblical sequence of events is accepted, still 'a young lad' (1 Kings 3:7), he makes a diplomatic marriage with the daughter of the pharaoh of Egypt, whom he installs in the city of Jerusalem until he has built a palace for her own use. From this, it has been surmised that she was his principal wife, for

> King Solomon loved many foreign women in addition to Pharaoh's daughter – Moabite, Ammonite, Edomite, Phoenician, and Hittite women, from the nations of which the Lord had said to the Israelites, 'None of you shall join [in marriage with] them and none of them shall join you, lest they turn your heart away to follow their gods.' Such Solomon clung to and loved. He had seven hundred royal wives and three hundred concubines.
>
> (1 Kings 11:1–3)

In this, as in much else, Solomon appears to have tended to excess. His building programme, which began in the fourth year of his reign (1 Kings 6:1), was enabled by an ambitious trade alliance with King Hiram of Tyre.

> So Hiram sent word to Solomon: 'I have your message; I will supply all the cedar and cypress logs you require. My servants will bring them down to the sea from the Lebanon; and at the sea I will make them into floats and deliver them to any place that you designate. There I shall break them up for you to carry away. You, in turn, will supply the food I require for my household.'
>
> (1 Kings 5:22–23; AV, NEB 1 Kings 5:8–9)

That was not all. The twenty-year project to build a temple as a permanent house for the Ark of the Covenant, and Solomon's palace complex, involved the employment of Phoenician carpenters and masons and a Phoenician craftsman in bronze. As David, too, had had to call on Hiram for carpenters and masons to build what must have been by comparison a very modest residence indeed, the inference is that the Israelites at this time were not skilled in building techniques. Whether their lack of aptitude in the more decorative arts was due to similar shortcomings or to a literal observance of the first part of the Second Commandment – 'You shall not make for yourself a sculptured image, or any likeness of what is in the heavens above, or on the earth below, or in the waters under the earth' (Exod. 20:4) – there is nothing in archaeology as splendid as the descriptions of the Phoenician-style carvings which adorned the Temple, described in 1 Kings 6.

The outline of the platform on which the Solomonic Temple stood has been traced. Entrance was through a porch at the east end flanked by two bronze standing pillars. Huge double doors of cypress opened into the Great Hall, from which a further flight of steps at the far end gave on to a screen of gold chains. Behind this were the doors of the Shrine, which was a perfect cube, each dimension being 9 metres. The portable Ark of the Covenant, an oblong chest probably of acacia wood, with two carrying-poles slotted into rings at its upper corners, was guarded by two cherubim, one at each side, facing the doors. These human-headed winged beasts, carved out of olive wood, were each 4.5 metres high. Together, their outstretched wings spanned the whole width of the room. An outer buttress wall round the north, west, and south of the Temple contained three storeys of rooms which were probably used for storage and as offices.

The description in 1 Kings 7 of Solomon's palace complex is nothing like as precise, but archaeologists suggest that it was built to the south of the Temple platform on a new site created by Solomon's extension of the city north of David's city wall, and that in design it had affinities with palaces said to have been built by Solomon at Megiddo, Hazor, and Gezer, remains of which have been discovered. It must, however, have been much more extensive than these if it incorporated his hall of judgement, courtyards, a residence for himself, and a palace for his principal wife (1 Kings 7:6–12), and, as would seem logical, administrative offices and possibly accommodation for the rest of his harem. It must also have been much more magnificent: to have his throne, inlaid with carved ivory, covered over then with 'refined gold' (1 Kings 10:18) was sheer pretentiousness.

It was possibly because he was not a fighting man himself that Solomon's military instinct was for defensive rather than offensive measures. Instead of employing a peasant army of part-time infantry, he built up a full-time mobile force of chariots, following the Canaanite tradition. These he stationed at strategic garrison towns throughout his realm, Hazor, Megiddo, Gezer, Lower Beth-horon, Baalath, and Tamar, with a contingent of reserves at Jerusalem. These places had first to be enlarged and fortified. That he also established 'garrison towns, chariot towns, and cavalry towns' (1 Kings 9:19) presupposes the maintenance of some kind of road network for communication and for the movement of troops.

All this building work required a vast labour force. It is true that Solomon was able to call on survivors of the original Amorites, Hittites, Perizzites, Hivites, and Jebusites who had peopled Canaan: these he enslaved (1 Kings 9:20–21). While the Deuteronomistic historian, writing at the end of the monarchal period and from a pro-monarchist perspective, goes on to state that 'he did not reduce any Israelites to slavery' (1 Kings 9:22), it is clear from other references that he resorted to the dreaded corvée, the forced-labour levy of his own people.

> King Solomon imposed forced labor on all Israel; the levy came to 30,000 men. He sent them to Lebanon in shifts of 10,000 a month: they would spend one month in the Lebanon and two months at home. Adoniram was in charge of the forced labor. Solomon also had 70,000 porters and 80,000 quarriers in the hills.
>
> (1 Kings 5:13–14; NEB 4:27–29)

If there was any distinction between slavery and forced labour, it was certainly lost on the Israelites themselves. On Solomon's death festering resentment turned to violence and then to revolution.

An extensive bureaucracy has to be paid for. A standing army had to be maintained, especially under a political system which made no provision for the seizure of booty by conquest, the standard fiscal method in the ancient world. Solomon divided his realm into twelve districts for administration and tax purposes (1 Kings 4), deliberately (no doubt) ensuring where he could that these cut across traditional tribal boundaries, so as further to reduce individual tribal influences. Each district had its own governor, among whose responsibilities was for one month in each year to supply all the provisions for 'the king and his household' (that is, the whole staff in his employment): 'Solomon's daily provisions consisted of 30 *kors* of semolina [*kor* being the largest measure of all], and 60 *kors* of flour, 10 fattened oxen, 20 pasture-fed oxen, and 100 sheep and goats, besides deer and gazelles, roebucks and fatted geese' (1 Kings 5:2–3; NEB 4:22–23). In addition each district in turn supplied all the fodder for the army's horses, which had to be delivered to wherever they were stationed: 12,000 horses had to be provided for. The population of each district has been calculated at around 100,000: that is, on today's figures, roughly that of the district of Stirling in Scotland, only a little more than that of the island of Grenada in the Caribbean, and rather less than that of the Isle of Wight off the south coast of England. There is a suggestion that Judah had its own administration, separate from the rest: thus the concept of a dual if not a divided monarchy persisted.

The opulence of Solomon's table was matched, if not also financed, by the extent and variety of his commercial activities. He built a seaport at Ezion-geber, at the head of the Red Sea, and, with Phoenician help, a fleet of merchant ships; a Phoenician source says that ten were built, from timber which had to be transported there on 8,000 camels. With largely Phoenician crews, these traded with the African coast, from which, once every three years, they returned, 'bearing gold and silver, ivory, apes and peacocks' (1 Kings 10:22). Needing from abroad both horses and chariots to police his realm and its borders, Solomon was forced to import the former from Cilicia in Asia Minor and the latter from Egypt. A chariot cost him 600 shekels of silver, and a horse 150, including delivery charges. He developed these transactions into a profitable international trade, with himself as exclusive agent, through his dealers selling on chariots complete with horses to 'all the kings of the Hittites and the kings of the Arameans' (1 Kings 10:29), who occupied the plains of Syria.

He developed trade links with southern Arabia through the extensive use of camel caravans. The Israelites themselves were not breeders of camels. The traditional donkey caravan was painstakingly slow, as frequent stops for water had to be made which might not be on the direct route. Camels are faster and can each carry a load of up to half a ton. They can go long distances and for several days without water, and can thus take the most direct (and shortest) route – the clichéd term 'ship of the desert' is said to derive from Arabic, in which the same root serves for both a sea and a land transport.

The south-west and southern coastal Arabian kingdoms of Saba (Sheba), Dhofar, and Hadhramaut were, together with Somalia, suppliers of frankincense and myrrh to the ancient world. These products, from the gum resin of trees found only in that particular area, brought in, according to the first-century BCE writer Diodorus Siculus, the greatest return for the lightest weight of goods. Frankincense featured in most offerings to the gods. Myrrh was employed in embalming, and also had numerous applications as a cosmetic – before being regarded

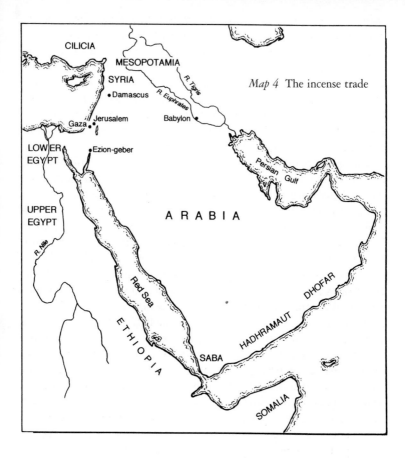

Map 4 The incense trade

as fit for the attentions of King Ahasuerus, Esther is prescribed a course of beauty treatment lasting twelve months, for six of which she was regularly rubbed down with oil of myrrh (Esther 2:12). Both commodities were widely used in medicine.

Several vital trade routes went through Solomon's territory: from Ezion-geber to Gaza, for Egypt overland or other Mediterranean ports by sea, and through Damascus and on to Mesopotamia by the northern route. Even if he did not also demand toll or a commission on the goods which passed through his domains, there was reason enough for a fact-finding state visit by the Queen of Sheba, who 'came to test him with hard questions' (1 Kings 10:1). Her reception was such that 'she was left breathless' (1 Kings 10:5). They exchanged royal gifts, and she got 'everything she wanted and asked for' (1 Kings 10:13). In the light of the practice of statecraft, it is impossible to suppose that the meeting did not conclude with an economic understanding if not a formal treaty. It also may have resulted in something else. It is central to Ethiopian national tradition, written from oral sources into the fourteenth-century saga *Kebra Negast* and enshrined in the revised (1955) state constitution, that the royal line of kings of Ethiopia descended from a son born to Solomon and the Queen of Sheba – certainly there was in about 1000 BCE a wave of Arabian immigration into Ethiopia, which suggests that it may at that time have been incorporated in the realm of Saba. The story reappears in various forms in Christian and Islamic legend, as well as in Jewish writings, in several of which there are references to Solomon, attracted by the queen's general appearance but appalled at her hairiness, inventing a depilatory to resolve the problem.

The Deuteronomistic account of Solomon's achievements, a selection from a lost book of the 'Annals of Solomon' with comment, tends to gloss over or attribute to his senescence the less glorious aspects of Solomon's rule. Urban prosperity for some meant the establishment of class distinctions, and for others rural poverty as well as forced labour. Solomon's massive indebtedness to Tyre brought such cashflow problems that in order to balance the books he was forced to sell, or to mortgage, to Hiram a strip of Israelite territory abutting on Phoenicia, including the twenty towns it contained. Even so, 'when Hiram came from Tyre to inspect the towns that Solomon had given him, he was not pleased with them' (1 Kings 9:12). He did, however, hand over 120 talents of gold as his part of the deal. Hiram seems to have driven a hard bargain, or else Solomon was in desperate financial trouble, for, if the Biblical account is correct in both cases, this is no more than the Queen of Sheba brought to Solomon *as a gift*, in addition to 'a large quantity of spices, and precious stones' (1 Kings 10:10).

Not only did the Israelites, within two generations, have to come to terms with a dynastic monarchy, they were also being asked to accept what was effectively a state religion with the king at its head. Solomon's indulgent attitude to the religious beliefs of his foreign wives did not help: he not only encouraged his wives to observe their own practices, but also built them individual shrines in which they and others could worship as they wished.

The main evidence for Solomon's claim to be the epitome of wisdom, and the patron if not the founder of the 'wisdom' movement in Israelite and Jewish literature as well as thought, is the folk tale of the two prostitutes, each of whom claims that the survivor of two new-born babies is hers. Solomon resolves the apparent impasse by ordering the child to be cut in two, and divided between them. He then awards judgement to the woman who renounces her claim rather than have the infant killed (1 Kings 3:16–27). While his reaction owes more to an appreciation of psychology than to what we understand as wisdom, to the Israelites wisdom was an attribute from God.

Wisdom in the sense of sage and often pithy advice on the conduct of daily life at home and in the community, on education and personal behaviour, and stark warnings against dishonesty, laziness, theft, adultery, arrogance, overindulgence in drink, and other human failings, is the moving force behind the Biblical book of Proverbs. While traditionally it is attributed to Solomon himself, who 'composed three thousand proverbs' (1 Kings 5:12; AV, NEB 4:32), many scholars have concluded that the book in its present form was written down or edited in the time of King Hezekiah of Judah, at the end of the seventh century BCE, and that parts of it, based on Egyptian and Canaanite lore, go back to a time before Solomon. There is no reason, however, why some of the material should not have been composed in the time of Solomon, or even recorded by him or one of his scribes.

Nor is there any doubt that the prosperity of some during the rule of Solomon was responsible for a flowering of literary endeavour. Even if two other Biblical books attributed to him, the philosophical Ecclesiastes and the erotic Song of Songs, are likely to be later additions to the Hebrew canon, and the Apocryphal Wisdom of Solomon to belong to the first century BCE, the Court History of the reign of David, as well as the matchless story of the origins of the Israelites composed by the 'Yahwist' which runs through the Pentateuch, are generally regarded as products of the Solomonic age.

The Deuteronomistic editor gives only a single hint of any internal opposition to Solomon's rule: the potential revolt of Jeroboam, a forced-labour overseer, encouraged by the prophet Ahijah of Shiloh (1 Kings 11:26–40). It proved to be an accurate portent of what was to come. Solomon died in what some scholars are agreed was 926/925 BCE (allowing for the new year being celebrated in the autumn, as it still is in the Jewish calendar). His policies had changed the nature of life for the Israelites and had brought a fragile political structure to breaking point. The united Israelite kingdom had only a few months to run.

DIVIDED ONCE AGAIN

Rehoboam, Solomon's son by an Ammonite wife (1 Kings 14:31), having assumed the throne in Jerusalem, travels to be formally acclaimed by the northern tribes at Shechem, a centre of historic tribal memories. As described in 1 Kings 12:1–24, the ceremony is a disaster. The people ask for a relaxation of the forced-labour laws and more recognition of the original tribal covenant in return for their allegiance. Rehoboam, heeding the advice of young hotheads in his court rather than his older councillors, not only arrogantly refuses but tactlessly sends Adoniram, his forced-labour supremo, to calm things down. Adoniram is stoned to death by the mob. Rehoboam retires to Jerusalem. The northern tribes secede from the union and proclaim Jeroboam ruler of the kingdom of Israel. Rehoboam, advised by the prophet Shemaiah not to resort to civil war, is left in possession just of the kingdom of Judah, with the prickly tribe of Benjamin occupying his vital strip of territory between Jerusalem and the southern border of the kingdom of Israel.

While the peoples of Israel (the northern kingdom is sometimes also referred to in the Bible as Ephraim, after the tribe to which Jeroboam belonged) and Judah retained identical cultures and traditions, the tension between them which had existed since even before the monarchy often flared into open hostility. Until the catastrophes that destroyed both kingdoms, the Israelites of the north and the Israelites of the south went their own political ways. Each kingdom was now much weaker than had been the case under the united monarchy, at a time when neighbouring powers were gathering strength again.

The empire went first. Damascus, which had already seized its independence in the time of Solomon (1 Kings 11:23–25), established a dominance over the Aramaean territories. Ammon and Moab were also lost. In about 920 BCE Sheshonk I, Biblical Shishak, the ruler of Egypt with whom Jeroboam had obtained asylum to avoid the attentions of Solomon, swept through Judah and Israel, capturing, according to an inscription on the wall of the Egyptian temple at Karnak, 156 towns, some of which archaeological evidence confirms he reduced to rubble. He then withdrew to attend to domestic matters, taking with him as tribute many of the holy treasures of Jerusalem. Among these were the solid gold shields of Solomon: it was a sad reflection on the times that these had to be replaced with shields of bronze, which the royal guards solemnly carried from the armoury to the Temple on occasions of state (1 Kings 14:25–28).

Contrary perhaps to expectation, the line of the House of David, with just one technical hiccup, ruled in Judah for as long as the kingdom of Judah itself survived. There was the inevitable dichotomy between the urban aristocracy of Jerusalem and the simple agriculturalists of the rural areas. There was tension between supporters of the pagan religions of the native Canaanites and those of the imported Yahwism. Otherwise the main excitements of the people of Judah in the first 150 years after the death of Solomon were sporadic and unnecessary conflicts with the kingdom of Israel.

In Israel, Jeroboam's immediate problem when he took office was that he had neither an administrative nor a religious centre. He made Shechem his capital, with an alternative residence at Penuel, on the other side of the river Jordan (1 Kings 12:25). He established two shrines, at Dan in the very north of his territory, and Bethel in the south, both places with strong religious traditions. Controversially, he set up in each a golden bull. Though the purpose of these may have been nothing less innocent than to symbolise a pedestal for the invisible God to stand on, in the same way as his enthronement on the Ark and in the Temple in Jerusalem was linked to a pair of cherubim, the Deuteronomistic history, which of course supports the line of David, is virulent about what it regards as a lapse into idolatry. In particular the prophet Ahijah, Jeroboam's original supporter, foresaw total disaster for the 'House of Jeroboam' and for Israel itself (1 Kings 14:14–16).

The line of Jeroboam was duly extinguished when his son Nadab, after not much more than a year's rule, was assassinated by Baasha, of the tribe of Issachar, who then 'struck down all the House of Jeroboam; he did not spare a single soul belonging to Jeroboam until he destroyed it – in accordance with the word that the Lord has spoken through His servant Ahijah' (1 Kings 15:29). Ahijah thus confirmed his place in the historical record, as did the prophet Shemaiah in his warnings to Rehoboam of the imminent descent of Shishak, and Nathan and Gad with David, and before them Samuel with Saul, in the same way as would other courageous prophetic participants in the traumatic events of the times.

PROPHETS AND HISTORY

There were as many different kinds of prophet as the backgrounds from which they emerged. To the Israelites a prophet was a messenger of God, such as was Moses – the description 'prophetess' is also attributed to two notable women leaders, Miriam (Exod. 15:20) and Deborah (Judg. 4:4). In the time of Samuel, bands of musical prophets haunted the high places and drove themselves into states of ecstasy in giving their pronouncements. Later, in the time of Elijah and Elisha, communities of disciples of leading prophets were established around the country. Nathan, Gad, and Shemaiah, as we have seen, acted as court advisers. Cultic prophets, such as Nahum, were attached to particular religious centres as members of the officiating staff. Elijah and his disciple and successor Elisha were the forerunners of a line of non-professional prophets who spoke out fearlessly, interpreting current events in terms of their predictable outcome in words which have come down to us.

Elijah the Tishbite materialised out of the harsh mountainsides of Gilead, in the northern kingdom, in about 860 BCE, as he was to do on other occasions when there was God's work to be done. His forthright style was legendary: 'When Ahab caught sight of Elijah, Ahab said to him, "Is that you, troubler of Israel?"' (1 Kings 18:17). So was his appearance: '"What sort of man was it," [King Ahaziah] asked them, "who came toward you and said these things to you?" "A hairy man," they replied, "with a leather belt tied around his waist." "That's Elijah the Tishbite!" he said' (2 Kings 1:7–8).

Elijah is equally celebrated for his courage, and for his athletic prowess. In 1 Kings 18:20–46, alone he faces, demoralises, and utterly confounds 450 prophets of Baal of the queen's household, whom he proceeds to slaughter, one by one. Then, in the downpour of rain which ends the state of famine which his original appearance presaged, he hitches up the skirts of his robe and runs before Ahab's chariot all the way from Mount Carmel to Jezreel, a distance roughly equivalent to a modern marathon. He finally disappears (2 Kings 2:11–12) even more mysteriously but much more spectacularly than he had arrived, leaving an awesome reputation as the upholder of the ancient religion of the Israelites and the conscience of the king and people alike.

His protegé and successor, Elisha, was the son of quite a well-to-do farmer of Abel-meholah in the valley of the river Jordan (1 Kings 19:19). To judge from the Biblical legends, he had more of the common touch than Elijah in that wonders big and small are attributed to him which illustrate his concern for individuals, such as the 'widow's cruse' (2 Kings 4:1–7), the decontamination of a pot of poisoned stew (2 Kings 4:38–41), and the healing of Naaman, commander of the Syrian army (2 Kings 5). He was also more active in the political arena. Whether or not, as is suggested in 1 Kings 19:15–16, it was the divinely inspired impulse of Elijah to effect a change of rule in Damascus which would cause an Aramaean invasion of the kingdom of Israel, and to foment a bloody revolution in Israel which would bring down the ruling house of Omri, it was Elisha who was responsible for carrying out the plans (2 Kings 8:7–15; 9:1–15). Even on his deathbed Elisha is concerned with affairs of state, as, with a bow and arrows and a touch of the theatricals, he advises the king on his forthcoming conquests (2 Kings 13:14–19).

With Amos, some thirty or so years later, we have the man's own testament, in the form of a collection of dicta compiled either by himself or by his disciples, out of which it is possible to tease a few biographical details. He was a countryman from Tekoa, in Judah, who combined the functions of shepherd on the uplands in winter and spring, with horticulturist on the plains in summer, when the fruit of the sycamore fig (*Ficus sycomorus*) ripens. His preaching is full of images of the fields and vineyards. When he got the call from God while looking after his flock (Amos 7:15), he went to the kingdom of Israel to perform his new task; though the two kingdoms were at regular loggerheads politically, their peoples were still joined by their common heritage and faith. According to rabbinical tradition, Amos shared with Moses either a speech impediment or, what is more likely, a lack of confidence in his ability to express himself spontaneously. This in no way inhibited him, however, when unannounced he began speaking his prophecies of doom in the royal sanctuary at Bethel (Amos 7:10–17), much to the understandable confusion of the chief priest, who sent a warning to the king, Jeroboam II. Jeroboam, whose reign was outwardly a prosperous one, might have done better to heed the prophecies. These are directed against social inequalities, and at a general malaise, diagnosed as unfaithfulness to the Mosaic Covenant, whose outcome would not simply be the destruction of the unrighteous, but of the kingdom of Israel itself.

That Hosea was from the northern kingdom has been deduced from the number of northern place-names he invokes; that he was an educated man is clear from his close understanding of the terms of the Mosaic Covenant. His oracles, delivered a few years after those of Amos, reflect the disturbed, murderous times that duly followed the death of Jeroboam II *c.* 746 BCE, when assassins are 'heated like an oven / and devour their rulers' (Hos. 7:7). They differ from those of Amos, however, in that Hosea offers the hope of an ultimate reconciliation. This is signposted in the course of his opening three chapters, a confessional account of a broken marriage which is ultimately patched up. Through his own bitter experience, he illustrates the relationship between God and the Israelites as a marriage made in the wilderness, a love match destroyed by the wife's unfaithfulness with countless lovers (she becomes a temple prostitute – a clear reference to the espousal of Canaanite religious practices) and finally renewed through repentance and forgiveness.

The eponymous writer whose works are incorporated in the first thirty-nine chapters of the book of the prophet Isaiah is known as Isaiah of Jerusalem or First Isaiah, to distinguish him from the unknown writer or writers of the other twenty-seven chapters; the latter, though composed in a similar intense poetic style, refer to events which happened later and specifically (Isa. 44:28 and 45:1) to Cyrus (557–529 BCE), king of Persia. Isaiah, the first and greatest of the prophets of the kingdom of Judah, describes being called to the prophecy in the Temple of Solomon 'in the year that King Uzziah died' (Isa. 6:1) – Uzziah (also known as Azariah) died in about 742 BCE, having suffered for some years from leprosy. Isaiah was a man of the teeming city of Jerusalem, who throughout times of continuous national crisis walked and talked with kings (and cured their illnesses), advised on matters of state, foreign affairs, and military tactics, openly attacked weak and corrupt government, spoke up for the poor and the oppressed, and vigorously upheld the rule of law and order.

Isaiah was married. His two sons, in the same way as Hosea's children, were given symbolic names: Shear-jashub ('[only] a remnant shall return', that is, repent, or turn to God) and Maher-shalal-hash-baz ('destruction hastens, looting speeds on'), indicating that two cities are to be pillaged in the near future. They turned out to be Aramaean Damascus, and Samaria, since about 880 BCE the capital of the kingdom of Israel, both of which fell to the Assyrians between 732 and 721 BCE. In the narrative portions of the writings, we catch an occasional glimpse of the man himself: taking his young son for a walk and waylaying King Ahaz, who was inspecting the city's water system, in order to speak his mind (Isa. 7:3–4); in protest against a projected alliance with Egypt, going around for three years wearing only the rudimentary mourners' gear of waistband of sackcloth, and sandals (Isa. 20:2–3).

It was political acumen as well as religious faith that inspired his advice to Ahaz. According to the accounts in 2 Kings 16 and Isaiah 7–8, an unlikely military alliance (c. 735 BCE) between the kingdom of Israel and the Aramaeans marches on Jerusalem, planning to replace Ahaz with a puppet king who will join their coalition, and thus also destroy the line of David. Ahaz offers vast bribes to the Assyrians in return for protection, with the inevitable loss of sovereignty that this would entail. Isaiah, seeing a way out of Ahaz's dilemma, wants him to cancel the arrangement and pursue a strategy of masterly inactivity. He is trusting that, with or without divine intervention, Assyria will nevertheless feel threatened enough by the Israel–Aramaean alliance to destroy it, leaving Judah a free agent still. So convinced is he that this is the only course of action, that he tells Ahaz to ask God for any sign that he likes as confirmation. Ahaz, who has already made up his mind, refuses to oblige him. An exasperated

Isaiah nominates his own sign, and then has his pronouncement written down, witnessed, and sealed.

This is part of his testimony:

> Assuredly, my Lord will give you a sign of His own accord!
> Look, the young woman is with child and about to give birth
> to a son. Let her name him Immanuel. (By the time he learns
> to reject the bad and choose the good, people will be feeding
> on curds and honey.) For before the lad knows to reject the
> bad and choose the good, the ground whose two kings you
> dread shall be abandoned.
>
> (Isaiah 7:14–16)

These words have been variously interpreted. Immanuel means 'with us is God'. The Jewish view is basically that before the unborn child has learned to distinguish between wholesome and harmful food, the kingdoms of Israel and Aram will have been destroyed and the threat to Judah removed. The child's name signifies that, unlike Ahaz, his mother believed that God would save the nation. Many Christians, though not necessarily Christian theologians, feel that this and other passages in Isaiah refer to Jesus of Nazareth.

Isaiah regarded the Assyrians as an instrument of the anger of God, which God could withdraw whenever he should choose to do so. Thus when King Hezekiah proposes not only to rebel against the arrangement his father made with the Assyrians, but also to join with Egypt and other powers in attacking Assyria, Isaiah reacts with fury. Not only has Hezekiah entered into 'a covenant with Death' (Isa. 28:15) which is invalid in terms of the precepts of God, but his advisers are drunken incompetents to whom the word of God is simply 'mutter upon mutter, / Murmur upon murmur' (Isa. 28:13).

We can, too, sense Isaiah's determination as well as his confidence in his God when, with the rest of the country in Assyrian hands, and an Assyrian army at the gates of Jerusalem itself, he counsels Hezekiah to resist rather than capitulate. This time his advice is taken. With spectacular results (Isa. 37:36)!

Isaiah enters history on the wings of a dramatic pronouncement: he drops out suddenly, age having done nothing to diminish his powers. There is a legend that when one day he chided Hezekiah for not marrying and having children, the king explained that he did not want to father an evil son. When Isaiah refused to accept this pretext, Hezekiah announced that in that case he would marry Isaiah's

Figure 5 Part of the inscription, reading from right to left in classical Early Hebrew script, from the lintel of a tomb cut out of the rock at Silwan, near ancient Siloam, across the Kidron Valley from Jerusalem. It states that the tomb belongs to the 'royal steward' and that there are no valuables inside, just his bones and those of his maidservant; at the end is a curse against anyone who breaks in. It is believed that the 'royal steward', or master of the palace, referred to is Shebna, who comes in for some personal criticism from Isaiah: 'What have you here, and whom have you here, / That you have hewn out a tomb for yourself here? / O you who have hewn your tomb on high; / O you who have hollowed out for yourself an abode in the cliff!' (Isa. 22:16). Shebna reappears in a different capacity in Isaiah 36:3, as the scribe of Hezekiah who parleys with Sennacherib's general before the walls of Jerusalem. (C. M. Dixon)

own daughter; hopefully such a union would ensure impeccable offspring. The eldest son turned out, unfortunately, to be Manasseh, who according to the legend compounded his wickednesses by accusing his grandfather of false prophecy, and when Isaiah fled and hid in a tree, killed him by having the tree cut down.

Micah, a countryman from Moresheth-gath in western Judah, was a contemporary of Isaiah with an even more uncompromising message. He saw the fall of Samaria and the Assyrian presence in Judah as the prelude to the veritable destruction of Jerusalem, brought about by corrupt administration and even corrupt priests and prophets, and by arrogance:

Yet they rely upon the Lord, saying,
'The Lord is in our midst;
No calamity shall overtake us.'
Assuredly, because of you
Zion shall be plowed as a field,
And Jerusalem shall become heaps of ruins,
And the Temple Mount
A shrine in the woods.

Micah 3:11–12

While there is no evidence for a blood relationship between Isaiah and King Manasseh or for Manasseh's responsibility for Isaiah's death, Manasseh was certainly, according to 2 Kings 21, the worst king ever of either Israel or Judah. Any prophetic rumblings during his reign did not, however, make themselves heard until later, about seventy-five years after the last of Isaiah's pronouncements, in the reign of the godly and charismatic reformer and statesman, Josiah. The prophet Zephaniah, certainly a man of Jerusalem and possibly a descendant of Hezekiah (Zeph. 1:1), foresaw the coming of the 'great day of the Lord' (Zeph. 1:14), 'a day of wrath, a day of trouble and distress . . .' (Zeph. 1:15), when 'the whole land shall be consumed; / For He will make a terrible end / Of all who dwell in the land' (Zeph. 1:18). In the same way as Isaiah, however, he allows for the survival of a 'poor humble folk' who 'shall find refuge in the name of the Lord. The remnant of Israel . . .' (Zeph. 3:12–13). The instrument of God's wrath is no longer the Assyrians, who are about to be destroyed themselves (Zeph. 2:13), but an unnamed power. Thus is God's purpose reflected from time to time in political events.

Though the name of Zephaniah's younger contemporary Jeremiah has passed into the English language as a teller of disaster and doom, it was his fate actually to live through the 'day of wrath' when Judah became extinct, to face up to the apparent inconsistency between the popular conception of Isaiah's assurance of Jerusalem's impregnability and his own conviction of God's purpose, and still to try and justify God's promise of an ultimate future for the faithful few. The gloomy prophet's advice by letter to those exiled to Babylon after the first transportations from Judah in 597 BCE was not to despair or refuse to cooperate with the authorities, but to build houses for themselves, plant gardens, marry, and multiply: 'and seek the welfare of the city . . . and pray to the Lord in its behalf; for in its prosperity you shall prosper' (Jer. 29:7). Alone of all the peoples forcibly transplanted during those grim times, the Judaeans maintained their identity as well as their dignity, and prospered: as Jews have tended to do in similar circumstances ever since.

The Biblical book of Jeremiah contains enough convincing detail positively to link the prophet with events and personalities of the time: in particular the autobiographical portions dictated to Baruch, his secretary, and the biographical sections written by Baruch in the form of vivid cameos, constitute the earliest surviving biographical study by a named writer. For his views, Jeremiah was derided, abused, flogged, imprisoned, dumped into a disused underground cistern, stinking with deep mud, and threatened with death.

Jeremiah 36 records how, when his inflammatory outbursts cause him to be banned from the Temple and to go into hiding, he dictates his pronouncements for Baruch to read out to the people, who are assembled in Jerusalem for a fast day. Baruch's scroll is duly confiscated and read aloud in the presence of King Jehoiakim, who sits warming himself by a charcoal burner. At the end of each section, the king leans over with his penknife and cuts it from the scroll, and then throws it into the flames, until the whole document is consumed. Jeremiah's response is to obtain a fresh scroll, and dictate the whole thing over again, with pointed editorial glosses!

The last stronghold in Judah to fall to the Babylonians before Jerusalem on their second punitive expedition in 588 BCE was the for-tified city of Lachish. A series of military letters, written in ink on potsherds in a language which is effectively the same as the Hebrew of Jeremiah, were discovered on the site in the 1930s. Referring to the current situation, one of them mentions that it is the object of prominent persons to 'weaken the hands' of the garrison and people in Jerusalem by spreading alarm and despondency. Virtually the same words are used of Jeremiah (Jer. 38:4), and this is certainly what he was doing. For his attitude was that it was pointless to fight against God.

According to Jeremiah 27 and 28, when Zedekiah, the last king of Judah, considers joining a rebellion of powers in the region to break the Babylonian stranglehold, Jeremiah walks the streets of Jerusalem wearing a yoke, the symbol of slavery, indicating what will happen to his people if Zedekiah goes ahead. There is a public confrontation in the Temple between Jeremiah and another prophet, Hananiah, during which Hananiah insists that God will 'break the yoke of the king of Babylon' within two years, and all the Judaean exiles of the first trans-portation and the treasures which were taken at the same time would then be returned.

'The prophets who lived before you and me from ancient times prophesied war, disaster, and pestilence against many lands and great kingdoms. So if a prophet prophesies good fortune, then only when the word of the prophet comes true can it be known that the Lord really sent him.'

(Jeremiah 28:8–9)

With that he whips the wooden yoke from Jeremiah's neck and breaks it in two. Jeremiah, unconvinced by this outburst, proceeds to make another yoke, of iron this time, indicating that God's purpose is unbreakable. Wearing his new yoke, he faces Hananiah again.

'Listen, Hananiah! The Lord did not send you, and you have given this people lying assurances. Assuredly, thus saith the Lord: I am going to banish you from off the earth. This year you shall die, for you have urged disloyalty to the Lord.' And the prophet Hananiah died that year, in the seventh month.

(Jeremiah 28:15–16)

Jeremiah lived during the reigns of seven kings of Judah. According to a grotesque legend, he inadvertently impregnated his own daughter when she took a bath in water into which a gang of hooligans had forced him to ejaculate. The resulting child, both his own son and grandson, was supposed to have been Ben Sirach, the second-century BCE sage and author of the Apocryphal book of Ecclesiasticus!

Nothing sums up the man and his perpetual predicament more vividly than the authentic story in Jeremiah 32. During the final days of the siege of Jerusalem, he is imprisoned for making subversive statements. Outside, the situation is not only desperate, but hopeless. Death is abroad in the streets: it 'has climbed through our windows' (Jer. 9:20). 'Little children beg for bread; / None gives them a morsel. / Those who feasted on dainties / Lie famished in the streets; / Those who were reared in purple / Have embraced refuse heaps' (Lam. 4:4–5). And most ghastly of all: 'With their own hands, tenderhearted women / Have cooked their children' (Lam. 4:10).

In an extraordinary demonstration of faith and vision Jeremiah now makes an astonishing decision. At this of all times he will take up the option to buy land left by his recently deceased uncle, so as to keep it in the family. What is more, the deal must be rigorously transacted according to the dictates of the laws of property: 'Take these documents, this deed of purchase, the sealed text and the open one, and put them into an earthen jar, so that they may last a long time. For thus said the Lord of Hosts, the God of Israel: "Houses, fields, and vineyards shall again be purchased in this land"' (Jer. 32:14–15).

Written contracts for the sale of land had long existed in Canaan and in other parts of the region. This is the only one mentioned in the Bible, but the process is described in such detail that the reference has become a significant source of information about the times. Also embodied in the chapter is a text reflecting the omnipotence of God which has stimulated much philosophical discussion: 'Behold I am the Lord, the God of all flesh. Is anything too wondrous for Me?' (Jer. 32:27).

The kingdoms of Israel and Judah

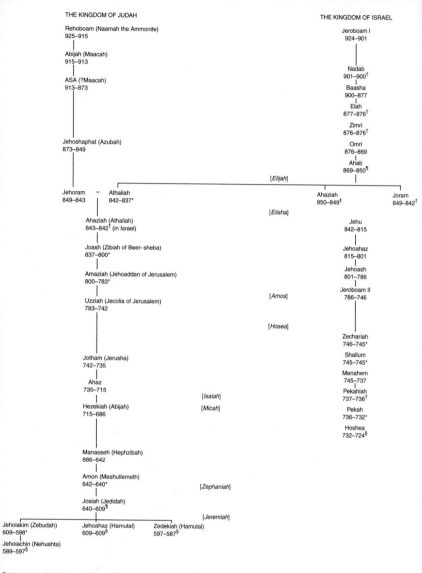

THE KINGDOM OF JUDAH

THE KINGDOM OF ISRAEL

Rehoboam (Naamah the Ammonite)
925–915

Jeroboam I
924–901

Abijah (Maacah)
915–913

ASA (?Maacah)
913–873

Nadab
901–900[†]

Baasha
900–877

Elah
877–876[†]

Zimri
876–876[†]

Jehoshaphat (Azubah)
873–849

Omri
876–869

Ahab
869–850[¶]

[Elijah]

Jehoram = Athaliah
849–843   842–837*

Ahaziah
850–849[‡]

Joram
849–842[†]

[Elisha]

Ahaziah (Athaliah)
843–842[†] (in Israel)

Jehu
842–815

Joash (Zibiah of Beer–sheba)
837–800*

Jehoahaz
815–801

Amaziah (Jehoaddan of Jerusalem)
800–783*

Jehoash
801–786

Uzziah (Jecolia of Jerusalem)
783–742

[Amos]

Jeroboam II
786–746

[Hosea]

Zechariah
746–745*

Jotham (Jerusha)
742–735

Shallum
745–745*

Ahaz
735–715

Menahem
745–737

Pekahiah
737–736[†]

[Isaiah]

Hezekiah (Abijah)
715–686

[Micah]

Pekah
736–732*

Hoshea
732–724[§]

Manasseh (Hephzibah)
686–642

Amon (Meshullemeth)
642–640*

[Zephaniah]

Josiah (Jedidah)
640–609[¶]

[Jeremiah]

Jehoiakim (Zebudah)
609–598*

Jehoahaz (Hamutal)
609–609[§]

Zedekiah (Hamutal)
597–587[§]

Jehoiachin (Nehushta)
589–597[§]

Dates are approximate but are consistent with others cited

(Mother's name)

* Assassinated in palace coup   [†] Assassinated in military coup   [¶] Killed in battle   [‡] Accidental death   [§] Died in captivity

4

THE TWO MONARCHIES

Of the nineteen monarchs who ruled the kingdom of Israel during its two hundred years of separate existence, eight were assassinated, one was killed in battle, one fell to his death, and one died in captivity. The kingdom of Judah had twenty rulers in a tenure that lasted 150 years longer; six were assassinated, one of them, Ahaziah, at the hands of the claimant to the throne of Israel, three died in captivity, and one was killed in battle.

THE KINGDOM OF ISRAEL *c.* 925–721 BCE

Baasha the usurper, having extinguished the 'House of Jeroboam', ruled the kingdom of Israel for some twenty years, after which his son and a further usurper met violent ends in quick succession. From the resulting confusion there emerged, in about 876 BCE, Omri, a man of such apparent stature that even after his dynasty had been brought down with the connivance of Elisha, the Assyrians continued to refer to Israel as the 'land of the House of Omri'.

The Deuteronomistic historians give Omri just six verses in 1 Kings 16, but then he was not of the line of David, he did not worship God in the way they thought he ought to, and they were not particularly interested in what he achieved for his people. However much he did that 'was displeasing to the Lord; he was worse than all who preceded him' (1 Kings 16:25), it would appear from the famous Moabite Stone that this was nothing compared to the displeasure that the Moabite god Chemosh felt for *his* people. This basalt slab, inscribed in a version of the Phoenician alphabet and erected in the middle of the ninth century BCE by Mesha, king of Moab, was discovered in 1868 by a German missionary. The inscription suggests that because of the anger of Chemosh, Omri had some years before been able to recover Moab as

Figure 6 An enigmatic-looking cherub, or sphinx, depicted in a thicket of lotus on a pierced ivory plaque, found at Samaria, and dating from the ninth century BCE. It probably decorated a piece of furniture, maybe in the 'ivory palace' of Omri and Ahab. It is certainly typical of the Phoenician style of art with which Solomon decorated the Temple some eighty years before. (Actual size)

his territory and as a buffer zone against incursions from the south-east; he also exacted useful tribute in kind (2 Kings 3:4).

At some point the capital of the kingdom of Israel was moved from Shechem to Tirzah, another Canaanite foundation about 7 miles to the north-east. Omri bought from its private owner an easily defensible hill (1 Kings 16:24), on which he built a new capital, Samaria, the only major city known to have been established by the Israelites. Archaeological evidence suggests that he abandoned building development at Tirzah in order to concentrate on the construction of an exclusive royal campus on the summit of the hill of Samaria: dwellings for the ordinary populace on the lower slopes are of a later date. The fact that the palace buildings were of stone, rather than the more normal mud-brick, has hindered rather than helped archaeologists – subsequent builders on a mud-brick site tend to use the razed buildings as foundations, while stone buildings are taken apart and the materials reused. It is clear, however, that Omri and his son Ahab had, in addition to living and administrative quarters with extensive courtyards, a pool (referred to in 1 Kings 22:38), and the 'ivory palace' (1 Kings 22:39), whose interior walls and furniture were overlaid with ivory carvings, fragments of some of which survived the Assyrian destruction of the city in 721 BCE and subsequent ravaging and rebuilding on the site.

More contentious was Omri's arrangement of the marriage of Ahab with Jezebel, daughter of the king of Tyre. To Omri, this was no doubt a useful international alliance. To Ahab, a hen-pecked husband who ultimately met a hero's death, and to the people of the kingdom of Israel, Jezebel was big trouble, a woman who did nothing by halves. Having been allowed, as had been the custom since the time of Solomon, to bring her pagan religion with her, and to worship in a temple specially built for her (1 Kings 16:31–33), nothing would satisfy her but to make the cult of Baal-Melqart the official court religion: to this end she imported from home 450 prophets of Baal and 400 of Asherah as part of her personal household (1 Kings 18:19), and organised a pogrom of the prophets of Yahweh (1 Kings 18:4). Her fury, when aroused, even scared Elijah (1 Kings 19:1–3).

The incident of Naboth's vineyard, which, at Jezebel's instigation, was appropriated by Ahab after she had had its owner stoned to death on a trumped-up charge of blasphemy and sedition, earned for Ahab, too, Elijah's implacable hatred (1 Kings 21). Ahab was killed fighting the Aramaeans (1 Kings 22:29–38) in about 850 BCE. His son Ahaziah fell from a window (2 Kings 1) after ruling only a short time, and died of his injuries. He was succeeded by his brother J(eh)oram, during whose reign the successful revolt against Israel took place which is referred to on the Moabite Stone. The combined forces of Israel and Judah who had mustered to put it down were so appalled at the action of King Mesha, when defeat seemed likely, in sacrificing his eldest son, and the heir to his throne, on the city wall as an offering to the Moabite god Chemosh, that they abandoned the campaign (2 Kings 3:27).

Joram also tried to right some of his parents' wrongs by removing pagan cult objects (2 Kings 3:2), but a people's revolution was always on the cards as long as Jezebel, the queen mother, remained alive.

The revolution, in the form of a military coup, was as bloody as it was comprehensive. According to the Biblical account (2 Kings 9–10), Jehu, commander of the army, having been anointed king by an emissary of Elisha on the prophet's instructions, embarks on a killing spree.

Figure 7 The Moabite Stone (2.2 m high) was discovered at Dibon, which features in Numbers, Joshua, Isaiah, and Jeremiah as a significant Moabite city. Fortunately a squeeze was taken of its surface, because Arabs of the locality, recognising its symbolic or its monetary value, broke it into pieces before it could be removed. Some of the fragments were subsequently retrieved and a version of the whole was constructed from the impression of the squeeze. It has been in the Louvre, Paris, since 1873. The inscription, the longest in Moabite so far discovered, and the oldest historical account in a dialect related to Hebrew, has been dated to about 830 BCE. The script is very similar to Early Hebrew. (C. M. Dixon)

Joram, recovering from wounds received in yet another encounter with the Aramaeans, is hunted down and shot – with a stroke of poetic justice, and possibly also with an eye to popular favour, Jehu has the body thrown into Naboth's vineyard. Then, for good measure, he kills King Ahaziah of Judah, the son of Joram's sister, who has come to pay a call on his sick uncle, and, meeting on the road to Samaria forty-two of Ahaziah's relatives, also on a goodwill visit, he slaughters them too. Jezebel, having put on eye make-up and had her hair dressed for the occasion, is at Jehu's command tossed out of the window by a couple of eunuchs, and kicked to death in the courtyard; then her body is torn to pieces. Later, in more calculated fashion, Jehu has all seventy of Ahab's sons decapitated and their heads brought to him in baskets. He completes the extirpation by massacring every single remaining member of Ahab's family and, for good measure, all his officials, and even his friends.

Finally, to justify his claim to be an instrument of divine retribution, Jehu proclaims a national convention of Baal-Melqart worshippers in Jezebel's temple. The place is surrounded by armed guards, who then butcher everyone inside. The sacred pillars are torn out and burned, and the temple itself is razed and turned into a public latrine.

That there had been at this time friendly relations between Israel and Judah is confirmed by the fact that at the battle in which Ahab lost his life, as on the subsequent occasion, which was commemorated on the Moabite Stone, the two kingdoms had formed a military alliance; in addition there had been the political alliance sealed by the marriage of Joram's sister Athaliah to King Jehoram of Judah. Now, as a result of the murder of the king of Judah and the members of his family, and of Jezebel and her priests, and the studied profanation of the Phoenician Baal, the foreign policy of the Omri dynasty was in ruins.

The first crisis for the now weakened kingdom of Israel was instigated by Hazael (c. 842–c. 806), a commoner whose coup against the king of the Aramaeans in Damascus was the other leg of the revolutionary double which the Bible attributes to the engineering of Elisha. The Assyrians, keen to enlarge their empire, posed another threat. The time-honoured tactics, later espoused by Isaiah, of hoping that one threat would eliminate the other, or that both would be too preoccupied with each other to bother about anyone else, failed. We have it from his own account that Shalmaneser III (858–824 BCE), king of Assyria, defeated the Aramaeans in battle, but could not take Damascus, in which Hazael had gone to ground. So Shalmaneser contented himself with uprooting the gardens of the Damascenes outside the city walls, and then marched south as far as the mountains of Hauran, destroying everything in sight. Then he wheeled westwards towards Phoenicia and the coast, presumably cutting a swathe through the northern part of the kingdom of Israel on his way. The inhabitants of Tyre and Sidon were glad to pay him tribute to go away. So was

Jehu: his humiliation before Shalmaneser is recorded pictorially and in writing on the Black Obelisk of Shalmaneser, a standing block of limestone discovered at Nimrud (Biblical Calah) which has been dated precisely to 841 BCE. The Assyrians then withdrew to their own lands, where they were for almost forty years too preoccupied with internal affairs to honour any obligations which they may or may not have owed to Jehu.

Hazael was now free to harass the kingdom of Israel, which he did so thoroughly that the armed forces available to Jehoahaz, Jehu's son and successor, were reduced to nominal figures (2 Kings 13:7). Relief came with a restoration of hostilities between the Assyrians and Aramaeans in about 805 BCE, in the wake of which Jehoash, the son of Jehoahaz, recovered the towns which had been lost to Hazael (2 Kings 13:25). He also soundly thrashed the army of Judah and humiliated its king, Amaziah, who had declared war against a reluctant Jehoash, after hiring mercenaries from the kingdom of Israel for a campaign against the Edomites, and then firing them before the expedition even set out. The disgruntled mercenaries vandalised various Judaean cities on their way home.

With the Assyrians once more attending to internal affairs, Jehoash's son and successor, Jeroboam II, in a forty-year reign, restored relations with Judah and embarked on the most sustained period of prosperity that the kingdom of Israel was ever to have, in the course of which its northern extent, including Damascus and the surrounding area, became roughly what it had been in the time of Solomon. That territorial gains were matched by material affluence is clear from archaeological evidence, especially from Megiddo and Samaria, and confirmed by the graphic allusions of the prophet: 'I will wreck the winter palace / Together with the summer palace; / The ivory palaces shall be demolished, / And the great houses shall be destroyed – declares the Lord' (Amos 3:15). Underlying the illusion of permanent prosperity, however, were the social injustices against which Amos railed, and the insidious pagan practices of the Canaanites referred to by Hosea, to which descendants of the children of Israel were reverting in the mistaken belief that it was Baal who had brought them the good life. Certainly, of the names of individuals in tax records from this period written on sixty-three fragments of pottery found at Samaria, almost half incorporate in some form the word 'Baal'.

The dynasty of Jehu was extinguished, about a hundred years after its establishment, with the assassination of Jeroboam's son Zechariah: he had ruled 'for six months' (2 Kings 15:8). The inevitable anarchy that ensued, from which even a weakened Damascus was able to secede, was no match for a revivified Assyria. The resurgence of Assyria was due to yet another military coup, as a result of which the throne was assumed by an army commander called Pulu (Biblical Pul), who took the name of Tiglath-pileser III (745–731 BCE), after the warrior king of that name who defeated the Babylonians in about 1100 BCE. Having set in train moves to subjugate the peoples of Urartu to the north and Babylonia to the south, and the Medes on his eastern borders, Tiglath-pileser turned his attentions to the kingdoms of the coastal regions to the west.

His policy was simple: pay up or face the consequences. The consequences were the deportation of up to half the population and the resettlement of the land with captives and colonists from elsewhere. Hamath, Damascus, Byblos, Tyre, and the kingdom of Israel duly paid up. Menahem, who had obtained the throne of Israel by murdering his predecessor Shallum, after 'one month' (2 Kings 15:13) in office, and then consolidated his position by committing inhuman acts of brutality against civilian populations of cities which opposed him, extracted the money from his subjects: 'every man of means had to pay fifty shekels of silver' (2 Kings 15:20). Menahem was succeeded by his son Pekahiah, who was killed in a palace coup by Pekah. It was also a political assassination in that Pekah represented a movement within the kingdom which was fomenting opposition to Assyria.

This was the background to the threat to the king of Judah, Ahaz, made by a coalition between the kingdoms of Israel and Damascus, supported also by the Edomites, which Isaiah pressed him to resist. Tiglath-pileser took Ahaz's bribes and then stage by stage embarked on a terrible campaign of retribution against the rebel kingdoms. Ammon, Moab, and Edom caved in. Then Tiglath-pileser moved against Israel 'and captured Ijon, Abel-beth-maacah, Janoah, Kedesh, Hazor [and] Gilead, Galilee, the entire region of Naphtali; and he deported the inhabitants to Assyria' (2 Kings 15:29). Archaeological evidence shows that Hazor, one of Solomon's garrison towns, having been destroyed by King Benhadad I of Damascus in about 885 BCE, was rebuilt shortly afterwards in the time of Ahab as a fortified city twice the original size, with an underground water system entered through a vast vertical shaft. Further changes, more hastily made, date to the period immediately before Tiglath-pileser's strike in 733/732 BCE. The destruction wrought by Tiglath-pileser is clear to see. According to Assyrian records, he also at this time exacted tribute, in the form of gold, silver, camels, spices, precious woods, and clothing, from rulers of cities in Arabia, including a Queen Zabibe. Another Arabian queen, Samsi, who had openly rebelled against him, was

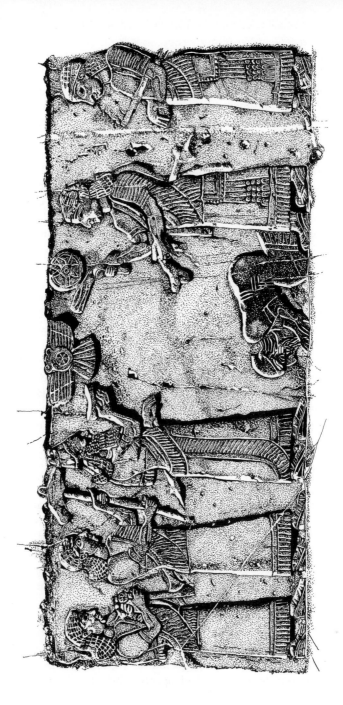

defeated and fled to eastern Arabia; she returned later, submitted to him, and was made to pay extra tribute.

Damascus was systematically destroyed (732 BCE), its king was killed, its territory annexed, and much of its population transported. The kingdom of Israel would have lost everything too had not Hoshea personally assassinated Pekah, seized the throne, and instantly submitted to Tiglath-pileser. The Assyrian king settled governors in the northern parts of the territory which he had overrun, transported key personnel, and diplomatically withdrew. His death, so far from easing the outcome, compounded it. Hoshea, seeing the accession of a new king, Shalmaneser V (727–722 BCE), as his chance to break free, withheld payment of his annual tribute, relying on the support of Egypt if there was any trouble. Shalmaneser correctly called Hoshea's bluff, and attacked. No Egyptian aid materialised. The Assyrians occupied what remained of the kingdom of Israel, except for the city of Samaria, which held out. Hoshea was called into the presence of Shalmaneser or went of his own accord to beg for mercy: either way, he ended up in chains and met an unknown death.

Astonishingly, Samaria held out for three years, until 722/721 BCE. The details of the battle are lost, but it must rank as one of the most heroic defences in the recorded history of the ancient world, even if it were not that only Carthage, besieged by the Romans in 149–146 BCE, held out for so long. The victory went to Shalmaneser, who died suddenly during the siege, but the credit was taken by his successor Sargon II (722–705 BCE). According to Sargon's account, 27,290 Israelites were taken captive to Assyria. Their properties and lands were

Figure 8 (*opposite*) One of the twenty pictorial panels from the four-sided, 2.25-metres-high, Black Obelisk of Shalmaneser III, in the British Museum. It shows the leader of the deputation from the kingdom of Israel, who may be Jehu himself, prostrated before the Assyrian king. He and the thirteen Israelite tribute bearers depicted on the other panels in this tier have on their heads a kind of hat known as a 'Phrygian cap', often worn in north Syria and Asia Minor. A caption inscribed in cuneiform above the panel describes the tribute as including silver, gold, a golden bowl and vase, gold cups and buckets, tin, and a royal sceptre. Shalmaneser is shown with four attendants, one of whom holds a sunshade over him. The two symbols top centre are the winged disc of the sun god Shamash and the star of Ishtar, Babylonian goddess of love and fertility, children of the moon god Sin. The unevenness of some of the carving suggests that stonemasons of varying skills worked on the panel. From the position of the eye, the mouth, and the left foot of the Assyrian on the far right, the sculptor would seem to be attempting a variation on the standard sideways-on figure.

resettled with colonists from 'Babylon, Cuthah, Avva, Hamath, and Sepharvaim' (2 Kings 17:24), who were a mixed bunch of Babylonian and Aramaean prisoners. The kingdom of Israel ceased to exist, even in name: it was now Samaria. The ominous prophecies of Amos, of Hosea, and of Isaiah of Jerusalem had been fulfilled.

THE LOST TEN TRIBES OF ISRAEL: A DIGRESSION

The fate of the members of the ten tribes (traditionally including Simeon) which constituted the kingdom of Israel is suggested in 2 Kings 18:11: 'And the king of Assyria deported the Israelites to Assyria. He settled them in Halah, along the Habor and the River Gozan, and in the towns of Media.' We hear no more about them, but some no doubt were assimilated into the people among whom they settled; others may have been able to retain their identity, and were ultimately joined by further immigrants or moved on with another migration. Certainly the original deportation was not wholesale. We read in 2 Chronicles 34:9 of members of the tribes of Manasseh and Ephraim contributing to King Josiah of Judah's fund for the refurbishment of the Temple at Jerusalem about a century later. Having intermarried with the new colonists, they resurface later as the Jewish sect of the Samaritans, who also called themselves Bene Israel (Children of Israel).

In legend, however, the ten tribes became the Lost Ten Tribes, dispersed far and wide, and a subject of deep speculation in the light of prophecies such as those in Ezekiel 37:16–17 and in the apocalyptic vision of Daniel 12, associating redemption with the reuniting of all the tribes of the Israelites. Thus the medieval world, Christian as well as Jewish, was astounded and fascinated by the revelations in 883 CE, in an open letter to the Jews of Spain from Eldad of the tribe of Dan, that he had located the lot: the tribes of Issachar, Zebulun, Reuben, Ephraim, Manasseh, and Simeon in various parts of Asia, and Naphtali, Gad, Asher, and Dan, together with the Levites, in Africa.

> In the tribe of Dan there is a tradition handed down from father to son that among all the tent dwellers in the land of Israel we were the bravest and mightiest in war. But when, after the death of Solomon, the kingdom of David was divided, we refused to fight against the people of Judah. So we took up our swords and lances and bows and decided instead to go and

fight against Egypt. Finally we were persuaded not to fight, but to march peacefully through Egypt and across the Lower Nile to Ethiopia. It was a fair land, with food and fields and gardens. The people could not stop us living there, because they had originally taken the land by force. They paid tribute to the Israelites, and we lived alongside them for many years, increasing in numbers and getting richer.

After the death of Sennacherib [the son of Sargon] the three tribes of Naphtali, Gad, and Asher, which had been held captive in Assyria, made their own way to Ethiopia, whose border they found after journeying for twenty days with their tents through the desert. These three tribes and the tribe of Dan now live on one side of the river Sambation, and the holy tribe of Levi on the other. The Sambation runs and rumbles with rocks and sand six days a week. Then it is still until the end of the Sabbath. There is a place where the Levites and the people of the four tribes can see each other and shout across. Otherwise, since no journeying is allowed on the Sabbath, when the Levites want anything important, they send messages across by carrier pigeon.

(Eldad the Danite)

Three hundred years later, the indefatigable traveller Benjamin of Tudela (*fl.* 1165–73) reported that the tribes of Dan, Zebulun, Asher, and Naphtali had settled in the mountains of Nishapur, near the border between Iran and Afghanistan. Indeed, many tales circulated in the Middle Ages of marauding bands of fighting Jews in central Asia, which gave much heart to their co-religionists who were facing oppression elsewhere.

An adventurer called David Reubeni (*d.* 1538) appeared in Venice in 1524, having, according to the diary of his travels, come via Ethiopia and Egypt as an emissary of his brother, who was king over three hundred thousand members of the tribes of Gad, Reuben, and Manasseh in the Arabian wilderness.

A crypto-Jewish traveller, Antonio de Montezinos, returned to Europe from South America to announce that in 1641, while exploring the region of the source of the river Amazon near Quito, in what is now Ecuador, he had come across American Indians who were of the tribe of Reuben. He swore affidavits to this. His evidence had an unexpected consequence, for it was taken up by the Dutch–Jewish scholar Manasseh ben Israel (1604–57), and formed the basis of his book, *The Hope of Israel* (1650), published in Hebrew, Spanish, Latin, and

English. In this, following the prophecy in Deuteronomy 28:64 that God would scatter his people 'from one end of the earth to the other', he argued that the Jews were even now scattered over the greater part of the world and that when they were allowed to enter the countries which still refused to admit them, the conditions would be met and the Messiah would appear.

His own hopes were fixed on England, which in medieval Jewish literature is described as *kenaf haaretz*, 'the end of the earth'. The Jews had been expelled from England in 1290 by Edward I. If they were readmitted, Manasseh was convinced that the prophecy would be fulfilled, even if other countries still refused to let them in. The timing was propitious. The Puritan-inspired commonwealth had been instituted by Oliver Cromwell, who ruled as Lord Protector from 1653 to 1658. The Puritans, more than any other Christian sect, regarded the Jews favourably as the ancient people of the Old Testament. Cromwell himself had not only delivered his people from what the Puritans saw as the tyranny of the Stuart monarchy, as his role models Gideon had liberated the Israelites from the desert raiders and in the second century BCE Judas Maccabaeus the Jews from the Syrians, but he was likely to respect the commercial advantages of recognising the skills of the tiny community of crypto-Jews from Spain which actually existed in London at this time.

The ultimate outcome was a testimony to diplomacy and legislation. While Cromwell was unable to get his proposals for the readmission through his council of state, it was established that Jews already in England were free to practise their own religion in private. When war was declared between England and Spain in 1655, and all Spanish property in England was confiscated, the Jews in England, who were still officially Spanish subjects, obtained a further concession, that they could be recognised instead as subjects of the Jewish nation. Now they were at least able to worship openly.

Manasseh died in Holland convinced that his campaign had ultimately failed. Two years after Cromwell's death, Charles II returned to England as king. He and his parliament set about cancelling the laws made by Cromwell's administration. When it came to the position of the Jews, there was nothing to cancel, since all that had been done was to acknowledge their existence. When the Jews asked the king for assurance that they could expect the same protection as his other subjects, the Privy Council issued a written note (22 August 1664) that they could 'promise themselves the effects of the same favour as formerly they have had, soe long as they demeane themselves peaceably & quietly with due obedience to his Majesties Lawes & without scandall to his Government'. Jews now felt free to come to England. It was some time before they had the same rights as other Britons, but then Manasseh had not asked for this. He knew it would be too much.

What of the original order expelling the Jews from England in 1290? Cromwell's lawyers had ruled that as it was a personal act of the king, it only applied to those Jews who were in England at the time. It therefore no longer had any validity.

As the known world grew larger, so tales of the lost tribes became wilder, claims being variously made on behalf of the Japanese, the American Indians, and certain African and Afghan tribes to be descended from one or more of them. The British Israelites, a religious sect some of whose doctrines are accepted by the Mormon church, became a worldwide organisation towards the end of the nineteenth century. They maintained that the British and their racial kinsfolk throughout the world were descended from the lost tribes, and that the Stone of Scone, on which British monarchs are crowned, was the stone on which Jacob rested his head on his journey from Canaan to Haran (Gen. 28:10–18); the latter tradition is reflected also in Celtic mythology, in which the stone is known as Lia Fáil. And as recently as 1973, the Sephardi chief rabbi of Israel issued a religious ruling, based on rabbinic conclusions reached over four hundred years earlier, that the Falasha Jews of Ethiopia were descended from the lost tribe of Dan.

One story which will not go away is that some of the Israelites who escaped being taken into captivity in Assyria in 721 BCE, in about 175 BCE, as a result of further hostile incursions by foreign foes, found their way to Bombay. Their ship was wrecked off shore. Only seven couples managed to swim to land, where their first task was to bury the bodies of their companions that had been washed ashore. The descendants of the survivors increased in numbers, calling themselves Bene Israel. One reason why this legend persists is that there was a considerable Bene Israel community in the area at the end of the eighteenth century, when it began to be joined by Jews from other parts, especially Baghdad. In recent times, Bombay Jews, in the company of those from the once also thriving Jewish communities in Cochin and Calcutta, have been on the move again, emigrating back to their roots in the state of Israel.

THE KINGDOM OF JUDAH *c.* 925–587 BCE

If Israel was a minor kingdom, then Judah, only about one-fifth of its size and one-third of its population, would have been a very minor kingdom indeed, were it not also that because of its mountainous terrain it commanded none of the great military highways, only an alternative trade route to Egypt, and had merely sporadic access to Arabia at times when relations with the Edomites allowed. Indeed, by keeping quiet, as sometimes it succeeded in doing, Judah might be overlooked by the major powers which sought to dominate the ancient world. Its Canaanite population was integrated rather than assimilated. There is little, however, to distinguish the one material culture from the other. Rehoboam and his successors, in common with their counterparts in the northern kingdom, generally pursued a policy of toleration of the indigenous Canaanite religion. This was anathema to the Deuteronomistic historians, in that inevitably there were wholesale defections from Yahwism on the part of those who were confused by the similarities between Canaanite and Yahwist festivals and sacrificial rituals, and tempted by more materialistic and less intellectualised beliefs: 'Judah did what was displeasing to the Lord, and angered Him more than their fathers had done by the sins that they committed. They too built for themselves shrines, pillars, and sacred posts on every high hill and under every leafy tree; there were also male prostitutes in the land. [Judah] imitated all the abhorrent practices of the nations that the Lord had dispossessed before the Israelites' (1 Kings 14:22–24).

Thus even when traditional attitudes prevailed, for example during the reigns of Rehoboam's grandson, Asa, and Asa's son, Jehoshaphat, the pagan 'shrines did not cease to function; the people still sacrificed and offered at the shrines' (1 Kings 22:44). Asa, who according to the conflicting Biblical genealogies could have been either the younger brother or one of the twenty-two sons from fourteen wives of his predecessor Abijah (Abijam), not only 'expelled the male prostitutes from the land, and removed all the idols that his ancestors had made', but dismissed the queen mother from office for erecting 'an abominable thing' to Asherah (1 Kings 15:12–13). His political initiatives were both good and bad news for the Israelites collectively of the northern and southern kingdoms. The armed squabbling between the kingdom of Israel and Judah had escalated to such an extent that King Baasha crossed the border and blockaded Jerusalem from the north. Asa, unable to shift him, appealed (by means of bribes) to King Benhadad of Damascus for help. Benhadad's response was as ingenious as it was effective: instead of marching to relieve Jerusalem, he overran and devastated Baasha's northern territories in Galilee (the occasion of the destruction of Hazor), causing Baasha to withdraw his troops from Judah. The uncertainty that now prevailed brought a sort of uneasy peace between north and south, but the confusion in the kingdom of

Israel was only resolved by the military coup which brought Omri to power.

Relations improved during the reign in Judah of Jehoshaphat: there were military alliances, albeit both unsuccessful, against the Aramaeans and the Moabites, and a political alliance whereby his son Jehoram married Athaliah, the daughter of King Ahab of Israel. There was at least an attempt (1 Kings 22:48–50 and 2 Chron. 20:35–37) at a joint venture between the two kingdoms to reactivate Solomon's seagoing trade from the port of Ezion-geber. There is also more than a suggestion that for a time Judah was subservient to Israel.

According to 2 Chronicles 21, Jehoram's first act as king was to murder all his brothers and senior members of their personal staffs. This sounds to have been at the instigation of his wife, Athaliah, a daughter of Jezebel, a Baal worshipper, a foreigner, and someone for whom regicide had been the means of her family achieving royalty. Be that as it may, Jehoram's own death was lingering, and painful: 'The Lord afflicted him with an incurable disease of the bowels. Some years later, when a period of two years had elapsed, his bowels dropped out because of his disease, and he died a gruesome death' (2 Chron. 21:18–19). Their son Ahaziah was the king of Judah murdered in Israel by Jehu, after a reign of only a few months. Athaliah broke the mould of the Davidic succession by promptly seizing the throne; she then 'killed off all who were of royal stock' (2 Kings 11:1). That is, all except one, for an infant son of Ahaziah, J(eh)oash, was spirited away with his nurse by Jehosheba, Ahaziah's sister and the wife of the High Priest Jehoiada, and hidden in the Temple – presumably in one of the numerous rooms in the buttress walls. The account of Joash's accession in 2 Kings 11 and 2 Chronicles 23 is sheer drama.

After waiting six years, Jehoiada presents Joash to both the on-duty and the off-duty watches of the royal bodyguard, from whom he extracts an oath of allegiance to the boy king. Then, with the approaches to the Temple blocked by guards, and the Temple itself protected inside and out, he produces Joash, and publicly crowns him and anoints him as king. There is wild enthusiasm, and cries of 'Long live the king'. Athaliah, hearing the commotion from the adjoining palace, comes out into the Temple courtyard, and sees Joash standing by the entrance pillar ('as was the custom'), with all the people cheering and blowing trumpets. Frantically crying, 'Treason, treason!', she is hustled out of the Temple precinct and through the horses' entrance of the palace, where she is 'put to the sword'.

It was natural that the long reign of Joash should begin with a reversion to traditional values. 'And Jehoiada solemnized the covenant between the Lord, on the one hand, and the king and the people, on the other – as well as between the king and the people – that they should be the people of the Lord' (2 Kings 11:17). Taking this as an invitation to mob violence, the people destroyed the local temple of Baal and lynched its high priest as he stood in front of the altar. Jehoiada also established a collection box, with a hole in its lid, in the Temple, for donations to the fabric fund; 'Money brought as a guilt offering or as a sin offering was not deposited in the House of the Lord; it went to the priests' (2 Kings 12:17). The money was not in the form of coins, which were not in use in Israel or Judah at this time. Contributors to the fund deposited lumps of silver in the box, according to what they could afford. These were melted down and redistributed in pieces of the appropriate weight.

Surprisingly, perhaps, Joash was one of the four legitimate rulers of Judah to be assassinated in a palace coup. The reason may have been that he had cravenly or diplomatically handed over national treasures to King Hazael of Damascus who, having swept down the west coast and captured the Philistine city of Gath, was threatening Jerusalem while on his way home by another route. It may, as 2 Chronicles 24 records, have also been connected with the suggestion that he ordered Jehoiada's son to be stoned to death for publicly pronouncing God's wrath on those who had abandoned him to 'serve the sacred posts and idols'. Joash was succeeded by his son Amaziah who, once he had assumed the reins of office, had his father's assassins executed, but spared their families. Having reconquered parts of Edom, he tried to incite King Jehoash of Israel to war. That he finally succeeded in doing so was due more to bad management than to military provocation: the result was a disaster both for him and for the city of Jerusalem (2 Chron. 25:5–24; 2 Kings 14:7–14). Subsequently he survived a plot against his life by taking refuge in Lachish. He was pursued there, and assassinated, being succeeded by his sixteen-year-old son Uzziah (also known as Azariah).

In 2 Chronicles 26 and a brief mention in 2 Kings 14:22, a glittering list is recorded of Uzziah's military and social reforms. He reorganised the administration of the army, and ensured that his soldiers were fully equipped 'with shields and spears, and helmets and mail, and bows and slingstones' (2 Chron. 26:14). He also made ingenious defensive devices for cities which either provided additional protection *against* missiles or represent the earliest written record of the use of artillery. He extended the kingdom into Philistia, took the Negeb, and completed the reconquest of Edom, where he rebuilt Elath (Eziongeber) as a trading port and naval base. On the agricultural front, he not only assisted existing farms and vineyards, but opened up arid regions, hewing water cisterns out of the rock and building forts for protection. These developments are confirmed by archaeological evidence. At Ezion-geber, among the ruins of a new town of this period was found a signet ring inscribed 'the property of [or belonging to] Jotham', the name of Uzziah's son; it has been hazarded that it was worn by the area governor. In the Negeb traces of some five hundred agricultural settlements have been discovered, many from the time of Uzziah, and also water cisterns, some of which are still in working order.

Uzziah was king of Judah for a long time. Latterly he fell a victim to leprosy and lived in retreat, with Jotham acting as regent. Jotham appears to have continued his father's expansionist policies at home and abroad, and to have extracted rich tribute in silver and cereals from the Ammonites. It was during Jotham's reign that the ill-fated revolt of the kingdoms of Damascus and Israel against Tiglath-pileser was conceived. Jotham would have none of it. His son and successor Ahaz reaped the consequences: against the advice of Isaiah he renounced the independence of the kingdom of Judah in return for protection from the Assyrians.

Ahaz, who was twenty when he came to the throne, perhaps had no choice: to him, but not to Isaiah, it appeared a case of giving in to the combined forces of Israel and Damascus and losing his throne, or submitting to Assyria. He is condemned also for his apostasy. 2 Kings 16:3–4 is specific about this. Ahaz merits not just the standard charge that 'he sacrificed and made offerings at the shrines, on the hills, and under every leafy tree'. He is brought to book also for child sacrifice: 'He even consigned his son to the fire, in the abhorrent fashion of the nations which the Lord had dispossessed before the Israelites.' Such a man was readily open to other influences. When he went formally to make his submission to Tiglath-pileser at the new provincial centre at Damascus, he was so impressed by, or pressed to show respect to, the altar which had been erected there to the Assyrian gods, that he sent back to Jerusalem a sketch and detailed plan of it, with orders that before he got home a replica should be constructed to replace his private altar in the Temple. When he was later asked what he wanted done with the original altar, he implied that he would think about it (2 Kings 16:15).

For general conditions in Judah at this time, we have the evidence in the prophetic utterances of Isaiah and Micah of dishonesty in public and private life, corruption among the priesthood, oppression of the less well off, debauchery, and unnecessary extravagance; the situation was much the same, if not rather worse, in the kingdom of Israel, as may be inferred from Amos and Hosea. The extinction of Israel occurred during the reign in Judah of Ahaz. That the kingdom of Judah had a temporary extension of its lease of existence was largely due to the reforms, policies, and energy of his son and successor Hezekiah.

Almost alone among those in the direct line of royal descent from David, Hezekiah gets full marks from the Deuteronomistic historians for religious zeal. He cleared the Canaanite shrines of their cult objects. He rededicated the Temple, removing all extraneous objects, including 'the bronze serpent that Moses had made, for until that time the Israelites had been offering sacrifices to it; it was called Nehushtan' (2 Kings 18:4). This purification of Yahwism was also in effect an intensification of nationalism, further fostered by Hezekiah's foreign policy, which included encouraging remnants of the peoples of the former kingdom of Israel not only to worship in Jerusalem but also to settle in Judah. Isaiah was right to urge him not to enter into a pact with the new Ethiopian dynasty in Egypt to foment a revolution against Assyrian domination in the region, for when the crunch came, Egypt backed away. The revolt began, and ended, in Philistia, several of whose cities were virtually wiped out in 712 BCE by the army of Sargon II, and which was then turned into an Assyrian province. The craven Egyptians even handed over to the Assyrians one of the cities' kings, who had sought refuge with them. To be fair, an informed guess as to the military strength of the Assyrians at this time has been made from a tablet found at the main fort at Nimrud, south of Nineveh, which lists the number of bowmen available for duty as 36,242. The total garrison has been estimated at up to a hundred thousand active personnel. Somehow Judah survived by not being deeply implicated after all.

Sargon died in battle in 705 BCE in a campaign away from home, and was succeeded by his son Sennacherib (705–681 BCE). This was the signal for a further, more widespread, and better-organised international revolt, instigated by Marduk-apal-iddina (Biblical Merodach-baladan), ruler of Babylonia, who despatched envoys to drum up support from all the other nations under Assyrian control, including Judah (2 Kings 20:12ff.). Against the advice of Isaiah, Hezekiah signed up not just as a participant, but as a principal. According to 2 Kings 18:8 he used force to encourage recalcitrant Philistine cities to join in; Sennacherib's own records reveal that the pro-Assyrian king of Ekron was deposed by his subjects, who objected to paying tribute, and handed over to Hezekiah, who imprisoned him in Jerusalem. The conspirators then withheld their allegiance to Assyria by refusing to pay up their dues.

While awaiting the inevitable retaliation, Hezekiah attended to the defences of his country, and particularly of Jerusalem. In addition to strengthening the walls, he initiated an astonishing feat of civil engineering to bring the main source of water at the Spring Gihon nearer to the city's inhabitants in the event of siege, by tunnelling 533 metres through solid rock. The inscription in stone, written in classical Hebrew prose and mounted inside the tunnel's entrance at the Pool of Siloam to celebrate its completion, hints at the excitement as the two gangs of labourers with their iron-headed picks, one working from each end, finally met, having been able to hear each other call during the last few hectic metres, but does less than justice to the achievement. To meet at all was a miracle, since the tunnel, which at one end is five metres high and is in places twenty metres below the surface, is not straight, but takes a meandering course.

Sennacherib first dealt with the Mesopotamian rebels. Then it was the turn of the rest. In 703 BCE he swept south along the Mediterranean coast. Tyre was obliterated. At Ekron, an Egyptian relief force was given the shortest of shrifts. Byron's image, 'The Assyrian came down like the wolf on the fold' ('The Destruction of Sennacherib'), is consistent with the Biblical and Assyrian accounts of what happened next, but there is some confusion as to the precise timing of events. The bare fact of Sennacherib's seizure of the fortified towns in Judah is recorded in 2 Kings 18:13–14: the sheer speed of the operation is reflected in Isaiah 10:28–32. Even the key fortress city of Lachish fell to the onslaught. In 701 BCE Hezekiah bowed to the inevitable, surrendered, and was made to pay punitive and exemplary compensation to his conqueror, in addition to the former statutory tribute.

For all this, there is graphic confirmation in Assyrian records of the time. The siege of Lachish is depicted on a frieze from Sennacherib's palace at Nineveh: the extent of the destruction is clear from Lachish, where a refuse pit was found also to contain the remains of 1,500 bodies in the form of singed bones and decapitated skeletons. Sennacherib's own account of the campaign, inscribed in cuneiform on a hexagonal clay cylinder, refers to his taking of forty-six cities of Judah, an unspecified number of walled forts, and numerous villages. As booty of war, he took '200,150 people, young and old, male and female, horses, mules, donkeys, camels, big and small cattle beyond counting'. As for Hezekiah, 'Himself I made a prisoner in Jerusalem, his royal residence, like a bird in a cage.' The gold and silver (to make up which required stripping the Temple), the precious stones, treasures of all kinds, and other commodities demanded from the kingdom of Judah were delivered to Nineveh by Hezekiah's personal representative, who was then required to become Sennacherib's slave. The consignment included some of Hezekiah's own daughters, it would seem as concubines.

The next stage of the operation is attributed in the Bible (2 Kings 18:19–37 and 19:1–36; also Isaiah 36, 37) to the same campaign. From Lachish Sennacherib sends an army right up to the walls of Jerusalem, where his representative demands to parley with the king. Hezekiah sends his palace major domo, his personal secretary, and a scribe, who, when the Assyrian starts laying down his conditions in Hebrew, beg him to speak instead in Aramaic, which was now the language of international diplomacy, so that those watching from the walls will not understand. This he flatly refuses to do, addressing himself directly to the people, warning them of the folly of resistance. Hezekiah, in despair, sends a deputation to Isaiah to ask for his advice, with the message: 'This day is a day of distress, of chastisement, and of disgrace.' There follows a vivid metaphor: 'The babes have reached the birthstool, but the strength to give birth is lacking' (2 Kings 19:3), indicating that the situation is desperate and he is helpless to do anything about it. Surprisingly, because hitherto he has always counselled caution, Isaiah recommends outright defiance. Equally surprisingly, because Hezekiah has never accepted his advice before, on this occasion he takes it.

'That night an angel of the Lord went out and struck down one hundred and eighty-five thousand in the Assyrian camp, and the following morning they were all dead corpses' (2 Kings 19:35). That the Assyrian army withdrew because of an epidemic (bubonic plague or a form of bacillary dysentery) in its ranks is perfectly feasible, especially in the light of the city's ability to hold out with its new water supply. So is the possibility that the actual cause of the withdrawal was a crisis on the Babylonian front which demanded the immediate presence back home of Sennacherib and his armies. Neither of these hypotheses, however, is consistent with Sennacherib having just accepted massive tribute in return for not attacking Jerusalem. This has led some critics to suggest that the Biblical account of failure of the siege of Jerusalem refers to a subsequent campaign, as much as ten years later, possibly as a result of a frustrated, or simply impoverished, Hezekiah failing to pay his dues. There is nothing in surviving Assyrian records of the times which approximates to any national setback, but then there probably wouldn't be, would there? There is, however, in the fifth-century BCE Greek historian Herodotus (II. 141), a reference, repeated by Josephus (*Antiquities of the Jews* X. 1. iv), to an unexpected defeat of Sennacherib at Pelusium, on the coast commanding entrance to Egypt, which was due to a different kind of providential disaster: a plague of field-mice, who gnawed through the Assyrian bowstrings and leather shield-straps.

Whatever happened, and whenever it happened, though Judah was devastated, Jerusalem was spared, and Hezekiah, unlike other kings in the region who had participated in the conspiracy, held on to his throne, which passed to his son Manasseh on his death soon afterwards. Sennacherib was assassinated in 681 BCE by two of his sons, but was succeeded by their younger brother, Esarhaddon (680–669 BCE), who returned from Babylonia, of which he was governor, to avenge his father's death.

Manasseh, who apparently reigned for longer than any other king of either Judah or Israel, continued the foreign policy of subservience to Assyria, while at home shocking conservative Yahwists with the intensity of his active encouragement of, as well as participation in, pagan cults, including the sacrifice of his own children, necromancy, and other mediumistic measures. While he died presumably in his bed, his 22-year-old son Amon was assassinated in a palace coup after ruling for just two years. 'But the people of the land put to death all who had conspired against King Amon, and the people of the land made his son Josiah king in his stead' (2 Kings 21:24).

Josiah was then eight years old. Whether the 'people of the land' were those who wanted independence from Assyria or a return to traditional Yahwism, Josiah's eventual nationalistic and religious reforms catered for the aspirations of both parties. Where Hezekiah had tried to purify the religion of his people by removing Assyrian and other influences, Josiah went much further. In the eighteenth year of his reign, when work had already begun on refurbishing the Temple, he sent Shaphan, his secretary, to supervise payments from Jehoiada's fabric fund which were due to the workmen and for materials. The High Priest showed Shaphan 'a scroll of the Teaching' (2 Kings 22:8), which had come to light during the repairs. The document was authenticated by the prophetess Huldah, wife of the keeper of the royal wardrobe, and read out aloud by Josiah from beginning to end to the people, assembled at the Temple. They in their turn, in a ceremony reminiscent of Joshua's covenant-making at Shechem almost six hundred years earlier, swore to uphold its decrees.

The scroll, which appears to have been a version of parts of the Mosaic law which are to be found particularly in chapters 12 to 26 of the book of Deuteronomy, galvanised Josiah into initiating, and the people accepting, a radical rethink of the national religion. Paganism, whether Canaanite, Assyrian, Ammonite, or whatever, was effectively abolished, and all material traces of its worship destroyed. Josiah's most fundamental measure, however, was to deconsecrate all local shrines, thereby putting out of business their attendant priests, and to centralise the worship of Yahweh at the Temple in Jerusalem. To emphasise and to celebrate the exercise of this policy, the festival of Passover, which had not been observed by the Israelites since before the days recorded in the book of Judges, was re-established as an annual event.

Most significantly, Josiah made a further assertion of national independence by extending his cleaning-up operations into the Assyrian-held former kingdom of Israel. It was thus ironic that he should meet his death in about 609 BCE at the pass of Megiddo, fighting to prevent an Egyptian army marching to the assistance of an Assyrian empire which was already collapsing under pressure from Babylonia.

Josiah's body was put in a chariot and brought to Jerusalem for burial. In a demonstration of democratic principles, the people passed over Josiah's untrustworthy eldest son Eliakim for Eliakim's younger half-brother Jehoahaz, whom they anointed king. Three months later Jehoahaz was summoned to meet Neco II (609–593 BCE), pharaoh of Egypt, at the latter's temporary headquarters at Riblah, north of Damascus. Neco, having broken through into Assyria after the battle at Megiddo, and found that the Babylonians had now established themselves as the new masters in the region, had decided to lay his hands on whatever lands and power he could while the going was good. He formally deposed Jehoahaz, who had presumably refused to submit to Neco's authority, and sent him a prisoner to Egypt, appointing Eliakim (now to be named Jehoiakim) king of Judah in his place. The final flicker of Judaean independence had been snuffed out.

Jehoiakim was nothing if not resourceful. He paid vast tribute in silver and gold, which he acquired by imposing a land tax on his subjects (2 Kings 23:35). At the same time, as Jeremiah 22:13–14 implies, he was using forced labour to build himself a luxurious palace, the remains of which are believed with sound reasons to be those of the building unearthed at Ramat Rahel, on a mountain ridge a few miles south of Jerusalem.

In 605 BCE, at Carchemish, Nebuchadnezzar II (605–562 BCE), heir apparent to the throne of Babylonia, finally unseated the Egyptians from what had formerly been Assyrian territory, and sent Neco packing. Dealing with the kingdom of Judah then had to wait while Nebuchadnezzar returned to Babylon to assume the throne on the death of his ailing father. The campaign was resumed at the end of 604 BCE with the destruction of Ashkelon in Philistia. Jehoiakim prudently signed on as a Babylonian vassal. Three years later, after Egypt and Babylonia had fought a bloody but indecisive battle on the Egyptian

Figure 9 The Holy of Holies in the Israelite temple at Arad, uncovered in 1964. The temple, which incorporates a court (with wash basin), altar, and sanctuary, beyond which is the Holy of Holies, is believed to have been constructed at the time of Solomon. If so, it could have been one of those 'shrines and altars Hezekiah did away with, telling Judah and Jerusalem, "You must worship only at this altar in Jerusalem"' (2 Kings 18:22), and would have been put completely out of commission by Josiah in the course of his religious reforms. Raised above the stone floor of the sanctuary by three steps, on the second of which the entrance is flanked by two stone incense altars, the niche contains two standing stones, or *masseboth* (singular: *massebah*). These cult objects, like the commemorative stones Jacob erected on his way to Haran (Gen. 28:18) and Joshua at Shechem (Josh. 24:26–27), were symbols of the divine presence, as probably also were the pillars which stood before the entrance to the Temple of Solomon in Jerusalem. (Richard Stoneman)

frontier, causing Nebuchadnezzar's army to withdraw home to recuperate, Jehoiakim imprudently withheld his tribute. Nebuchadnezzar's hold on the region was such that he did not need to march until he had time to work Judah over properly. In the meantime he harried the kingdom at long distance by sending in contingents of Babylonian, Aramaean, Moabite, and Ammonite commandos. While this was going on Jehoiakim died, most probably at the hands of members of his own court hoping for preferential treatment from the Babylonians. His eighteen-year-old son Jehoiachin had been nominally on the throne for just three months when in 597 BCE Nebuchadnezzar himself arrived at the gates of Jerusalem.

Jehoiachin, his mother, and the senior members of his court and of his army surrendered, and were packed off to Babylon, together with other key civil and military personnel and skilled workers. Temple and palace were stripped of everything of value. Surprisingly perhaps, we do hear something more of Jehoiachin, both in the Bible and in Babylonian records. Ration lists on tablets found in a palace storeroom and dating to around 592 BCE refer to a monthly allocation of oil to Jehoiachin 'and his sons'. 2 Kings 25:27–30 reports that when Jehoiachin was about fifty-five, King Evil-merodach, who was Nebuchadnezzar's successor, released him from prison and treated him with respect and kindness, giving him regular supplies of food and, according to AV and NEB, an allowance out of the royal purse.

Having also removed from Jerusalem all the anti-Babylonian elements, Nebuchadnezzar appointed as king Mattaniah, Jehoiachin's 21-year-old uncle, full brother to Jehoahaz, and had him renamed Zedekiah. From the references to him in the book of Jeremiah, Zedekiah comes over as a pleasant and kindly man, ready to ask for and listen to advice, but often not courageous enough to take it or discriminating enough about the reliability of its source. He was finally persuaded or panicked into renouncing his allegiance to Babylonia, presumably by the time-honoured method of failing to pay his dues. The massed forces of the Babylonian army duly materialised in Judah in 588 BCE. Finally, only the fortress cities of Azekah and Lachish, and Jerusalem itself, remained.

There is a graphic reference to the military situation in the letters discovered at Lachish. An outpost reports that it can no longer see the fire signals from Azekah and is now watching for those from Lachish! Jerusalem was surrounded, and held out for eighteen months (Jer. 39:1–2), with a temporary reprieve when the Egyptians finally came to someone's aid, but were predictably and summarily repulsed. This action coincided with a revealing sequence of events within the city, reflected in Jeremiah 34.

Zedekiah, wishing to avert the wrath of God which Jeremiah has promised will be visited upon the city and its occupants, invokes Mosaic law on the release from enslavement after seven years for members of their own race (Deut. 15:12ff.), a provision which had fallen into disuse: 'everyone should free his Hebrew slaves, both male and female, and that no one should keep his fellow Judean enslaved' (Jer. 34:9). It is not stated, but it may be implied, that people were pleased to do this, because it meant fewer mouths for them to feed at a time of great shortage. 'But afterward they turned about and brought back the men and women they had set free, and forced them into slavery again' (Jer. 34:11), that is when things looked up for a time.

With the Egyptian relief force disposed of, the siege resumed in earnest. Conditions inside the walls deteriorated. Finally, the wall was breached. As the Babylonians surged into the city, Zedekiah tried to get away, but was pursued and caught before he could cross the river Jordan. There was some sort of trial. His children were killed in front of him. Then his eyes were put out and he was transported to Babylon in chains.

Jerusalem was razed and put to the torch. Certain leading military, administrative, and religious officials, 'and sixty of the common people who were inside the city' (2 Kings 25:19), were rounded up, taken to Riblah, where Nebucchadnezzar was holding court, and executed. All the rest of the principal survivors were exiled to Babylon: all, that is, except apparently Jeremiah, who was released from the dungeon to which his forebodings had caused him to be consigned, given an allowance of food, and set free to join the remaining people of Judah, who were resettled in the fertile plain around Mizpah. These, 'some of the poorest people who owned nothing', were given 'vineyards and fields' (Jer. 39:10). Appointed by Nebuchadnezzar in charge of this pathetic remnant was Gedaliah, a former member of Zedekiah's cabinet, who managed to build up a small agricultural colony, which included survivors from outlying parts of the countryside and returning refugees who had sought safety outside Judah. Then came the final bloodbath. Gedaliah, his garrison of Babylonian guards, his Judaean associates, and a party of holy men who happened by on their way to make offerings at the ruined Temple in Jerusalem, were massacred by a distant scion of the House of David. Terrified of reprisals from Babylon, the surviving Judaeans fled to Egypt, taking with them an unwilling Jeremiah.

5

THE ISRAELITES: SOCIETY, CULTURE, RELIGION

The Israelites who settled in Canaan and ultimately made of the land two kingdoms were originally of semi-nomadic stock. They came out of the desert bringing patterns of society and codes of behaviour which are common among such peoples: tribal organisation, the defence of territorial rights, conventions of hospitality and of family ties. Above all they brought their unique faith, forged and confirmed under desert conditions, with its relevance to the conduct of family and daily life. As incomers, they were also influenced by the practices and habits and basic skills of the peoples among whom they settled.

The Israelites were and remained primarily an agricultural people, rearing and keeping cattle, sheep, and goats, and growing cereal crops and a variety of vegetables and fruit. Where necessary, from early times they stored water in cisterns hewed out of the rock below ground level, some of which they lined with plaster. They lived in villages, in flat-roofed houses built to, and arranged in, a recognisable pattern, such as survived into monarchic times. Centralised government, and the demands of a national economy, and of international trade as well as of international warfare, seem not so much to have disturbed this model as to have created an urban as well as a rural dichotomy between rich and poor.

FAMILY LIFE

The family unit, in its extended form, was a microcosm of a male-dominated society, but though the laws that governed family life were written by men, at least there were laws, and the status of a woman at various stages of her development was respected if restricted. The father was the head of a self-supporting household which could include his own father, his uncles, his brothers, his sons, and his grandsons, with their childbearing consorts. The family included also workers who lived on the premises, slaves, widows and orphans, guests, and 'strangers'. These strangers appear to have been aliens who were resident by virtue of being immigrants from other lands, or residents who were regarded as aliens because they were not Israelites. The latter class included former inhabitants of the land who had not intermarried with Israelites or converted to Yahwism. They were still technically free citizens, subject to the same laws and penalties as the Israelites; they were to observe the laws of cleanliness, the Sabbath, and the Day of Atonement fast, and could participate in other religious rituals, including, provided they are circumcised, the festival of Passover.

The head of the family had absolute power over the household, but he also had the responsibility of protecting and providing for its members, for managing its land, employing workers, negotiating marriages and other settlements, and acting as host to those who sought hospitality.

Arranged marriages were the norm, but there is no reason to suggest that there was no place also for romance, or that a loving as well as a socially desirable relationship was a rarity, any more than it is today among cultures which still favour the practice. While the list of forbidden degrees of marriage, such as that in Leviticus 18, is in line with modern legislation, it was not always so among the Israelites. Abraham's wife Sarah is also his half-sister (Gen. 20:12), and thus when in Egypt he passes her off as his sister for reasons of personal security (Gen. 12:10–20), he is not dissembling, merely being economical with the truth. Endogenous marriages between close cousins were encouraged especially where the heads of the two households were brothers. This is reflected in the genuine delight at the outcome of his assignment expressed by Abraham's servant in Genesis 24. Despatched back to the ancestral homeland with a small string of camels to find a wife for Abraham's son Isaac, the beautiful maiden he happens upon is the granddaughter of Abraham's brother. She is also a paragon of hardworking womanhood; she has just voluntarily watered at the trough by the spring all ten of his camels – a thirsty camel can drink at one time 28 gallons of water, which she presumably had to carry from spring to trough in her household jar.

Israelite society was theoretically polygamous, and remained so at least until the Middle Ages, but in practice the acquisition of an additional wife, or additional wives, was most likely to be undertaken for reasons of expediency or international politics. In any case, as a bride price had to be found on each occasion, it was a prerogative of the rich, or, such as in the case of Jacob, who worked off the cost of two wives over fourteen years with his own hands (Gen. 29:1–30), the very industrious. Opinions differ as to whether the bride price was a cash purchase or compensation for the loss of a daughter's services: either way it constituted a bond between the families. Under a law in Deuteronomy 25:5–10 known as the levirate, where two or more brothers belonged to the same household and one died childless, one of the other brothers was required to take on the widow as his wife; the first son of this mating was regarded for legal purposes as the child of the dead man. If the surviving brother refused the office, he was haled before the town elders, where the widow tore off one of his sandals, spat in his face, and publicly declared that he was unworthy.

Once the bride price had been paid, the couple were regarded as being formally engaged, and the fiancé, if conscripted for army service, was excused battle, 'lest he die . . . and another marry her' (Deut. 20:7). If an engaged woman was raped in a built-up area, both she and her assailant were to be stoned to death, she on the grounds that if she had called for help, she would have been saved. If the assault took place out in the country, only the man was to die. If the victim was not engaged, the man must pay her father fifty shekels of silver and marry her; in which case he could never divorce her.

The marriage ceremony itself was a civil affair. That there was some form of written document may be assumed – detailed marriage contracts on papyrus, written between 459 and 440 BCE, survive from Elephantine on the river Nile, where there was a Jewish colony of mercenaries and their families. The occasion brought forth 'the sound of mirth and gladness, the voice of bridegroom and bride' (Jer. 16:9). There were processions and music and singing, and a feast which could go on for a week or even a fortnight. It would appear, however, that the marriage was consummated on the first night, and that the bride did not remove her veil until then: thus it was possible for Laban to deceive Jacob by substituting his elder daughter Leah for Rachel (Gen. 29:21–27). The blood-stained evidence was kept by the bride's family in the event of the husband ever claiming that she was not a virgin at the time. 'In such a case, the girl's father and mother . . . shall spread out the cloth before the elders of the town [at the gate]' (Deut. 23:15–17).

Whatever the legal position of the wife and whatever authority she possessed in the home, a woman's vestigial legal rights were subsumed within a system in which she was regarded as a commodity, essential to the smooth functioning and regeneration of the community, but a commodity nevertheless. A wife could be disposed of by her husband writing out and handing to her a 'bill of divorcement' (Deut. 24:1), and though she had no redress she could at least remarry. A wife had no rights of inheritance, though daughters could inherit a man's estate if he had no son. No formal commitment made by a woman was valid unless it was endorsed by her father or, if she was married, by her husband. Though a man might sell his daughter as a slave, he could not sell his wife.

A mother could expect, however, the same respect from her children, and by inference from other members of the household, as was due to the father. Proverbs 31:10–31 is a dazzling catalogue of the qualities and also responsibilities of a good wife. The wife of the head of the family was a kind of chief executive, herself performing a wide range of domestic tasks at the same time as supervising the supply and maintenance of food and other consumables, marketing her own produce, and dealing with the minutiae of daily life, while managing her own as well as others' pregnancies and births, and being the resident childcare expert and teacher of basic morality and tribal traditions. Help and advice before the birth, and sometimes before intercourse, and during and after birth was given by professional midwives. Circumcision was performed on boys on the eighth day after birth by the father, with a flint knife.

It was the mother who usually named the child, as Bathsheba named Solomon (2 Sam. 12:24). It was hoped that children with names of animals or, more rarely, plants would reflect the positive characteristics of their namesake. Most common were names associated with God, such as Michael ('Who is like God?') or Nathan ('He has given', shortened from Nathanyahu, 'Yahweh has given'), or with qualities, such as Rebecca ('Captivating beauty') or Naomi ('Pleasant'). At some point the education of boys passed to the father: 'My son, heed the discipline of your father, / And do not forsake the instruction of your mother' (Prov. 1:8). The mother also gave the child its initial training and education, and introduction to stories: 'Her mouth is full of wisdom, / Her tongue with kindly teaching' (Prov. 31:26). Genesis 2–3 are examples of texts which have been identified as belonging to the oral tradition; in Israelite literature the oral and written traditions developed alongside each other, so much so that Moses is believed to have received on Mount Sinai not just the written Torah, but an elaboration of it known as the oral Torah. The oral Torah was not allowed to be written down, and according to one tradition this was only done when Roman persecution threatened to destroy the scholars who were perpetuating its teaching.

The father was responsible for his children's religious education.

From references in Jeremiah 6 and Zechariah 8, it is clear that young children played, and older children congregated, in the streets and other public places. Sons were taught the skills or trades of their fathers, daughters the responsibilities of motherhood: thus were the cycles of the survival of society maintained in the ancient world, and until modern times.

The writer of Psalm 90, which is attributed to Moses, nominates seventy or even eighty as a normal old age, representing an enormous span of life by the standards of the ancient world. According to a Jewish tradition of the second century CE, recorded in *Avot* (Ethics of the Fathers) 5. 21, there are fourteen (as opposed to the Shakespearean seven) ages of mankind, ranging from five to a hundred years old – since Moses himself is said (Deut. 34:7) to have died at 120, it is customary, when someone says how old they are, to respond, 'May you live to 120.'

Death among the Israelites was an occasion for the ritual expression of grief, such as was also observed at times of national disaster. Clothes were torn (it is still the custom among Orthodox Jews for the nearest relative to make a rip in their outer garment), and then replaced by a vestigial piece of sackcloth. Mourners debased themselves by covering their heads with earth or ashes, or even lying in the ashes. There are suggestions that while mourning, people were not allowed to wash. At the funeral itself, the basic cries of grief were stark: mourners exclaimed 'as sadly as the jackals, / As mournfully as the ostriches' (Micah 1:8). The address was a formal lament, like that of David for Saul and Jonathan, but composed for the occasion from a variety of stock texts, and sung by male and female professional singers. It would appear from Jeremiah 9:17–19 that daughters followed their mothers into the profession of public lamentation. The occasion was strictly secular. Priests were forbidden to risk defilement by association with a corpse, except when it was of an especially close relative – today, in Orthodox Jewish circles, a Cohen (a lay functionary who is by tradition a descendant of the priestly Aaron, brother of Moses) must keep as far away as possible from the coffin when attending a funeral of anyone to whom he is not closely related.

Coffins were not used among the Israelites. The dead were buried fully clothed in single or communal graves, or in a burial cave or a tomb, accompanied by various offerings, which might be in the form of pottery vessels or other objects. Such a burial allowed the shade of the dead soul to have an existence in the underworld of Sheol, and, by a later tradition, for the bones to be available for resurrection after the Messiah has restored the Israelites to their proper land.

HOUSE AND HOME

The tents of the original Israelites were of black goatskin, supported by guy ropes pegged or staked into the ground. They might be divided by hangings into two or more rooms; women and guests sometimes had separate tents. In later times tents were used by herdsmen and by the army on active service. The ascetic Israelite sect, the Rechabites, who were strictly teetotal and did not own property or cultivate the fields, maintained the ancient tradition by living in tents away from urban areas. Claiming descent from Jonadab, son of Rechab, who was Jehu's travelling companion when the surviving kin of Ahab were slaughtered, they were still active in their way of life in the time of Jeremiah 250 years later.

The houses of the Israelites were simple affairs of mud bricks and wood, on solid foundations of stones or broken rock, with flat roofs of clay on brushwood, reached by an outside ladder or staircase and maintained by periodic flattening with a cylindrical stone roller. The roof was an excellent place to dry the washing, to congregate in the cool of the evening, and to converse with your neighbours across the narrow street. That safety precautions were required is attested by Deuteronomy 22:8: 'When you build a new house, you shall make a parapet for your roof, so that you do not bring bloodguilt on your house if anyone should fall from it.' Cooking would have been done as far as possible out of doors, because of the smoke from the fire. Animals bedded down with the humans or, in larger houses, which might also have an upper floor, were stabled behind a line of pillars down each side. Beds were only for special guests. Thus when the rich woman of Shunem prepares to have Elisha as a periodic lodger, she puts in his room 'a bed, a table, a chair and a lampstand' (2 Kings 4:10). Normal seating was the floor or a stone ledge along an inside wall of the house, such as was used by Saul and leading members of his household (1 Sam. 20:25). There is archaeological evidence that some rural houses had individual underground water cisterns, dug out of the rock.

Town houses for the rich were suitably palatial and were sometimes built round a courtyard. Poorer citizens lived in separate quarters of the town in standardised boxes, crammed together. Problems were heat, cold, winter rains, insects, and dirt.

Biblical homilies about cleanliness, however, are not confined to the spiritual implications of the term. Indeed the scholarly rabbis whose contributions to the exegesis of the Torah, collected between about 400 and 500 CE, comprise the Talmud, interpret references in Leviticus 11 to include also things which are naturally distasteful, such as unwashed bodies, dirty platters, and putrescent food, as well as the eating of flesh which may be objectionable for other reasons. The soothing and cleansing of feet by bathing them on entering a tent or house was a tradition with a practical application when the standard footwear was a simple sandal and roads, where they existed, were thick with dust or mud. Built-in washbasins have been discovered, notably one at Debir in what was probably an official guest-house. Later tradition prescribes the washing of one's hands before a meal, before praying, on getting out of bed, after being in the vicinity of a corpse, and after going to the lavatory. It probably derives from the time of Hillel, the first-century BCE philosopher and religious teacher, who, when asked by his disciples where he was off to, replied, 'To perform a religious duty.' 'Where?' they asked. 'In the bath-house,' he said. 'Is that a religious duty?' 'Yes, indeed,' replied the sage, as he strode purposefully on his way. 'If the statues of the emperors of Rome are regularly washed to keep them clean, how much more important is it that a human being, created in the image of God, should wash and keep clean.'

That housewives in Biblical times concerned themselves with the supply of soap, possibly in liquid form, is suggested in the Bible itself: 'The stain of your sin is still there and I see it, though you wash with soda and do not stint the soap' (NEB Jer. 2:22).

The detailed instructions in Deuteronomy 23:13–14 about dealing with the end product of bodily functions while on active service suggest that similar care was exercised around the home.

Isolation and subsequent re-examination of the patient are prescribed in Leviticus 13 for cases of suspected leprosy and related diseases, with cleansing or incineration of any of their clothing which may be infected. Whatever the extent of scientific knowledge at the time, the Old Testament contains references to fifty or so different medical conditions. We know less about attempts to cure them, though Isaiah successfully prescribed a fig poultice for Hezekiah, who was dangerously ill with a rash, or a boil, or possibly an ulcer (2 Kings 20:1–7).

Some of the dietary laws which derive from Leviticus 11 and Deuteronomy 14:3–21 may have some basis in terms of ancient standards of hygiene or have been born of practical experience. The injunction against pork in all its manifestations may go back to nomadic times in that unlike cattle, sheep, and goats, which are among the kosher (that is, fit or permitted) animals which have cloven hooves and chew the cud, pigs cannot be herded for long distances and, if they are, they become too muscular to eat. Another tradition is that the pig is especially liable to contract scabies. The wisdom of not eating any animal, bird, or fish which has died a natural death is self-evident. To eat only the flesh of animals and birds which have been ritually slaughtered to allow as much blood as possible to drain away and then treated by soaking in water and salting to remove blood that remains, has a religious significance: 'For the life of the flesh is in the blood, and I have assigned it to you for making expiation for your lives upon the altar; it is the blood, as life, that effects expiation. Therefore I say to the Israelite people: No person among you shall partake of blood' (Lev. 17:11–12). When all is said and done, while self-discipline in eating can generate self-discipline in other things, and rules made by God can bring one nearer to God, those who are careful about what they eat tend to be more healthy than those who are not, for which the particular fecundity of the Jewish people at the time of the early Roman empire in the first and second centuries CE has been cited as evidence.

The diet of the ordinary people tended to be simple anyway: bread in various forms, porridge, bits of fowl or fish (meat was generally eaten only as part of a sacrificial ritual), a form of cheese, vegetables of many kinds, and fresh and dried fruit, with milk and wine to drink. Spiced food was probably a prerogative of the rich.

Clothing was simple, too. The basic garment was a long- or short-sleeved ankle-length tunic of wool or linen: Deuteronomy 22:10 specifically forbids the wearing of cloth which is a mixture of the two. Linen was obviously superior, to judge from Samson's wager with the Philistines involving 'thirty linen tunics and thirty sets of clothing' (Judg. 14:12–13). It might be of more than one colour, as was Joseph's in Genesis 37 (though the meaning may be embroidered or ornamented). The tunic was belted, which enabled its skirt to be tucked up for working or running – alternative working or military dress was a short loin-cloth or kilt, secured by a belt. Apart from sandals, the only additional wear was the cloak or mantle, a blanket-like garment which in the case of women could be drawn over the head. This cloak, as vital to the Israelite as was the plaid to the Scottish Highlander, was used also as a rug for sitting on and as bedclothes at night. Its significance in daily life was such that it was forbidden to take a widow's cloak in pawn; if it was taken from anyone else as a pledge, it must be returned by nightfall (Deut. 24:13, 17). One of the earliest letters which has been found, written in ink on a piece of pottery and dating from the reign in Judah of Josiah (c. 640–c. 609 BCE), is a plea for justice to someone in authority about a cloak which, in front of witnesses, a named culprit has taken, whether justifiably or not, and failed to return. There must have been some clear distinction between men's and women's clothing, because cross-dressing by either sex is specifically forbidden (Deut. 22:5). Both men and women usually kept their hair long. Men went bearded and when not bareheaded wore turbans; women wore head-cloths.

AGRICULTURE AND INDUSTRY

Local politics and law were controlled by elders of the village or town, such as those convened by Boaz in Ruth 4 to resolve a case which involved both property rights and the levirate. So, the husband of the wife in Proverbs 31 'is prominent in the gates, / As he sits among the elders of the land' (Prov. 31:23). Elders of a town sat at the town gates: elders in rural districts met on the threshing-floor on the outskirts of the village. Both venues were symbolic as well as practical meeting-places, in that they represented a frontier between the settled order of things within the town or village and the supposed chaos outside.

The common threshing-floor was also the focal point of village activity during the spring, when first the barley and then the wheat were reaped backbreakingly with an iron sickle, gathered into sheaves, and taken by donkey or in carts to be threshed underfoot by oxen driven round the floor or by means of a threshing sledge dragged by oxen. The grain was then tossed into the air with a shovel to allow the wind to blow away the straw and chaff, passed through a wooden sieve with a leather mesh, and then stored in jars or in underground silos.

Hillsides were terraced and cleared of scrub and stones to take the fruitful vines that gave the grapes; these were trodden in a winepress to make wine, or eaten fresh or dried in the sun to make raisins. Psalms 104:14–15 refers to the making of 'wine that cheers the hearts of men, / oil that makes the face to shine', as well as 'bread that sustains man's life'. The rubbing on of olive oil as a cosmetic was just one of several uses of the pressing of this versatile fruit. It was also employed for cooking, lighting, ritual anointing, and in religious offerings; it was applied to 'bruises, and welts, and festering sores' (Isa. 1:6); it was eaten, when mixed with unleavened bread to make a rich cake, or spread on unleavened wafers. Another multi-purpose fruit was the fig, eaten fresh or dried, and used, by Isaiah at least, as a poultice. There was also a poor people's fig, the fruit of the local sycamore fig tree, which grew on the plains; it was this that the prophet Amos tended in the interval betweeen helping with the herding. The almond and other nut trees were cultivated for their fruits. The palm trees mentioned in the Bible presumably provided fruit, in the form of dates, as well as shade, as would have done what AV translates as mulberry trees. Pomegranates were widely appreciated for their fruit and also for their luscious, refreshing juice.

'Fair Zion is left / Like a booth in a vineyard, / Like a hut in a cucumber field, / Like a city beleaguered' (Isa. 1:8). The booth, a temporary shelter of poles and thatch, still retains its significance in Jewish tradition as a symbol of the protection God gave to the Israelites in the wilderness years. Here the watchman had his post, a protection against the sun and rain while he guarded the ripening grapes against thieves and marauding animals. In the same way the custodian of the cucumber field operated from a hut. The cucumber is one of the vegetables cited with longing by the Israelites in the wilderness (Num. 11:5), together with leeks, onions, garlic, and also melons, and though it is the only one of these to be mentioned elsewhere in the Old Testament, it is reasonable to assume that the others too were grown by the Israelites of later times, and were included because the writers of the account in Numbers were familiar with them. There are several references to the cultivation by the Israelites of beans and lentils, and one (Eccles. 12:5) to the caper.

Farming was a communal occupation, in which everyone in the village helped each other. Some farmers also kept sheep, goats, and cattle, from which they got milk, wool, and meat. There were those who prospered by supplying the rich with what sounds suspiciously like veal: 'They lie on ivory beds, / Lolling on their couches, / Feasting on lambs from the flock / And on calves from the stalls' (Amos 6:4). It was not uncommon for such an animal to be kept for a special occasion, such as Saul's visit to the medium: 'The woman had a stall-fed calf in the house; she hastily slaughtered it' (1 Sam. 28:24).

Where herding was a separate operation, the herders still depended on farmers to supply the land for grazing, fodder for the animals, and fresh water. Herding contracts on tablets recovered from the Late Bronze Age (*c.* 1500–*c.* 1250 BCE) Mesopotamian city of Nuzi suggest that a standard herd consisted of about twenty-six sheep and twelve goats. This mixture provided economic grazing, since goats only eat the leaves of grass, while sheep devour the entire plant, and profitable breeding, and made the best use of wool and goat hair, meat, and milk products.

While there were state industries involved in the king's building programmes and in enhancing his households, urban industriousness was in the hands of individual craftsmen, who tended to live and work in a particular part of the town: bakers, barbers, carpenters, dyers, fullers, goldsmiths, metal workers, potters, stonemasons, weavers.

Goods were sold direct to members of the local public in the market square or at the city gates, where farmers and peasants also displayed their animals and produce for sale. There was virtually no merchant class: trading on a big scale was the province of foreigners, or of the king.

SLAVES AND LABOUR

The employment of Israelite forced labour by Solomon for his extensive building programme is described in I Kings 5 and attested by the existence at least in his and his son Rehoboam's reigns of a minister in charge of it. Twenty or so years later Asa 'mustered all Judah, with no exemptions' (I Kings 15:22) to lift the stones and timber with which King Baasha of Israel had blockaded Jerusalem and use them to fortify Geba and Mizpah. Whether Hezekiah used volunteer or conscripted Israelite workmen to hack the underground water tunnel through the rock while awaiting the inevitable Assyrian siege of Jerusalem, or whether it was slave labour, is not clear, but the upbeat tone of the celebratory inscription would suggest that they were native Israelites. Certainly the necessary skills, learned perhaps from the indigenous Canaanites, would have been developed from the cutting out of the rock of underground cisterns and silos.

It is equally certain that, as was common practice in the ancient world, prisoners of war comprised a state force of slaves to do heavy work. Whatever the conditions of these particular unfortunates, laws governed the treatment of private slaves obtained by conquest, or purchase, or in lieu of a debt, of which the injunction in the Fourth Commandment that slaves too shall rest on the Sabbath is the first. Admittedly, if an ox which is known to be dangerous gores an adult or child to death, both animal and owner are killed; if the victim is a slave, the animal is still killed, but its owner simply pays thirty shekels of silver to the slave's proprietor. It is a criminal offence to beat a male or female slave to death, but not if the slave lives for a day or two; this is because, as the law adds ingenuously, the slave 'is the other's property' (Exod. 21:20–21). If a man has designs on a female prisoner captured in war, she must remain in his house for a month, wearing her ordinary clothes, not prisoner's dress, and trim her hair and cut her nails, after which he can have her as his wife. When she has served her purpose, she must be let go absolutely. 'You must not sell her for money; since you had your will of her, you must not enslave her' (Deut. 21:14).

Israelites were allowed to buy and deal in foreign slaves or slaves who were children of resident aliens. Israelites who became slaves through poverty or debt, or convicted thieves unable to make restitu-　tion, were subject to special treatment. If they were in the service of a resident alien, they could be redeemed at any time by a member of their own family, or could redeem themselves if they could afford to do so. It was in any case the law that after six years a debt was written off. While it appears that an Israelite debt slave could be sold on to another owner, after six years he had not only to be freed, but provided for 'out of the flock, threshing floor, and vat' (Deut. 15:14). If he was married when he became a slave, then his wife was to be freed too. If his owner supplied the wife, then she and any children remained the property of the owner. If in this, or any other circumstance, the slave opted to stay, then he had to remain in the service of that household for life.

SOLDIERS AND SOLDIERING

Notwithstanding the political insight and grasp of military strategy attributed to David, the defensive tactics of Solomon in retaining the empire that David had carved out, and the practical experience gained from these activities, the collective survival of the Israelites had little to do with military expertise at least until the second century BCE. Especially allowing for the statutory exaggeration and inconsistency of military reportage of the region in that period, it would appear that only against peoples less endowed with organisational skills, or against each other, did they have any long-term success in battle. Certainly, when matched against the Philistines in open conflict, the result could be disaster, as is reflected in 1 Samuel 4:1–2 and 31:1–7.

In the period covered by Judges, the individual tribal levies oper-ated as private armies, in the same way as did later the American Indian tribes and the Scottish Highland clans. Saul was able to muster anyway what passed for a national call-up against the Amalekites and the Philistines, ill-armed as it seems to have been. He later established a permanent corps of picked men. David employed mercenaries, including Philistines, as his household guard and also to bolster the tribal levies. The basis of Solomon's permanent military defences were his chariots, which because of their disposition would largely have become part of the army of the kingdom of Israel. The two-horse chariots of the time were light and highly manoeuvrable, with spoked wheels of bent wood, and carried a crew of two, of which one seems to have been the driver and shield-bearer, and the other the bowman.

According to the account of the Assyrian king, Shalmaneser III, Ahab contributed two thousand chariots (in addition to ten thousand foot) to an unsuccessful military alliance against him in about 853 BCE. By the end of the ninth century BCE, the chariots of the kingdom of Israel had been reduced, by Hazael, king of the Aramaeans in Damascus, to just ten. The Israelites did not use mounted men, except as scouts or dispatch riders. Thus, a century later, Sennacherib's representative can publicly taunt the kingdom of Judah: 'Come now, make this wager with my master, the king of Assyria: I'll give you two thousand horses if you can produce riders to mount them' (2 Kings 18:23).

Peasant armies in the ancient world, and in subsequent eras, fought when the harvest had been gathered in. The service of tribal levies according to clan relationships was still standard practice in the kingdom of Judah in the time of Jehoshaphat (2 Chron. 17:13–18), but a century or so later, under Amaziah, conscripts seem to have been redistributed into a more coherent force (2 Chron. 25:5). A senior officer, his adjutant, and a 'scribe' were responsible for mustering a 'battle-ready' army of men over twenty years of age; there was also an elite force of 2,600 'valiants', who appear to have been hereditary heroes who held land from the king (2 Chron. 26:11–12). Every man over the age of twenty was expected to respond to the call to arms, probably made by means of trumpet calls and word of mouth. Exceptions to serving were then granted to those who had built a new house and 'not dedicated it' (that is, occupied it), not yet picked their grape harvest, were engaged but not yet married, and 'anyone afraid and disheartened', 'lest the courage of his comrades flag like his' (Deut. 20:8).

At what point conscripts were no longer required to supply their own arms is not clear, but 'Uzziah provided them – the whole army – with shields and spears, and helmets and mail, and bows and sling-stones' (2 Chron. 26:14). This is a far cry from Saul going out against the Philistines with only himself and his son Jonathan properly armed with the latest weapons. Since Uzziah's standard issue does not include any sword or dagger, for which the Hebrew Bible uses the same word, it is possible that each soldier had his own implement, which could serve also as a cutting or digging tool on the farm as well as on active service. Both large and small shields were employed, made of wood or basket-work and covered with leather, which for battle were greased with fat or oil. The Israelites may have used the larger shield in the manner of the Assyrians: held by a shield-bearer to protect one or more archers. The design of spears varied, according to whether they were for stabbing or throwing. Bows are generally understood to have been of wood, but the advanced technology which produced the shorter and much more powerful composite bow, of wood with a strip of gut on the outer side and thin strips of bone on the inner, had been known in the ancient world since the middle of the second millennium BCE. Bows were strung with cords of flax, plaited hair, or animal gut. Wooden arrows were tipped with heads of various designs made of bronze, and later of iron. The other personal long-range offensive device, the sling, consisted of a leather pocket attached to cords, one of which was let go at the point of release. To judge from examples of stone slingshot balls which have been unearthed, between five and eight centimetres in diameter, it could be a fearsome weapon in the hands of skilled slingers such as the seven hundred left-handed Benjaminites, each of whom 'could sling a stone at a hair and not miss' (Judg. 20:16). Their successors may have been the contingent of slingers who in the reign of Ahaziah so hemmed in the king of Moab in his fortified capital that he was unable even with 'seven hundred swordsmen to break a way through' (2 Kings 3:26).

RITUAL AND WORSHIP

Sociological factors alone could not account for the emergence and survival of the unique spirituality of the Israelites, or explain their history. For centuries desert tribes had settled on the fringes of cultivated lands and had become assimilated, first with rural and then with urban groups of people of different and more entrenched cultures, such as the Ammonites and the Moabites. What was extraordinary in the case of the Israelites is that their culture became the dominant one, and that it was characterised by its spiritual force. It survived because of the ethical, legal, and sociological dimensions of that force. This was to happen again, but not for another 1,500 years, when the original Muslim empire was created out of the spiritual, as well as military, impetus of the religious culture of Islam.

In addition to the three great annual festivals, the feast of unleavened bread (Passover) in the spring, the feast of weeks at the beginning of the wheat harvest in the summer, and the feast of ingathering in the autumn, the Israelites held feasts to celebrate many events in the domestic and agricultural calendar: birth, weaning, a wedding, a funeral, sheep-shearing, the first harvestings of the various crops and fruits, the first lambs, the first pressings of oil, and the first wine of the new vintage. Some anyway of these events had a religious significance too: 'You shall take some of every first fruit of the soil, which you harvest from the land that the Lord your God is giving you, put it in a

basket and go to the place where the Lord your God will choose to establish His name' (Deut. 26:2). The basket is to be handed to the priest in front of the altar, and a particular prayer recited.

This suggests the existence of individual village shrines as well as central places of worship such as those which are specifically mentioned in the stories of Samuel, David, and Saul: Bethel, Gilgal, Gibeon, Hebron, Mizpah, Nob, and the House of the Lord and the Mount of Olives in Jerusalem. These permanent places of worship were imitations of the existing sanctuaries or 'high places' of the Canaanites, or were originally Canaanite sanctuaries. Hilltop sites were favoured where there was a convenient hill. Otherwise a mound would serve, such as the raised oval platform uncovered at Megiddo, which was in use in 1900 BCE and may date from about 2500 BCE. Constructed of large stones, it measures 35 feet 8 inches by 31 feet at the top, which is reached by a flight of seven steps. Animal bones and the remains of jars testify to its function as a place of offerings and sacrifice.

Altars were of different makes, sizes, and shapes. The platform at Megiddo was effectively itself a vast altar. At Petra altars were hewn out of the solid rock. A vast rectangular block of stone, weighing 5 tons, with a hollow in one of its faces, has been found at Hazor. The substantial altar in the Israelite temple at Arad, built probably in the time of Solomon and following the design of the Temple at Jerusalem, was made of unshaped stones, following the Biblical precept: 'If you make for Me an altar of stones, do not build it of hewn stones; for by wielding your tool upon them you have profaned them' (Exod. 20:22). Whatever its form, the altar symbolised the presence of God. It was also the place of sacrifice, the central element of worship among the Israelites.

Sacrifice in the ancient world, as exercised by the Canaanites before and after the arrival of the Israelites, and later by the Greeks and Romans, was believed to be a form of magic, by which a deity would be encouraged to give services in return for the offering. To the

Figure 10 (*opposite*) The High Place of the Nabataeans at Petra, from the north-east. The extensive forecourt, in which stands an offering table, is hewn out of the rock face. Beyond the table, four steps lead up to the altar (right centre). The sacrificial animal was slain to the left of the altar, on a rock with a trough cut into it, along which the blood drained into a basin beside the altar. The sanctuary was probably dedicated to a deity known as Dushara, meaning the god of Shara, which is the area in which Petra is situated. Dushara, who is associated with fertility and vegetation, was the supreme god of the Nabataeans between about 3000 BCE and 500 CE. (C. M. Dixon)

Israelites, sacrifice was a means of communication with God, and in particular of healing a broken relationship and enabling a sinner to be seen to atone, and thus have the hope of being received into God's presence. The ritual shedding of blood signified the existence of a covenant between two parties, sealed by the sharing of food:

> Then Laban spoke up . . . . 'Come, then let us make a pact, you and I, that there may be a witness between you and me.' Thereupon Jacob took a stone and set it up as a pillar. And Jacob said to his kinsmen, 'Gather stones.' So they took stones and made a mound; and they partook of a meal there by the mound.
>
> (Genesis 31:43–46)

Priests made daily offerings, and also offerings to celebrate the Sabbath and other special occasions on behalf of the community or a family or an individual. Depending on the circumstances, the sacrifice could be an animal or a bird, choice flour mixed with oil and frankincense, or oven-baked cakes or wafers. There were also various degrees of sacrifice, of which the most comprehensive, involving the burning up of the entire victim, is translated into English as holocaust – it is not known who was the first to apply the term to the destruction of six million Jews by the Nazis in World War II. In other cases, the animal, having been ritually slaughtered, was divided up: one part was burnt on the altar, two sections were retained by the priest, and the rest was eaten by the person making the offering, his family, and guests.

Those who belonged to the priestly class of Levi (said to be descended from the third son of the patriarch Jacob) or Cohen (descendants of Aaron, brother of Moses) had public functions which went beyond tending the shrine, offering sacrifices, observing the rituals of worship, making prayers, and generally acting as the mediator between God and mankind. They were expositors of the law represented by the Torah, and also, according to some scholars, were required through the system of tithes due to them to redistribute produce to the state treasury as taxes, or within the community as loans. Jehoshaphat appointed 'Levites and priests . . . for rendering judgment in matters of the Lord, and for disputes' (2 Chron. 19:8).

The Temple of Solomon at Jerusalem was the national shrine of his kingdom, and remained the religious centre to which those also in the northern kingdom of Israel looked after the division, even in the period immediately after its destruction. It was, quite simply, the place where God had his divine presence, signified by the dense cloud which enveloped its interior when the Ark was first put in position (I Kings 8:10–13). This was where he had chosen to live. The juxtaposition of Temple and Solomon's royal palace was deliberate: it symbolised the bonds which originally linked religious faith with the exercise of statecraft.

Solomon had been charged with building the Temple by his father David, who then took a census of the Levites according to their current occupations: 'There were 24,000 in charge of the work of the House of the Lord, 6,000 officers and magistrates, 4,000 gatekeepers, and 4,000 for praising the Lord "with instruments I devised for singing praises"' (1 Chron. 23:4–5). Once the Ark had a permanent resting-place, the Levites were excused from acting as its porters. The author of Chronicles, in recasting the much earlier accounts in the books of Samuel and Kings, gives so much attention to the Levites in general and their musical functions in the Temple in particular, that it has been surmised that he may have been a musician himself in the latter era of the Temple.

About sixteen different musical instruments are mentioned in the Old Testament. David's own instrument was, of course, the lyre. When he brings the Ark of God to Jerusalem, he and all the Israelites dance to the sound of 'lyres, harps, timbrels, sistrums, and cymbals' (2 Sam. 6:5) – the timbrel was an ancient form of tambourine, such as Miriam and her accompanists banged to celebrate the destruction of the Egyptian chariot army; the sistrum was made of wires or rings on a wooden frame, which tinkled when shaken. Psalm 150, which presumably refers to the accompaniment of hymns in the Temple, lists horns, harps, lyres, timbrels, lutes, pipes, and 'resounding' and 'loud-clashing' cymbals. The Talmudic *Arakhin* (Valuations) refers (2:3–4) to between twenty-one and forty blasts of the trumpet being sounded in the Temple, to music of between two and six harps and two and twelve flutes, and to the soft tone of a reed pipe closing a tune. Even the sacrificial ritual had a musical accompaniment: 'When the Levites were in place with the instruments of David, and the priests with their trumpets, Hezekiah gave the order to offer the burnt offering on the altar. When the burnt offering began, the song of the Lord and the trumpets began also, together with the instruments of King David of Israel' (2 Chron. 29:26–27).

When Solomon was anointed king, 'They sounded the horn and all the people shouted, "Long live King Solomon!" All the people then marched up behind him, playing on flutes and making merry till the earth was split open by the uproar' (I Kings 1:39–40). The actual anointing of the infant Joash was a stealthy ceremony, but once it was completed there was pandemonium, 'and all the people of the land rejoicing and blowing trumpets' (2 Kings 11:14). Solomon, among other trappings of wealth, acquired for himself 'male and female singers' (Eccles. 2:8). Doubtless these enlivened his banquets, though such entertainment was not to everyone's taste. A generation earlier, the eighty-year-old Barzillai excused himself from David's invitation to dine: 'Can your servant taste what he eats and drinks? Can I still listen to the singing of men and women?' (2 Sam. 19:36). Or maybe his problem was similar to that of the elderly man, chosen to be the chair at a feast, whom Ben Sirach addresses: 'Speak, if you are old – it is your privilege – but come to the point and do not interrupt the music' (NEB Ecclesiasticus 32:3).

It is difficult not to conclude that more than other ancient cultures which could lay claim to an artistic temperament, such as the Egyptians, Greeks, and Romans, the Israelites enjoyed music for its own sake, and that their music was generally noisy and tuneful. They may for one reason or another have been inhibited from producing works of art, but in addition to establishing a musical tradition, the Israelites of the pre-exilic period left literary works in prose and poetry which have profoundly influenced the course of world history.

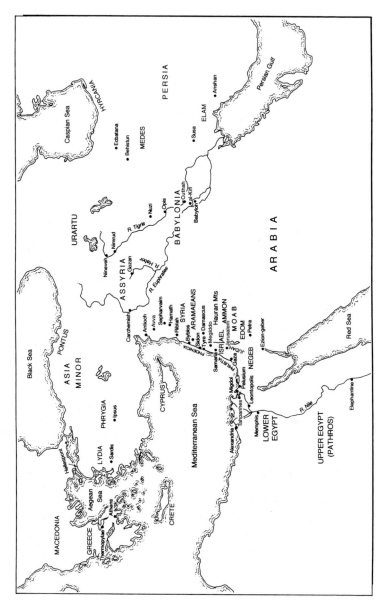

Map 5 Peoples and places in the Assyrian, Babylonian, Persian, and Hellenistic empires

6

THE JUDAEANS: BABYLONIAN EXILE 586–538 BCE, AND THE PERSIAN YEARS 538–332 BCE

The singers of psalms and prayers in the Temple went into exile in Babylonia with the rest of their people, but kept alive their musical tradition in the hope one day of being able to exercise it again in the holy place in Jerusalem designated for it. Today in places throughout the world to which the diaspora (Greek, 'scattering' or 'dispersion') brought them or their ancestors, many Jews celebrate the annual fast of Tisha b'Av: a feature of the synagogue service is a reading, or chanting to a mournful melody, from the book of Lamentations. The fast was instituted after the exile to remember the original destruction of the Temple. Subsequently its scope was extended to be a reminder also of the destruction by the Romans in 70 CE of its successor, and of other tragic communal disasters which occurred at about the same time of the year.

Lamentations comprises five poems expressing shame and despair at the fall of Jerusalem and the destruction of the Temple in 587/586 BCE. There is a tradition that they were written by Jeremiah: whether or not this is so, it is generally agreed that the author or authors lived at the time the events happened. The form is unusual. Each of the twenty-two verses in 1, 2, and 4 begins with a different letter of the Hebrew alphabet in sequence from *aleph* to *tav*: 3 is a triple alphabetical acrostic, in that there are three verses for each letter. Chapter 5, also of twenty-two verses, ends with an expression of penitence and faith which exemplifies the resilience of the Children of Israel and their ability to survive.

But You, O Lord, are enthroned for ever,
Your throne endures through the ages.
Why have You forgotten us utterly,

Forsaken us for all time?
Take us back, O Lord, to Yourself,
And let us come back;
Renew our days as of old!
For truly, You have rejected us,
Bitterly raged against us.

(Lamentations 5:19–22)

What conditions were like in Judah at this time can only be guessed. The diaspora, which later became a drift and then a ceaseless flood of humanity, had effectively begun with the deportations to Assyria from the kingdom of Israel by Tiglath-pileser in 733/732 BCE; it continued with the mass forced exodus after the fall of Samaria in 722/721. The next major movement was the selective transportation of personnel from Jerusalem by Nebuchadnezzar in 597 BCE, followed by the more general one in 587/586, and an additional one, consisting of '745 Judeans' (Jer. 52:30) in 581. From the account in Jeremiah 40 of the aftermath of the final destruction of the city, it is clear that between times refugees had fled to places such as Moab, Ammon, Edom, or even farther afield. After the murder of Gedaliah, there was a further exodus, to Egypt, where settlements are referred to as being established, or having earlier been established, at 'Migdol, Tahpanhes, and Noph, and in the land of Pathros' (Jer. 44:1). These places are some distance apart. Migdol is cited by Ezekiel as representing Egypt's northernmost point. Tahpanhes was in the Nile delta, and Noph (Memphis) some way up the Nile itself. Pathros is another term for Upper (that is, southern) Egypt, where at Elephantine the evidence has been found in the form of documents and letters, written in Aramaic and dating from the fifth century BCE, of the existence there of a Jewish colony: this seems to have been established originally as a garrison of mercenaries from Judah charged with protecting Egypt's borderlands in that region, and with general duties to do with the supervision of land and river trade routes to and from the south. From a reference in the copy of a request (407 BCE) to Jerusalem from the elders of the settlement for permission to rebuild their temple, which had been destroyed by an Egyptian military mob, it would appear that it had originally been built before 525 BCE, when the Persian king Cambyses II (530–522 BCE) conquered Egypt. It is of some interest also that though the Persians 'knocked down all the temples of the gods of Egypt', no damage was done on that occasion to the temple of the Elephantine community. Further evidence of the diaspora of the Judaeans is in Isaiah 11:11, which cites Assyria, and 'Egypt, Pathros,

Nubia, Elam, Shinar, Hamath, and the coastlands' as places where they have settled – Nubia is Ethiopia and Shinar is Babylonia.

The Babylonia of the exile, and in particular the city of Babylon itself, had been transformed by Nabopolassar (626–605 BCE), who had wrested the Babylonian empire from the Assyrians, and his son Nebuchadnezzar, who, to judge from his cuneiform inscriptions, was as proud of his architectural as of his military achievements. The canals and dykes of the river Euphrates were refurbished, new canals and a vast reservoir, upstream from Babylon and 40 miles in circumference, excavated, whole cities reconstructed, and every temple in the land rebuilt. Nebuchadnezzar also liked to put his personal stamp on everything he built: bricks have been unearthed bearing the imprint, 'I am Nebuchadnezzar, king of Babylon, rebuilder of Esagila and Ezida, elder son of Nabopolassar.' Ezida and Esagila were temples, the latter being the principal temple of Marduk, chief deity of Babylonia. Within the temple complex was the great ziggurat Etemenanki ('House of the foundation of heaven and earth'). Herodotus (484–420 BCE), the Greek traveller and historian, saw it about a century later. He describes it as eight towers, one on top of the other, the bottom one being one furlong square: the topmost tower was a temple, reached by a winding exterior staircase, with a resting-place with seats halfway up. He also noticed an unusual custom in the city. Since, he says, there are no doctors in Babylon, anyone who is ill is laid out in the public square. Pedestrians are required to ask the patient what the problem is, and if they have suffered from it, pass on advice as to how to deal with it (I. 181, 197).

Surprisingly, perhaps, the Judaeans deported to Babylonia seem to have been better off than those who remained in Judah. From references in the Bible and in Mesopotamian inscriptions, they were settled in various cities, in new (or rebuilt) towns, and in agricultural districts. The reference to the 'rivers of Babylon, / there we sat, / sat and wept, / as we thought of Zion' (Psalm 137:1) implies that there were Judaean communities in the rich lands beside the tributaries and canals of the Euphrates. It also suggests, in spite of evidence especially in the book of Ezra that the exiles were free to congregate, to organise their own affairs, and to keep servants, the extent of the culture shock of being transported from a small-town or subsistence-farming existence to a cosmopolitan society such as Babylonia. At the same time, the extent of the assimilation of Judaeans into Babylonian ways may be inferred from the fact that Aramaic began to supersede Hebrew as their spoken language.

The cultural identity of the Judaean exiles was further undermined in that they had been cut off from not just the central, but the sole embodiment of their religious faith, the Temple at Jerusalem, whose destruction many of them had witnessed. Hence the significance of the question, 'How can we sing a song of the Lord on alien soil?' (Psalm 137:4). Yet it was during the exile in Babylonia that the final editing was done of the Deuteronomistic history comprising effectively the books of Joshua, Judges, 1 and 2 Samuel, and 1 and 2 Kings, and the texts of the priestly tradition were interwoven with the Yahwist and Elohist versions of earlier events, described in the Pentateuch. This was the work of priestly scholars and scribes steeped in the oral tradition; some may also have brought with them precious manuscripts in which the teachings had been preserved.

That, astonishingly, the faith of the people remained intact, and in some respects emerged strengthened, was due partly to their insistence on maintaining the combination of traditional practices – observance of the Sabbath, dietary laws, and circumcision – and partly to the inspirational leadership of Ezekiel and the anonymous author or authors of the latter books of Isaiah. These prophets followed Jeremiah, who, by his words as well as by his actions, had already given notice that the exile was simply part of God's scheme of things, and that there would be a return to Judah and a rebuilding of the land: 'For I will restore the fortunes of the land as of old – said the Lord' (Jer. 33:11).

Ezekiel, a man of sublime eccentricity, was in the first wave of exiles from Jerusalem in 597 BCE, and, according to his own account, began his prophetic career in 593 BCE in the sensational manner which he describes in Ezekiel 1. Broadly speaking, his message is that the destruction of Jerusalem and the deportations (and much worse in the form of personal indignities) are God's punishment, through which will come the knowledge of how Divine judgement is exercised: the realisation of God's purpose will be the physical redemption of his people to a rebuilt land 'out of the countries where you have been scattered' (Ezek. 11:17), and the renewal there of God's Covenant with them. The extent of the projected reorganisation of the land as well as of the reconstruction programme is described in considerable detail in Ezekiel 40–48.

What is said to be the tomb of Ezekiel is at al-Kifl, Iraq, 20 miles north of Babylon. It was visited in about 1180 CE by Rabbi Petachia of Ratisbon, whose travels were recorded by Rabbi Judah the Pious bar Samuel.

> Round the tomb is a wide space, enclosed by a wall. The gate in the wall is so low that you have to crawl through on hands

and knees. At the festival of Tabernacles, when people flock there from all parts, the entrance expands so that they can pass through even on camelback. Afterwards it shrinks back to its normal size. . . . While the Rabbi was at the tomb itself, he saw in the building a bird with a human face [probably an owl]. The guide was distraught. 'It's a tradition here that any house in which such a bird is found will collapse,' he explained. Just then the bird flew towards the window, but dropped dead just before it got there. 'If the bird dies, it doesn't count,' breathed the guide with relief.

The poems of Second Isaiah, or Deutero-Isaiah, begin at chapter 40 of the book of Isaiah, and can be said to represent a reinterpretation and elaboration, in the light of circumstances, of the earlier chapters. Written during the decline of the Babylonian empire (with the possibility that chapters 50–66 were composed after the return from exile), they offer a more positive message of delivery and redemption, in which the Persian king Cyrus (Isa. 45:1) is nominated as God's agent in the exercise of his Divine programme for his people. Certain passages, and particularly chapters 52:13 to 53:12, collectively known as the Suffering Servant poems, are interpreted by most Jewish commentators as referring to the Jewish people: many Christians understand them as a prediction of the Passion of Jesus.

The colourful stories and elaborate visions of the apocalyptic book of Daniel are set in the Babylon of the exile, but they are more likely to have been written in the second century BCE deliberately to reflect the situation of the Jews under Syrian oppression. The heroic Daniel, however, cited in Ezekiel 14:14, together with Noah and Job, as a paragon of righteousness, has been associated with an even earlier tradition, in which he features as the father of the protagonist in the tale of Aqhat, a Canaanite epic in verse, dating from before 1400 BCE, which was discovered in the excavations at Ugarit. The impressionable and temperamental Nebuchadnezzar of the book of Daniel, who goes mad and is restored to sanity, is an image introduced by a later writer or editor; the historical Nebuchadnezzar was a formidable empire-builder, after whose death in 562 BCE the kingdom, bereft of his personality, began to fall apart. According to the king list discovered at Uruk (Erech), he had reigned for forty-three years. His successor Amel-Marduk (Biblical Evil-merodach) lasted only two years, but his release of Jehoiachin, the penultimate king of Judah, from custody, described with humanity at the very end of 2 Kings, provides a fitting climax to the Deuteronomistic history of the kingdoms of Israel and Judah while also suggesting the date shortly after which its editing was completed.

There is no account in the Bible of the confused years that followed, which have, however, been pieced together largely from Babylonian inscriptions. After three years of Amel-Marduk's successor, Neriglissar, and three months of Neriglissar's infant son, the throne was assumed in about 556 BCE by Nabonidus, who presided, sometimes at long distance, over the final seventeen years of the short-lived Babylonian empire – we also have an extensive tomb inscription of Nabonidus' mother, who 'died a natural death' in the ninth year of his reign at the age of 104, sound in sight, hearing, and speech, steady with her hands and on her feet, and with a good appetite for food and drink. Both she and her son were devotees of the Babylonian moon god Sin rather than of Marduk, the national deity, and this and Nabonidus' extended absences, leaving the government in the hands of his son Belshazzar, further destabilised a situation which, in the light of what was happening elsewhere in the region, hardly needed a prophet to predict the outcome.

THE RISE OF PERSIA

The end of Babylonia, however, when it came, was more the result of a takeover than a conquest. Cyrus (557–529 BCE), a vassal of the Medes and king of the Persian city of Anshan in Elam, had in 553 BCE rebelled against his masters, whose ruler he defeated and whose empire he annexed three years later. He then, in an astonishing campaign, advanced north and east, bypassing Babylonia itself for the moment but overrunning some of its territories, and striking at Sardis, capital of Lydia, which he incorporated into his burgeoning Persian empire. He then seems to have left Babylon to stew for the time being, while he enlarged his acquisitions to the east, as far as what are today Afghanistan and Kazakhstan.

In 539 BCE, after some token resistance at Opis, on the river Tigris, Babylonia capitulated and Cyrus entered the city of Babylon in triumph, which he claimed was as much a victory for the Babylonian god Marduk as it was for himself. While his own account of his magnanimous behaviour, written in cuneiform lengthwise on a convex cylinder of clay, may necessarily reflect a certain amount of bias, the Babylonian chronicle of the times confirms the suggestion that Nabonidus, in spite of failing to worship Marduk, was merely arrested when he returned to Babylon, not executed, as was common practice for defeated kings: it also states that Nabonidus put himself further in the wrong by massacring confused Babylonian citizens who had rebelled against him after the Opis fiasco.

The most significant portion of Cyrus' message has been translated thus: 'I restored to the sacred cities on the other side of the Tigris, the sanctuaries of which have been ruins for a long time, the images which used to belong there and established permanent shrines for them. I gathered all the former inhabitants of those places and returned them to their homes.'

There are two versions in the Biblical book of Ezra of that part of Cyrus' general edict which concerned the Judaean exiles. The one (Ezra 1:2–4), written in Hebrew, confirms that he will rebuild the Temple in Jerusalem, and states that any who wish to return are free to go: those who prefer to stay should still make a voluntary contribution to the rebuilding programme. The other (Ezra 6:3–5) is one of several official documents in Aramaic inserted into chapters 4–6: it is in the form of a 'memorandum' on the original edict, stating the dimensions of the new Temple, confirming that the 'palace' will defray the cost, and ordering the return of the 'gold and silver vessels of the House of God which Nebuchadnezzar had taken away from the temple in Jerusalem'.

So those who wished were free to go home to Judah, though home was a part now of the Persian empire, which would last for two hundred years. With the destruction by the Assyrians of the northern kingdom of Israel, the dispersal of its inhabitants, and its partial re-emergence as Samaria, effectively the term Israelite no longer applies. On the one hand there is the Persian province of Judah (later, in its Hellenistic–Roman years, known as Judaea), whose inhabitants can therefore continue to be called Judaeans. On the other are the exiles and their descendants, 'the servants of the God of heaven and earth' (Ezra 5:11), who believed in God's special relationship with them and were faithful to their religious traditions, notably keeping the Sabbath and the food laws, and practising circumcision: they now became known as Jews (Hebrew *Yehudim*, Aramaic *Yehudin*). Thus the people of Judah went into exile as Judaeans, and returned also as Jews: as Jews, too, they were to disperse ever more widely throughout the known world.

The Persian empire was the greatest in the ancient world until Roman times. For the period of Persian control of Judah, which ended in 332 BCE when the young Macedonian king, Alexander the Great (born 356, ruled 335–323 BCE), overran the territory as part of his campaign of global conquest, we have a number of literary sources. The Biblical books of Ezra and Nehemiah, originally a single unit put together in about 350 BCE by the editor of 1 and 2 Chronicles (known as the 'Chronicler'), both incorporate autobiographical material. The prophetic books of Haggai and Zechariah also allude to events during the early years of Persian rule. Further references are in the Apocryphal 1 Esdras (most likely compiled in the first century BCE) and the apocalyptic 2 Esdras, which has been dated to the years immediately following the destruction by the Romans in 70 CE of the rebuilt Temple. The Jewish-born historian Flavius Josephus, who witnessed the destruction on that occasion, covers the period of Persian control in Book XI of his *Antiquities of the Jews*. Much of our knowledge of the Persians themselves derives from the Greek historian Herodotus, whose account of the Persian wars against the Greeks culminates with the defeat of the Persians in 479 BCE, which happened in his lifetime. Herodotus clearly admired the Persians, as did his countryman Xenophon (*c.* 430–*c.* 355 BCE), who wrote a racy personal account, known as *Anabasis*, of a disastrous expedition in 401 BCE to aid the rebellion against Artaxerxes II by his younger brother Cyrus, and his own heroic part in it; the mission at least opened Greek eyes to a potential Persian military weakness, which was duly exploited by Alexander.

The sparseness of archaeological evidence within Judah may partly be explained by the fact that during this period at least three separate waves of wholesale destruction have been detected: in the territory of Benjamin in about 480 BCE, along the coast and in the Negeb about a hundred years later as a result of Egypt's struggle for independence against Persia, and a more widely spread devastation, including several major towns, in the latter half of the fourth century BCE, connected with a number of revolts against the prevailing rule. Where the remains of houses have been found, however, these suggest that they followed a uniform plan based on the Mesopotamian and Assyrian design of an open courtyard with rooms round it. Peculiar to the region of Judah is a type of underground tomb, dug out of the soft limestone rock, provided with rock benches on which the bodies were laid, and often containing local pottery. Tombs were also depositories of metalware in the form of bowls, jugs, ladles, and strainers, alabaster vessels, jewellery, cosmetic materials (especially mirrors), and glass amulets.

THE EXILES RETURN

The chief concern of the Chronicler was to complete the account of the central worship at Jerusalem which begins in the time of David; less priority is given to matters of chronological consistency and historical probability. However tempting it is to envisage a massive crocodile of fifty thousand adults and eight thousand animals slowly assembling from the various parts of Babylonia where they had settled, and then setting out on the long, dusty walk to a land which most had never seen, to the accompaniment of the '200 male and female singers' (Ezra 2:65), and once home dispersing 'each to his own city' (Ezra 2:1), the reality is likely to have been more prosaic. As leader of the expedition and governor of the embryo province Cyrus chose Sheshbazzar, 'prince of Judah' (Ezra 1:8), which, if it means that Sheshbazzar was of the royal house of David, constitutes an enlightened appointment. Sheshbazzar's principal responsibility was to re-establish Jerusalem as the focus of worship; he would have been accompanied initially by a comparatively small entourage comprising enthusiastic pioneers and members of the priestly class. There is no reason to doubt the veracity of Josephus' source for his statement that many of the exiles were 'unwilling to leave their possessions' (*Antiquities* XI. 1. iii).

It was either Sheshbazzar or his successor Zerubbabel who set up the altar in Jerusalem, laid the foundations of the new Temple, and formally reinstalled the Levites in their spiritual home. That the building operation did not proceed smoothly was due to a combination of the appalling weather conditions referred to in the two books of Haggai, which impoverished many of the new immigrants, and conflicts from within and outside the community. The descendants of the remnant who had remained in Judah resented the presence of newcomers who regarded themselves as the privileged people of God and the rightful owners of their ancient properties. The Samaritans to the north, descendants of the former inhabitants of the kingdom of Israel who had intermarried with foreigners settled there by the Assyrians, but who still regarded themselves as worthy worshippers of Yahweh, offered to help build the Temple. When their offer was turned down by Zerubbabel on the somewhat specious grounds that Cyrus' instructions were that it was a job exclusively for the former exiles, the Samaritans took the huff and mounted a campaign to disrupt the operation.

Work was not resumed in earnest until about 520 BCE, some eighteen years after it had begun. By this time Cyrus had been succeeded by his eldest son Cambyses II, the Persian king who conquered Egypt but spared the Jewish temple at Elephantine, on whose death in 522 the throne had been appropriated by Darius I (522–486 BCE). Jerusalem was still in ruins. The population of the tiny Persian province of Judah (only about 30 miles from north to south and the same from east to west) had been bolstered by the return of further

Babylonian exiles, but has been estimated to have been no more than about twenty thousand.

The building of the Temple was completed in 515 BCE. The urgings of Haggai and Zechariah for the people to get on with it were inspired by political as well as by spiritual motives. An extraordinary monument, carved into the sheer rock face at Behistun about 100 metres above the ancient caravan route from Babylon to Ecbatana, the former capital of the Medes, records, in Persian, Elamite, and Akkadian, Darius' success in dealing mercilessly with a series of rebellions which rocked his empire. To the Jews in Judah, it seemed that the explosion into violence of nationalistic ideals elsewhere could more peaceably be reflected in their own activity. They responded in the only way they could, and by doing so established a community whose focus was the Temple and whose faith was messianic.

Not that this activity went unnoticed by their Persian overlords. According to Herodotus (III. 89), Darius divided his empire into twenty regions (or satrapies), each of which contained several provinces: the book of Esther, a romance with historical trappings, refers to the empire comprising 'over a hundred and twenty-seven provinces from India to Ethiopia' (Esther 1:1). The province of Judah was part of the fifth satrapy, called 'Beyond the River' (Ezra 5:6). The book of Ezra 5:6 to 6:13 records how when the satrap (regional governor) queried with Darius whether permission had been given for the building, he was told that written confirmation of Cyrus' original order had been found in the archives at Ecbatana.

The Jews now had a Temple, a solid enough structure if in splendour nothing like that of Solomon. Meanwhile Darius consolidated his empire, establishing an elaborate network of communications, reforming the legal system, rationalising the coinage, and encouraging industry and trade. He failed to conquer Greece, a state of affairs which his son Xerxes (486–465 BCE) compounded. Having built two pontoon bridges across the Hellespont from Asia Minor to the Greek mainland, Xerxes crossed with a huge army in 480 BCE. After a heroic Spartan defence at the pass of Thermopylae, the Athenians abandoned their city to its fate and put their trust in their fleet. Xerxes retired in dismay, having lost two hundred ships. He left an army behind, but after this was beaten in 479 BCE by a combined force of Athenians and Spartans, no Persian force ever set foot again on the mainland of Greece. Though the Persian empire still had many years to run, its invincibility was even further questioned during the reign of Artaxerxes I (465–424 BCE), when he was forced to agree terms with the Greek states.

After Zerubbabel, the position in Judah seems to have been that administration was conducted from Samaria, with local affairs being in the hands of the High Priest. Though further returning exiles increased the population perhaps to about fifty thousand, and the city of Jerusalem 'was broad and large, the people in it were few, and houses were not built' (Neh. 7:4). Apart from continued sniping by 'the adversaries of Judah and Benjamin' (Ezra 4:1), as well as by the Samaritans, it would appear from the prophecies of Obadiah that the neighbouring Edomites were a constant nuisance. Morale within Judah was low. According to the prophecies attributed to Malachi, no respect was being shown to parents or masters, unwholesome animals were being sacrificed at the altar, men were divorcing their own kind and marrying Gentile wives, the practice of giving tithes had fallen into disrepute, sorcery, adultery, and perjury were rife, labourers were being cheated, and widows, orphans, and visiting strangers were being deprived of their due.

The situation was taken in hand not from within Judah itself, but through two enlightened appointments by the Persian king.

EZRA AND NEHEMIAH

Nehemiah was a Jew who had attained the office of cupbearer to Artaxerxes, a post, according to Herodotus (III. 34), of considerable importance which gave him personal access to the royal family. If he was a eunuch, as his position suggests, his autobiographical memoir might be seen as a memorial such as is reflected by the prophet:

> For thus said the Lord:
> 'As for the eunuchs who keep My sabbaths,
> Who have chosen what I desire
> And hold fast to My covenant –
> I will give them, in My House
> And within My walls,
> A monument and a name
> Better than sons or daughters.'
>
> (Isaiah 56:4–5)

In the month of Kislev (which roughly equates to December) of 445 BCE, a year which has been confirmed by archaeological evidence, Nehemiah's brother returned from Judah to the Persian capital of Susa with a small party of Judaeans. They brought disturbing news of the circumstances of the former exiles and in particular of the devastated condition of the walls and other fortifications of Jerusalem. Four months later, a distressed Nehemiah persuaded Artaxerxes to appoint him to the task of organising the necessary repairs, and to provide the materials. Not only did Artaxerxes accede to this request and speed it on by cutting through the inevitable red tape, but at some point he also created Nehemiah governor of Judah. The job called for diplomacy as well as energy, for concerted hostility and mounting sabotage came from Sanballat, governor of Samaria, Tobiah the Ammonite (possibly Sanballat's regional deputy), and sundry Arabs, Ammonites, and Ashdodites (Philistines). So it was that three days after his arrival in Jerusalem, Nehemiah slipped out in the night with a handful of helpers to make a secret reconnaissance of the city walls and gates.

Where Nehemiah is regarded as one of the great Jewish political leaders, who also ensured the continued development of Judaism, Ezra, according to rabbinical tradition, ranks alongside Moses as a teacher of the Torah. Ezra is also believed to have been responsible for changing the running script, in which the Torah was first written down, into the square Hebrew script which is used today. He was a member of the priestly family of Zadok, employed as a Persian government scribe. While the terms of his royal commission are clearly defined, involving the regulation of all matters appertaining to Jewish religious law, the actual timing and dates of his assignment have generated endless discussion. Suffice to say, in spite of inconsistencies within and between the accounts of the Chronicler, the traditional view is that Ezra arrived in Jerusalem in 458 BCE, having journeyed for four months as leader of a considerable caravan of further returning exiles. Even though, according to his own autobiographical account, Nehemiah was in 433 BCE recalled by Artaxerxes to Babylon, subsequently returning to Jerusalem for a further brief term as governor, it may thus be assumed that at some points their careers in Judah coincided, even if there is no hard evidence that two such forceful personalities, with closely related missions, collaborated to achieve them.

Whether the rebuilding of the wall and fortifications of Jerusalem took fifty-two days (Neh. 6:15) or two years four months (Josephus, *Antiquities* XI. 5. viii), it was a remarkable feat of organisation and mechanics, of which traces, confirming the Biblical account, have been discovered. First, Nehemiah divided the wall into sections, each of which he assigned to a particular group of people to work on, some of them being responsible for two sections. In such a way were the great boundary lines in Britain, Hadrian's and the Antonine walls, constructed by Roman legions in the second century CE. Nehemiah employed a particularly ingenious tactic: where possible, the person in charge of a group was responsible for the stretch of wall protecting his own house! When the wall had been completed all round to half its height, Sanballat and company woke up to what was happening. From psychological warfare, they turned to open abuse and then to violence, as a result of which, according to Josephus, many Jews were killed. Nehemiah responded by dividing his building force into two. Half stood guard, while the other half worked: 'The basket carriers were burdened, doing work with one hand while the other held a weapon. As for the builders, each had his sword girded at his side as he was building' (Neh. 4:11–12; NEB 17–18). Those who lived outside Jerusalem were required, with their servants, to stay in the city overnight to guard the work. Nehemiah and his own entourage kept their clothes on and their weapons at the ready the whole time. The conspirators now resorted to treachery. After trying in vain four times to lure Nehemiah out of the city to his death, they threatened to accuse him openly of sedition against Persia. Nehemiah ignored their communications, as he did intimidation from Tobiah, who claimed, through his and his son's Judaean wives, to have inside knowledge of malpractice by Nehemiah.

An irascible man with a deep sense of conscience, Nehemiah dealt with the spiral of debt into which the poor had sunk by exacting a solemn promise from their creditors to cancel all debts and restore all dispossessed lands and property. He balanced the population by restricting the number of people in Jerusalem, by lot, to one in ten. He enforced the payment of tithes to the Temple and recalled the Levites from the fields, to which they had dispersed to find work in the absence of payment from the public. He ensured that the Sabbath was observed by having the city gates closed throughout the whole time, from sunset to sunset, so that merchants and tradesmen could not get in. Above all he railed against mixed marriages, being so incensed to find that children of these alliances spoke in foreign tongues that he reprimanded the fathers, tore out their hair, had them flogged, and made them promise that no son or daughter of theirs would marry anyone who was not Jewish.

Ezra's brief from the Persian king, complete with budget from the imperial treasury, is detailed in the book of Ezra 7:12–26. His powers to teach the Law and to uphold its precepts extended beyond Judah: 'to appoint magistrates and judges to judge all the people in the province of Beyond the River who know the laws of your God, and to teach those who do not know them', that is Jews settled in other parts of the territory. According to the book of Nehemiah (8:9), Nehemiah himself was present on the momentous and moving occasion when Ezra, mounted on a wooden dais, read and expounded, with the assistance of the Levites, the Teaching of Moses to 'the entire people assembled as one man in the square before the Water Gate' (Neh. 8:1), though in the parallel account in 1 Esdras, the personage is simply referred to as the 'governor' (NEB 9:49). At first, the people wept in remorse, but the diplomacy of the Levites won the day and their hearts: '"Hush, for the day is holy; do not be sad." Then all the people went to eat and drink and send portions [to whoever had nothing prepared] and make great merriment, for they understood the things that were told' (Neh. 8:11–12).

'On the second day, the heads of the clans of all the people and the priests and the Levites gathered to Ezra the scribe to study the words of the Teaching. They found written in the Teaching that the Lord had commanded Moses that the Israelites must dwell in booths during the festival of the seventh month' (Neh. 8:13–14). So the people went out and collected leafy branches and made themselves booths on roofs, in courtyards, and in other open spaces in the city. Ezra 'read from the scroll of the Teaching of God each day, from the first to the last day. They celebrated the festival seven days, and there was a solemn gathering on the eighth, as prescribed' (Neh. 8:18). They were recreating the ancient festival of ingathering, known as Sukkot (tabernacles or booths), celebrated today from the fifteenth to the twenty-first day of Tishri, the seventh month of the Jewish year. The eighth day (the twenty-second of the month) is the festival of Shemini Atzeret, which in Israel and among less traditional communities in other parts of the world is combined with the celebration of Simchat Torah, which otherwise falls on the twenty-third day of the month.

The ensuing sequence of events appears to have been that two months later Ezra called 'all the men of Judah and Benjamin' (Ezra 10:9) to come to Jerusalem, on pain of being expelled from the congregation and having their property confiscated, to discuss the problem of foreign wives, which was still so deeply rooted that even members of the priestly class were involved. The convocation, which opened in a rainstorm, was subjected to a tirade from Ezra, to which the trembling assembly responded positively but meekly, and with the suggestion that a commission be appointed to study each case. The investigation, behind closed doors, lasted three months, and on the first day of the first month of the following year reached its inevitable conclusion: all mixed marriages were annulled.

On the twenty-fourth day of that month, the people reassembled, 'fasting, in sackcloth, and with earth upon them' (Neh. 9:1). After readings from the Torah, they confessed their sins and formally re-affirmed the Covenant. This pledge was put down in writing and witnessed, signed, and sealed, by leading members of the priestly class and the community. There, effectively, Old Testament history comes to an end. The exclusive, some might say drastic, policies of Nehemiah and Ezra, imposed with the blessing of the Persian empire, had however confirmed the principles which stabilised the community and ensured that Judaism, wherever it might be practised, would somehow survive. These principles reflect the inspiring words of the prophets: 'And they shall beat their swords into plowshares [that is the iron tips of the wooden plough] / And their spears into pruning hooks: / Nation shall not take up / Sword against nation; / They shall never again know war' (Isa. 2:4); 'Spare Me the sound of your hymns, / And let Me not hear the music of your lutes. / But let justice well up like water, / Righteousness like an unfailing stream' (Amos 5:23–24); 'And what the Lord requires of you: / Only to do justice / And to love goodness, / And to walk modestly with your God' (Micah 6:8). They spring from the central belief and declaration of faith of Judaism: 'Hear O Israel, the Lord our God, the Lord is One.'

As far as Judah is concerned, the rest of the Persian era is obscure, apart from archaeological finds in the form of potsherds inscribed in Aramaic, Hebrew, and Phoenician with lists of names or receipts for goods, and coins, based on the design of of the Athenian coinage which was standard throughout the western Persian empire, but bearing the legend *Yehud*. Samaritan papyri from the years 375 to 332 BCE found in 1962 at Wadi Daliyeh, about 14 kilometres north of Jericho, comprise in the main legal documents. The cave in which the documents were discovered extends over 70 metres into the hillside. From the fact that the cave also revealed over two hundred skeletons, personal jewellery, fragments of cloth, remains of food, and pottery, it has been concluded that the guardians of the documents were among a party of probably wealthy refugees from the destruction of Samaria in the aftermath of Alexander's conquest.

That a Jewish life could subsist under unusual circumstances, and without access to the Temple at Jerusalem, at the end of the fifth century BCE is attested by the documents from Elephantine. They include, in addition to the request to rebuild the community's temple, details of rations for both men and women, prices of goods and soldiers' pay, and family archives. Persian rule in Egypt ended at some point between the beginning of 401 and the middle of 400 BCE, when a local ruler, Amyrteus, took charge. According to a letter to a Jew at Elephantine called Islah, dated 1 October 399 BCE, Amyrteus was killed and succeeded by Nepherites I, who then established the twenty-ninth Egyptian dynasty. It is the last piece of evidence for the existence of the Jewish community at Elephantine, which disappears from history. Meanwhile the balance of world power was shifting from the Middle East to the European mainland.

7

JUDAEA: HELLENISTIC AND HASMONAEAN YEARS 332–63 BCE

In a legend cited by Josephus (*Antiquities* XI. 8. v), Alexander the Great, in the course of his lightning conquest of the mainland and islands of Greece, and of Asia Minor, Libya, Egypt, Syria, Persia, Afghanistan, and the lands in between, as far as India, took the Philistine city of Gaza (after a two-month siege) and then advanced upon a quaking Jerusalem. Instead of resisting, the inhabitants opened the city gates and poured out behind the priests in a procession headed by the High Priest in purple and scarlet, on whose headdress was a gold plate inscribed with the name of God. Alexander, recognising the name in the inscription, gave the High Priest obeisance and accompanied him into the city, where he personally performed the ritual sacrifices in the Temple. He then gave the Jews, wherever they might be, in Babylonia and Persia, as well as in Judaea, the right to obey their own laws and to be exempt from paying taxes every seventh year. When the Samaritans asked for the same privileges, on the grounds that they too were Jews, Alexander deferred his decision.

All this may mean simply that Alexander, who is unlikely to have had time to make a detour to Jerusalem on what historical sources suggest was a seven-day march from Gaza to Egypt, was agreeable to the Jews retaining their own traditions. The reference to Samaria may reflect the violent reprisals there, as a consequence of an uprising against Alexander's governor.

Alexander died of a fever in Babylon at the age of thirty-three, having changed the course of history and initiated yet another beginning for the Jews. While Jews continued to drift away from Judaea and settle along the coasts of the Mediterranean, on the Greek islands, and on the shores of the Black Sea, a significant number made their homes in Alexandria, the Egyptian port which had been founded in honour of Alexander, where they formed a community which rivalled that of Babylon in significance. Here, according to the legend, seventy-two scholars, sent from Jerusalem, translated the Pentateuch into Greek at the request of the librarian of Ptolemy II (283–246 BCE), for the benefit of the Alexandrian literary establishment. The Septuagint (LXX), as it is called (seventy being the nearest round number), probably *was* compiled at this time, but by Alexandrian Jews themselves for those of their number who no longer understood Hebrew. The rest of the Hebrew Bible was translated into Greek in the same way, at various times up to about 150 BCE.

The Hellenisation (the spread of Greek culture and civilisation) of the empire of Alexander the Great was a gradual process, but it affected, to different degrees, even the Jews of Judaea, whichever ruling party of the successors of Alexander happened to be in charge. At his death no one commanded sufficient power or charisma to assume the succession, which devolved on his generals, from whom, Alexander's legal heirs having been liquidated, three emerged as the ultimate contenders, without ever establishing their influence over the whole territory, however hard they tried: Antigonus (*d*. 301 BCE), 'the One-Eyed', who started with Asia Minor and northern Syria, Ptolemy (*d*. 283 BCE), ruler of Egypt and southern Syria, and Seleucus (*d*. 280 BCE), satrap of Babylonia and founder of the Seleucid dynasty. As so often before and since, the narrow corridor of land incorporating Judaea was fiercely contended for, though Judaea itself was of such political insignificance that it is hardly mentioned by the Greek historians who covered this period. Ptolemy, recognising its strategic significance as a springboard for an invasion of Egypt, made the first successful armed bid, only to lose the area to Antigonus, from whose supporters he regained it in 312 BCE.

Six months later, Antigonus himself annexed the land of which Judaea was part, only to be defeated and killed in 301 BCE at Ipsus in Phrygia. It was then claimed by Seleucus. Ptolemy, who had not been involved at Ipsus, forestalled him by occupying the territory. It may be of this campaign that it is said that Ptolemy took Jerusalem by sending in his troops on the Sabbath – a tactic similar to that employed with less success by Egypt and Syria against the state of Israel in 1973 CE, when they attacked on the holy Day of Atonement. The defenders, loyal to the precepts of Ezra, refused to take up arms. Ptolemy then deported 100,000 Judaeans to Egypt, where they considerably bolstered the membership of the local diaspora.

For almost exactly a hundred years the Judaeans remained subject to the Ptolemies. They had to pay annual tribute, but they were ruled by their own High Priest, whose office was generally hereditary, with a council of seventy 'elders', and they were free to practise their religion. During the latter half of the third century BCE, however, there arose a conflict in Judaea which reflected the continual rivalries between the Ptolemies and the Seleucids elsewhere in the region. The High Priest Onias II, who was pro-Seleucid in his tendencies, decided to withhold the annual tribute to Ptolemy III (246–221 BCE) of twenty talents of silver. Ptolemy sent a deputation to demand it, threatening to put the country under armed occupation if it was not paid. Joseph, the son of Onias' sister and of Tobias, a powerful Jew with lands and a stronghold east of the river Jordan, stood up as spokesman for an opposition party, offering personally to negotiate with Ptolemy. His subsequent success, and appointment as tax collector over the whole of Coele-Syria (effectively southern Syria), Phoenicia, Samaria, and Judaea, an office he held for twenty-two years, represented the initial victory of the Tobiads over the Oniads.

The wealth that Joseph and his son Hyrcanus amassed by fair means and foul brought them and their party political power, and put them in the forefront of those who advocated the Hellenism under whose influence they had profited in the first place. It made no difference that just in time the Council of Elders voted to transfer their allegiance from Ptolemy V (204–181 BCE) of Egypt to the Seleucid Antiochus III (223–187 BCE) of Syria: the chief protagonists of the motion were Hyrcanus' disaffected half-brothers. It proved to be a wise, if short-lived, measure. When Antiochus finally captured Judaea from Egypt in 198 BCE, he generously rewarded the Jews for their support, according to decrees reproduced by Josephus (*Antiquities* XII. 3. iii–iv), by restoring the city of Jerusalem and repairing the Temple, reducing taxation and tribute, forbidding non-Jews to enter the Temple precinct, and banning the introduction into the city of non-kosher meat.

The High Priest at this time was Simon II (held office *c*. 220–*c*. 190 BCE), son of Onias II. A reference to the restoration of the Temple and the description of a service conducted by him, with libations, trumpet fanfares, and full choral accompaniment, are in Ecclesiasticus 50, written in Hebrew between the time of the death of Simon and 175 BCE by Ben Sirach and translated into Greek in 132 BCE by his grandson. The book, also known as The Wisdom of Ben Sirach, or of Jesus the Son of Sirach, is an expression of traditional Jewish values, written at a time when these were under threat from Hellenism. It covers a range of topics from the nature and philosophy of wisdom, the doctrine of creation, and the origin of evil, to table manners, when to call the doctor, and how to control your flighty daughter.

As long as the influence of Hellenism was confined to the principles of democratic government, architecture, and the appreciation of philosophy, literature, science, and art, then the Jews had as much to learn, and learn also to reject if they wished, as people of any other culture. Bitter and deep conflict, however, arose over the more controversial and, to many, degenerate aspects of Hellenism, which embraced athletics, with its religious connotations, the theatre, dress, rich food and wine, and religion itself. It is said that a Jewish athlete, embarrassed to have to appear circumcised when running in the nude, as was the custom, had his operation reversed. The conflict was social as well as cultural: it was the wealthy aristocrats of Jerusalem, and the leading priestly families, who had most to gain from Hellenism, and had gained most from it. While there was religious toleration under both Ptolemies and Seleucids, the adoption of Hellenistic ways was still to a certain extent a matter of personal choice. When Antiochus IV (175–164 BCE), with some support from within Jerusalem, used violent means to impose his brand of extreme Hellenism on Judaea, armed revolution became inevitable.

THE REVOLT OF THE MACCABEES

The fourth and final vision in the book of Daniel contains, in chapter 11, a remarkable summary, couched in prophetic terms, of the situation in the region from Alexander's victory over Persia to the death of Antiochus IV. From the fact that the only historical error concerns the manner and place of Antiochus' death, it has been deduced that

Figure 11 Silver tetradrachm (= one shekel) of Antiochus IV. On the reverse side the king is represented as Zeus, head of the Greek pantheon. He has a royal staff in his left hand, and balances on his right hand the winged figure of Nike, goddess of victory. The inscription is in Greek: (from the right) King Antiochus; (from the left) God manifest; (bottom) Bringer of victory. Antiochus IV formally assumed the title Epiphanes, '(God) Manifest', in about 169 BCE. Other Hellenistic kings before him had claimed divine privileges, as Alexander had done, but to impose his divinity on the Jews was deliberate provocation. (Actual size)

the passage was written between 168 and 164 BCE, that is after the beginning of the Maccabaean revolt and just before he died. By a similar kind of reckoning, the Apocryphal 1 Maccabees, covering 175 to 134 BCE, can be dated as having been compiled not later than 104 BCE. 2 Maccabees, dealing with events approximately from 180 to 161 BCE and incorporating an abridged version of a lost history of the revolt by Jason of Cyrene, has been calculated to have been composed in about 123 BCE.

Both Hellenism and personal greed contributed to a deterioration of the general situation in Jerusalem. Simon II was succeeded as High Priest by Onias III, who held office from about 190 to 174 BCE. Onias was in Antioch, making a report to Seleucus IV (187–175 BCE), when the latter was assassinated by one of his ministers and replaced by Antiochus IV. Onias never returned to Jerusalem and was in due course murdered. In his absence his office was appropriated by his brother, formerly Joshua but now called by the old Greek name of Jason, who had his appointment confirmed by Antiochus on the basis of a large bribe, an increase in taxes on the population, and a further sum in respect of the franchise to build a Greek-style sports stadium and gymnasium. In 171 BCE Jason sent Menelaus (originally Menahem), an even more fanatic Helleniser than he was, to Antioch with the latest instalment of tribute. On arrival Menelaus outbid Jason for the office of High Priest, which Antiochus gave him. Jason had at least belonged to the high-priestly family. For a successor who was not of a priestly family at all to be appointed to the highest religious office in the land by a non-Jewish king was too much for the Jews of Jerusalem, who rioted. Menelaus got into arrears with his extra payments. While Menelaus was away, explaining himself to the king, his brother, with Menelaus' connivance, relieved the Temple of some of its treasures and was in the course of further rioting lynched by the mob.

Antiochus, believing that the answer to his Jewish problem was the abolition of the practice of Judaism altogether, twice reacted with extreme and repulsive brutality, graphic examples of which are in 2 Maccabees 6, 7. The time was ripe for organised resistance.

The revolution began in 167 BCE, either just before or soon after the Seleucids' crowning insult, the defiling of the Temple itself with a sacrifice of pigs' flesh on an altar newly dedicated to Zeus, the head of the Greek pantheon. It was the first conflict in history to be fought, and won, on the issue of religious freedom: when it finally ended in 142 BCE, it had become also a war of national independence. It originated not in Jerusalem, but out in the country, 28 kilometres away, in the village of Modein, home of the priest Mattathias, of the Hasmonaean family, and his five stalwart sons, John, Simon, Judas, Eleazar, and Jonathan. Mattathias, called upon by visiting agents of Antiochus to take the lead in publicly abandoning his faith, and so qualify with his sons for special privileges as 'Friends of the King', not only refused, but hacked to death a Jew who offered to take his place, killed the Syrian supervisor, and tipped over the altar. He and his sons then melted into the surrounding hills to plan the next stage of the operation.

The first skirmish of the campaign involved an intensely pious group of Jews known as Hasidim (Biblical Hasideans). As passionately devoted to the Law of God as to the cause of freedom, when hunted down by forces of Antiochus, they refused to come out of their caves or even to defend themselves on the Sabbath, and were all massacred with their families. Mattathias' first strategic decision was to announce that, if attacked, Jews would fight on the Sabbath; his second, made just before he died in 166 BCE, was to appoint his third son Judas as leader of the revolt. Judas, known as 'Maccabee' (The Hammer), was not just a worthy fighter, but also a military genius. Clearly, he trained his rustic army in guerrilla warfare, and established an armoury of weapons captured from the enemy. What tactics he employed in the field against armies of regular troops, comprising heavy and light infantry and cavalry, chariots, and elephant battalions, all equipped with the latest weaponry, including artillery, can only be guessed at. He had, however, some advantages. His men, though always heavily outnumbered, were dedicated to their cause and fighting for their country, their religious beliefs, their freedom, and their families, whereas their opponents were mainly mercenaries. Judas knew the terrain and was able to choose when and where to fight. And he had obviously worked out how to combat the standard battle formation of the Greeks, the heavy infantry massed phalanx, the Seleucid version of which comprised blocks of pikemen, each thirty-two men deep and fifty abreast, which he did presumably by attacking on the flanks and causing the line to roll up on itself.

A victory over Apollonius, the regional governor based in Samaria, who was killed in the fighting and had his sword taken by Judas, was followed by the ambush at the pass of Beth-horon of an army despatched from Syria. It was now 165 BCE. Antiochus, about to embark on a campaign in the east against rebellious elements in Persia, divided his forces in two and appointed Lysias viceroy over the west of his empire, with special responsibilities for putting down the insurrection in Judaea. Lysias sent three generals, with twenty thousand troops, into Judaea, where they set up a main encampment at

Emmaus, in the foothills above the valley of Aijalon, some 25 kilometres from Jerusalem. Such was the confidence of the Syrians on this occasion that slave-dealers were invited to join the company, to handle, at a preset price, the expected influx of Jewish prisoners-of-war.

The Jewish victory, this time fought largely on ground selected by their enemy, was a triumph for Judas' imaginative tactics and the discipline of his troops. The surviving Syrians fled towards the coast, leaving booty galore in the form of gold and silver, cloth, and military equipment. The next attempt at putting down the revolution was made by Lysias himself, whose hastily mobilised army approached from the south-east of Judaea through Idumaean territory, and was severely mauled among the passes and dried-up watercourses in the region of Beth-zur. Lysias' withdrawal to Antioch, however, could have been due to his realisation that the campaign was doomed without a better-prepared army, or to affairs of state, of which the illness of Antiochus is the most likely.

This was the signal for which Judas had been waiting. Gathering supporters from the hills along the way, he and his army marched to Jerusalem. Having shut the Syrian garrison up in the Akra, their fortress citadel on a ridge of Mount Zion, he and his men set to work to repair the desolation of the Temple and clean away all traces of the filth and the profane uses to which it had been put. On 14 December 164 BCE, three years to the day after it had been desecrated, the Temple was rededicated 'with hymns of thanksgiving, to the music of harps and lutes and cymbals. All the people prostrated themselves, worshipping and praising heaven that their cause had prospered' (NEB 1 Macc. 4:54–55). The eight-day festival that followed has been celebrated ever since as Hanukkah. According to tradition, there was only enough oil available on the first occasion for the Temple lights to burn for one day. They burned for eight, and Jews from miles around came to gaze at the miraculous flames.

There was something providential too about the subsequent course of events. Antiochus, just before his death in 164 BCE, named a commander called Philip as regent for his eight-year-old son, Antiochus V (164–162 BCE). Lysias, whom Antiochus IV had previously appointed guardian of the young prince, took no notice and continued to prosecute the conflict with the Jews. In 163 BCE, he advanced against Judaea by the same route as before, and was met by Judas at Beth-zecharia. The Syrian elephants, stimulated by a heady mixture of grape and mulberry juice, caused much consternation among the Jewish ranks. At the height of the battle Judas' brother Eleazar, seeing an elephant bearing the royal crest on its body armour, fought his way towards it, got underneath its belly, and thrust upwards with his sword, only for the dying animal to collapse on top of him and kill him. Shortly afterwards, Judas withdrew his troops and retreated to Jerusalem, where he stationed a garrison on the Temple Mount before taking the rest of his army into the Gophna hills to the north, to fight another day.

Lysias, as expected, made for Jerusalem, found the Temple Mount too tough a nut to crack, and settled in for a siege. At this crucial point word came that Philip, who had been engaged on the Seleucid eastern front, was approaching Antioch, bent on taking over the government. Lysias abandoned the siege and offered peace terms. In return for accepting Syrian control and a permanent Syrian garrison in Jerusalem, the Jews were given freedom of worship once again. Lysias hastened back to Antioch, where his efforts to secure his position were short-lived. Demetrius I (162–150 BCE), nephew of Antiochus IV, escaped from Rome, where he had been a hostage for fifteen years, had Antiochus V and Lysias killed by the army, and assumed the throne.

In obtaining freedom of worship, the Jews had simply reverted to the situation of four years before. Judas would be satisfied with nothing short of national independence, towards which he was spurred also by Demetrius' continued insistence on appointing the High Priest. The armed conflict between Judaea and Syria continued. At the same time Judas pursued a policy of protecting the Jews in areas outside Judaea by armed intervention, which also had the effect of extending the area over which he had control. He was also active in the field of diplomacy, despatching two envoys to Rome to negotiate an alliance against the Hellenistic powers. The Romans, whose policy of 'divide and rule' involved supporting anyone against the power of the Seleucids, sent a stiff note to Demetrius.

In the meantime Demetrius had despatched yet another army to Judaea. The two sides met at Elasa in 160 BCE. According to 1 Maccabees 9, against the Syrians' twenty thousand infantry and two thousand cavalry, Judas had only three thousand troops, many of whom deserted when they saw the size of the opposition, leaving him with just eight hundred. Though his left flank, in which he positioned himself, put the opposition right to flight, his other flank could not contain the enemy, who then wheeled round and took the Judaean left in the rear. Judas Maccabaeus was one of the last to fall.

By popular acclaim, the role of leader of the nationalistic Jews was given to Judas' youngest brother, Jonathan. He and his supporters soon found themselves so harassed both by the Seleucids and by the Hellenisers among their own countrymen, that they took to the desert. It was during an armed skirmish that John, the eldest Maccabee, was kidnapped and killed by a group of Jambrite raiders from Moab while attending to the baggage train. After a full-scale defeat of the Seleucids in a desert encounter in 157 BCE, there was a formal cessation of hostilities and a return of Jewish hostages. Jonathan set up his headquarters at Michmash, north of Jerusalem, from where he 'began to govern the people, rooting the godless out' (NEB 1 Maccabees 9:73). The situation changed for the better in 152 BCE, with the emergence of an alternative candidate for the throne of Syria, Alexander Balas, who claimed to be another son of Antiochus IV; because he was a disruptive influence on the status quo, needless to say he had the support of the Roman senate.

For the next two years Jonathan played off Alexander Balas and Demetrius I against each other in their attempts to gain the support of the Jewish people. Balas appointed Jonathan High Priest, a post which had been vacant for several years, and nominated him a 'Friend of the King', an honour which immediately confounded the Hellenistic faction in Judaea and effectively silenced them as an opposition party. In spite of the offer from Demetrius of additional blandishments, Jonathan threw in his lot with Balas, which turned out to be a wise choice when Demetrius was killed in battle against Balas in 150 BCE. When Alexander Balas (150–145 BCE) was assassinated after being defeated by Demetrius II (145–138 BCE), son of Demetrius I, Jonathan's control both of the military and of the diplomatic reins of his nation was sufficient to enable him to extend his influence further under the new arrangement. By a combination of bold military tactics and diplomacy, he obtained exemption from certain taxes for Judaea and for three districts of Samaria which he asked to be brought under his control, and an undertaking that the Syrian garrison would be withdrawn from the Akra.

Jonathan's single recorded diplomatic miscalculation led to his being captured and subsequently murdered in 142 BCE by Diodotus Tryphon, a former general of Balas, whom he had decided to support against Demetrius. By that time Jonathan had made further overtures to Rome, and he and his elder brother Simon had strengthened the defences of Judaea and undertaken military expeditions which ranged from Gaza to Galilee. Simon, whom the Jews had appointed Jonathan's successor, further consolidated the position of Judaea by occupying the port of Joppa, thus securing his overseas links. The people of Joppa were an untrustworthy lot, having in the time of Judas Maccabaeus drowned the entire Jewish community of the town.

Jonathan had obtained religious independence for Judaea; Simon now had the basis from which to negotiate political independence. He achieved this by demanding from Demetrius complete exemption from taxation for the people of Judaea in return for their loyalty and support. Demetrius, beset with the problem of Tryphon, who had in the meantime murdered Antiochus VI, his own candidate for the throne, and was claiming it for himself, had no choice but to agree. So, 'In the year 170' [of the Seleucid dynasty, that is 142 BCE] 'Israel was released from the gentile yoke. The people began to write on their contracts and agreements, "In the first year of Simon, the great high priest, general, and leader of the Jews"' (NEB 1 Macc. 13:41–42).

JUDAEA LIBERATA

With the surrender in 141 BCE of the garrison in the Akra, the ultimate symbol of Syrian rule was removed. While the Hellenistic faction in Judaea ceased to exist as a political and military power, Judaea itself was still part of the Hellenistic world and subject to its cultural influences, not least in the opulence with which its Hasmonaean rulers surrounded themselves. Though the Jews had confirmed Simon as hereditary High Priest, the appointment was only 'until a true prophet should appear' (NEB 1 Macc. 14:41), suggesting a compromise between the political aspirations of the Maccabees and their Hasmonaean descendants and the demands of the traditional, devout Jews, of whom various distinctive groups had begun to emerge.

Events in Syria, while further weakening the Seleucids' claim to world power, ensured that the path of independence was far from smooth. Demetrius, having in 138 BCE undertaken a campaign against the Persians and been rendered obsolete by being captured, was succeeded by his brother Antiochus VII (138–128 BCE). As long as Tryphon still remained a threat, Antiochus was only too keen to confirm all the rights which Simon had extracted from Demetrius, and in addition to award him the privilege of minting his own coins, of which Simon does not appear to have availed himself. Once he had sent Tryphon packing, Antiochus changed his tune. He demanded the return of the cities of Joppa and Gezer, the reinstatement of the Akra as a Syrian garrison, and either taxes to be levied on places captured outside Judaea or a sum of one thousand talents paid in lieu. Simon, the wealth of whose establishment amazed Antiochus' emissary, rejected all demands and offered one hundred talents in respect of just Joppa and Gezer. Antiochus responded by sending in an army, which was soundly defeated near Modein by Simon's sons, John and Judas.

All five Maccabees died violently: Simon, who is regarded also as the first of the Hasmonaean rulers, was assassinated in 134 BCE by his son-in-law Ptolemy, whom Simon had appointed governor of Jericho. Ptolemy invited Simon, with Judas and his brother Mattathias, to his fortress at Dok, and killed them at dinner. He then sent word to Antiochus VII, offering his full cooperation in return for troops and for authority to take over the government. Simon's son John was at Gezer. Forewarned of the plot, he captured and killed the Ptolemy aides who had been sent to kill him, and then raced Ptolemy to Jerusalem, whose inhabitants, disgusted at Ptolemy's actions, gave John a royal welcome. That Ptolemy ultimately escaped was due to a further piece of dastardly behaviour. He took refuge in another of his Jericho forts, where he had already locked up John's mother and his two other brothers. Whenever John's assault on the place seemed to be succeeding, he brought them out on to the ramparts and publicly tortured them. In this way, according to Josephus (*The Jewish War* I. 2. iv), Ptolemy managed to spin out the siege until the sabbatical year came round, which, like the Sabbath itself, was a Jewish time of rest. John was forced to withdraw, whereupon Ptolemy killed his captives and escaped to the Ammonite city of Philadelphia.

The account in 1 Maccabees ends with the death of Simon. From this point on, the works of Josephus, writing between 70 and 93 CE, represent the main source of information about the Hasmonaeans. John (134–104 BCE), called 'Hyrcanus' from Hyrcania to the south of the Caspian Sea, where a Jewish settlement had been established in about 345 BCE by prisoners of the Persians, was duly confirmed as High Priest and ruler of the people. Syrian interference continued until about 125 BCE, when protracted wranglings over the succession, other foreign enemies, and a further warning from Rome at last left Judaea in a position to give priority to its own affairs. For Hyrcanus this meant extending his borders. He crossed the Jordan and subdued the significant Moabite city of Medeba. He invaded Samaria, destroyed Shechem, and razed the Samaritan temple on Mount Gerizim, thus ensuring the continuity of enmity between Samaritan and Judaean Jews. In a further campaign he captured the Hellenistic city of Samaria, which he then demolished by digging out its foundations so that it was swept away by the mountain torrents, and took Scythopolis (Beth-shan), within the territory of Galilee. In the south, he marched into Idumaea, imposing Judaism on its population and forcibly circumcising its males.

In order to further his military campaigns, Hyrcanus employed foreign mercenaries, to pay whom he broke into the tomb of King David and removed three thousand talents of silver. It was no doubt this, as well as his military ambitions and Hellenistic high-handedness, which caused members of the party of the Pharisees, who had openly supported the Maccabees, to suggest that he should give up the office of High Priest and concentrate on matters of practical government. Hyrcanus, who had none of the charisma or humility of King David, took offence and transferred his patronage to the Sadducees, whose members were largely of the rich priestly nobility and were less likely to look askance at worldly aspirations.

Be that as it may, Hyrcanus instructed that on his death his widow should assume the government of the country, and his eldest son Aristobulus should be High Priest. Instead, Aristobulus incarcerated his mother and starved her to death, and imprisoned his brothers except for his favourite, Antigonus, whom he first nominated as joint ruler with him, and then, when objections were raised, put to death. Aristobulus died in 103 BCE after being in charge for just one year, during which it would appear that the rest of Galilee was brought under Judaean control and the Jewish faith.

Aristobulus' widow, Salome Alexandra, released his surviving brothers from prison, and married Jonathan (Jannai), the eldest of them and Hyrcanus' third son, for whom she secured the office of High Priest. Alexander Jannaeus (103–76 BCE), as he is known, went further than either his brother or father, claiming also the title of king, which he inscribed on some of his coins. That he was free to pursue a militant expansionist policy was largely due to the Romans being preoccupied with the expansionist policies of Mithridates VI (120–63 BCE), king of Pontus, and to the Egyptian queen, Cleopatra III (107–101 BCE), who had two Jewish generals, being more sympathetic to Alexander than to her son Ptolemy IX (101–88 BCE).

Alexander began with a territory which effectively embraced Judaea, Idumaea, Samaria, and Galilee. By conquest and forcible conversion, he extended it along the coastal plain (all except for the city of Ashkelon) and across the river Jordan, until it matched in extent the kingdom of David and Solomon. Matters at home, where the Pharisees and other devout Jews were unhappy about his military activities and incensed at his breaking the Law (Lev. 21:14) which expressly states that no priest, let alone the High Priest, shall marry a widow, reached breaking-point in about 96 BCE when, at the Feast of Tabernacles (Sukkot), the congregation pelted him with lemons, which they were carrying as part of the seasonal ritual, and hurled insults at him. According to Josephus (*Antiquities* XIV. 8. v), he retaliated by massacring six thousand of his own people, and built a wooden partition round the altar as a defence against further missiles when he was performing the sacrifice.

Resentment erupted into open rebellion in about 94 BCE, when Alexander was forced to flee back to Jerusalem in the wake of an ignominious encounter with the Nabataeans. After six years of civil war, and the loss of fifty thousand Jewish lives, the Pharasaic element among the rebels appealed to the Seleucid king, Demetrius III (95–87 BCE), to intervene. Alexander, having been defeated at Shechem and lost all his mercenaries, took refuge in the mountains with the remains of his Judaean forces, where he was joined by six thousand rebel Jews who obviously felt that life under Alexander was preferable to a return to Seleucid occupation. Demetrius returned home. Once back in control, Alexander wreaked terrible vengeance. As he feasted with his concubines, eight hundred of his opponents were publicly crucified, and then, while they were still alive, the throats of their wives and children were cut before their eyes. The commentary on the book of Nahum among the Dead Sea Scrolls identifies certain verses in chapter 2 as referring to these events, and mentions Demetrius by name. In a chilling gloss on verse 13 (NEB 12), hanging up men alive is described as never having been done before in the land of the Israelites.

Alexander died during yet another campaign across the river Jordan, having according to Josephus had a drink problem which caused a recurrent fever. He was succeeded, by what means it is not clear, by his 64-year-old widow, Salome Alexandra (76–67 BCE), who appointed their elder but less able son, Hyrcanus, High Priest, and put the younger, Aristobulus, in charge of the army. It says a lot for her capabilities that she was able for the most part to restrain the ambitions of Aristobulus, and by diplomatic means to keep a balance between the Pharisees, to whom Hyrcanus belonged and of which, according to tradition, her brother was a significant leader, and the now less favoured Sadducees, who were supported by Aristobulus. Only during her final illness was Aristobulus able to secure a power base by obtaining the backing of twenty-two strategic fortresses in Judaea.

On Salome Alexandra's death, Hyrcanus was duly sidelined after a military encounter with his brother's supporters, as a result of which he relinquished his office of High Priest and his claim to be ruler, in return for retaining his possessions and income. The royal ambitions of Aristobulus II (67–63 BCE) now came under threat from an unexpected quarter. Antipater (*d.* 43 BCE) was a rich Idumaean who had assumed the role of governor of Idumaea which had originally been granted to his father by Alexander Jannaeus. A born political schemer who trusted Hyrcanus more than he did Aristobulus, he encouraged Hyrcanus to emerge from premature retirement by brokering an arrangement between him and Aretas III (*c.* 85–62 BCE), king of the Nabataeans, whereby in return for military support against Aristobulus, Hyrcanus would restore cities and lands which Alexander Jannaeus had taken from Nabataea.

Aristobulus was defeated and escaped to Jerusalem, where in 65 BCE he was besieged in the Temple precinct. Both sides now appealed to Rome, whose massed forces, under their general Pompey 'the Great' (106–48 BCE), had since the previous year been occupied in causing the collapse of the Seleucid dynasty and adding Syria to the Roman empire, and were now eyeing Judaea as the next acquisition. The Roman governor of the new province of Syria, having received deputations, and bribes, from both Aristobulus and Hyrcanus, settled the dispute in favour of Aristobulus and ordered Aretas to withdraw his troops from Judaea. Aristobulus confirmed his success by pursuing the retreating Nabataeans and inflicting on them a heavy defeat.

He was not quite out of the wood, however. In 63 BCE he was forced to send a further delegation to Pompey himself, who was being approached not only by Hyrcanus demanding his right to be recognised as the legitimate ruler, but also by representatives of the more devout Jews of Judaea, who wanted the Hasmonaean royal dynasty abolished and for there to be a return to rule by priests.

Pompey undertook to announce his decision at a later date. The headstrong Aristobulus made plans to bring military force to bear. Pompey invaded Judaea. Aristobulus surrendered to him. Pompey advanced on Jerusalem. The supporters of Hyrcanus opened the gates to him, while those of Aristobulus blockaded themselves inside the Temple precinct and prepared for a siege. They held out for three months. When the Romans finally broke through, there was a terrible massacre. Josephus (*Antiquities* XIV. 4. iii–iv) reports that twelve thousand Jews died, including priests, even as they performed their offices, as they had done throughout the siege. Pompey shocked all right-thinking people by forcing his way through the curtained sanctuary into the Holy of Holies, which only the High Priest was allowed to enter. He touched nothing, however, and gave instructions that the Temple should be cleansed and normal offices resumed.

Numerous Jewish prisoners were taken back to Rome, including Aristobulus and his two daughters and two sons, of whom the elder contrived to escape on the way. In 61 BCE, Aristobulus and other royal families captured during the campaign were made to walk in front of Pompey's chariot in the procession celebrating his triumph in Asia, though on this occasion Pompey waived the custom that they should do so in chains. Aristobulus escaped in 56 BCE with his second son, Antigonus, and raised a rebellion against Rome, but was defeated and put back in captivity. Released in 49 BCE and given two legions with which to secure Syria for the Roman party opposed to Pompey, he was poisoned, presumably by adherents to Pompey's cause. His body was preserved in honey until it could be returned to Judaea for a royal burial.

In the meantime Hyrcanus II was confirmed as High Priest (63–40 BCE) and appointed ethnarch of Judaea, a term for a ruler which implies that he is subservient to another authority, in this case the Roman governor of Syria. Judaean independence was at an end.

PEOPLES AND PLACES OF WORSHIP

Simon II, 'the Just', the High Priest who in Ecclesiasticus 50 administers the rituals in the Second Temple, is referred to in the Talmud as stating that the world is upheld by the Torah, the Temple service, and acts of loving kindness. The Temple is mentioned by the Greek philosopher Hecataeus of Abdera (*fl. c.* 300 BCE), writing about a century before Ben Sirach. Hecataeus, according to Josephus (*Against Apion* I. 22), describes Judaea as having numerous fortresses and villages but only one fortified city, Jerusalem, with a population of 120,000: a sacred building stands in the centre of the city, bare except for a golden altar and lampstand, in which a light burns perpetually, while throughout night and day priests perform rites of purification.

There were traditionally (1 Chron. 24:7–19) twenty-four teams of priests, operating on a rota system. The members of each team came to Jerusalem from wherever their homes were to perform the various offices, and undertake the administrative duties, for one week, beginning on the Sabbath. A priest normally wore a white tunic, a broad sash wound three times round his waist, and a conical hat. Formal wear when officiating in the Temple was broad trousers, a tunic made from a single piece of cloth, a waist-band four fingers wide, and a turban. Priests on duty went barefoot, a perilous business on stone floors perpetually wet with blood from the sacrifice and with running water used in ritual ablutions and for washing away the sacrificial blood – a contemporary from Alexandria, writing under the name of Aristeas probably during the second century BCE, was particularly impressed by the Temple water system and refers to a series of hidden vents round the base of the great altar through which the blood and water drained away. Temple physicians were on hand to treat priests who caught diseases, which were usually of the dysentery variety.

The Levites were the priestly assistants: doorkeepers, musicians, ushers, security officers, secretaries, clerks. They also jointed and skinned the animals for sacrifice, prepared the incense, and baked the shewbread, the twelve cakes of pure wheat flour (reflecting the twelve months of the year, and also the twelve tribes of the Israelites) laid out on a table in the sanctuary in two lines and renewed each Sabbath. Levites were subject to military discipline: a Levite found asleep on guard duty was beaten, and might also have his tunic set on fire. The Talmud records that loud cries in the courtyard were ignored as being of no significance: 'Just a Levite being thrashed!' It has been estimated that a staff of twenty thousand was required to administer the organisation and offices of the Temple, paid for out of the tithes and from contributions made by Jewish communities outside Judaea in the form of a statutory tax.

The Temple ritual and its significance are described in some detail, mainly in two works on *The Special Laws*, by Philo of Alexandria (*c.* 20 BCE–*c.* 45 CE), a Hellenistic Jewish philosopher who visited the Jerusalem Temple at least once and participated in its rites. To him, the Temple symbolises the universe, within which the High Priest is a link between earth and heaven, and the public sacrifices are acts of obeisance on the part of the human race. The High Priest wears a full-length violet robe, whose hem is embroidered with symbolic golden bells, pomegranates, and flowers. Over this is the ephod, a kind of waistcoat, in gold, blue, purple, and scarlet, with epaulettes each of which has sewn on to it an emerald engraved with the names of six of the twelve tribes. Set into a square breastplate are twelve gemstones of different colours, in four rows of three, representing the circle of the zodiac and the four seasons. The High Priest's headdress resembles the tall Persian hat worn by royalty.

Every day, two lambs are sacrificed on the great stone altar before the sanctuary, one in the morning and one in the early evening, supplemented by a further two on the Sabbath. The sacrifice is accompanied by the burning of incense immediately within the sanctuary, on an altar of pure gold on which stands the *menorah*, the seven-branched candlestick. On the far side of the altar, behind a curtain, is the Holy of Holies itself. Philo refers to ten special days, or festivals; by his reckoning every day is a special day in terms of worship, the second special day being the Sabbath, and the third the new moon. In addition to the traditional festivals of Pesach (Passover), Shavuot (Weeks, which he calls Pentecost, signifying fifty days after Pesach), and Sukkot

Hear, O Israel, the Lord
our God, the Lord is One.

Blessed be his name,
whose glorious kingdom is
for ever and ever.

And thou shalt love the
Lord thy God with all thine
heart, and with all thy soul,
and with all thy might.
And these words, which I
command thee this day,
shall be upon thine heart ;
and thou shalt teach them
diligently unto thy children,
and shalt talk of them
when thou sittest in thine
house, and when thou
walkest by the way, and
when thou liest down, and
when thou risest up. And
thou shalt bind them for
a sign upon thine hand, and
they shall be for frontlets
between thine eyes. And
thou shalt write them upon
the door posts of thine
house, and upon thy gates.

שְׁמַע יִשְׂרָאֵל יְיָ אֱלֹהֵינוּ
יְיָ אֶחָד :
בָּרוּךְ שֵׁם כְּבוֹד מַלְכוּתוֹ
לְעוֹלָם וָעֶד :

וְאָהַבְתָּ אֵת יְיָ אֱלֹהֶיךָ
בְּכָל־לְבָבְךָ וּבְכָל־נַפְשְׁךָ
וּבְכָל־מְאֹדֶךָ : וְהָיוּ הַדְּבָרִים
הָאֵלֶּה אֲשֶׁר אָנֹכִי מְצַוְּךָ
הַיּוֹם עַל־לְבָבֶךָ : וְשִׁנַּנְתָּם
לְבָנֶיךָ וְדִבַּרְתָּ בָּם בְּשִׁבְתְּךָ
בְּבֵיתֶךָ וּבְלֶכְתְּךָ בַדֶּרֶךְ
וּבְשָׁכְבְּךָ וּבְקוּמֶךָ : וּקְשַׁרְתָּם
לְאוֹת עַל־יָדֶךָ וְהָיוּ לְטֹטָפֹת
בֵּין עֵינֶיךָ : וּכְתַבְתָּם עַל־
מְזֻזוֹת בֵּיתֶךָ וּבִשְׁעָרֶיךָ :

Figure 12 The opening of the Shema (meaning 'Hear . . .'), which it became
customary to recite morning and evening in the Temple. This passage, which starts with what is, after the existence of God, the
most fundamental affirmation of Judaism, derives from
Deuteronomy 6:4–9. 'When thou liest down . . .' indicates the
times of day when the Shema should be recited. The following sen-
tences refer to *tefillin*, the little boxes attached to the head and arm
on leather straps at prayers, in which are extracts from the
Scriptures, and to the *mezuzah*, verses from Deuteronomy 6 and 11
written on parchment and enclosed in a case which is nailed or
glued to a door-frame.

The Hebrew reads from right to left. The modern Hebrew
alphabet comprises twenty-two consonants, with no capitals.
Vowel sounds, where these are included as here, are shown by
arrangements of indicators above, below, or within a letter.

(Tabernacles), there were also at this time in the Jewish calendar feasts of Unleavened Bread (now celebrated concurrently with Pesach), Sheafs (the people's offerings of their first-fruits), Trumpets (now Rosh Hashanah, the Jewish Day of New Year), and the Fast (Yom Kippur, the Day of Atonement), when, for the only time in the whole year, the High Priest enters the Holy of Holies.

Other sources reflect the awesome solemnity of the worship: the recital of the Shema, the Jewish declaration of faith ('Hear, O Israel, the Lord our God, the Lord is One . . .'), and of the Ten Commandments, the burning of the incense, the blessing of the congregation, the sacrifice, and the singing by the Levitical choir of the psalms prescribed for the day, to the accompaniment of musical instruments with trumpets and cymbals.

The Temple was also the state treasury, and sometimes served as a safe deposit for the wealth of private citizens. Its immediate surroundings constituted the central site in the city for buying and selling of goods, and for financial dealings. Here also the money-changers exchanged foreign coins for the shekels which were the required currency for contributions to the Temple, and traders sold unblemished animals for private sacrifices – birds, in the form of turtle-doves or pigeons, were available for those who could not afford a beast. The Samaritans had a central temple, and temples were built by the Jewish community in Elephantine and in about 160 BCE in Leontopolis in Egypt by Onias, who had fled there in the wake of the events following the succession of Antiochus IV which resulted in the removal from the office of High Priest of his father, Onias III. The Temple in Jerusalem, however, was the focal point of the practice of the Jewish faith. This was true even when Jews had 'entered every city, to the extent that it is difficult to find anywhere in the civilised world which has not taken them in and where they have not made their presence felt', an observation of the Hellenistic geographer Strabo (64 BCE–24 CE) referring to the year 85 BCE (quoted in Josephus, *Antiquities* XIV. 7. ii).

Worship in the local synagogue, an institution which some believe originated during the Babylonian exile, reflected the rhythm of the Temple rituals but was not a substitute for them. Synagogue is a Greek term meaning 'assembly'. It was a house of prayer and for the reading of the Law, but it was also an institute of study.

> On the Sabbath in every city, countless places of learning open their doors for the study of practical wisdom, sound and lively thought, justice, and other intellectual virtues. Here

men sit quietly in rows, giving their full attention, with ears pricked, eagerly to imbibe the flow of words from a scholar of great experience, who stands at the front and instructs them in what is most useful and beneficial towards the improvement of life as a whole.

(Philo, *The Special Laws* II. 62)

The Sadducees and Pharisees, and also the Essenes, represented different movements within the Jewish faith at this time. All Jews accepted the fundamental belief in the one God, and in the authority of the Torah as the basis of their religion and community life. Differences of opinion, often amounting to open conflict, arose in the interpretation and application of the Torah.

Sadducees seem in the main to have been the wealthy and aristocratic clerical and lay members of the community. They were traditionalists, to whom the complex of religious and administrative machinery centred on the Temple had more significance than messianic, apocalyptic, or prophetic statements which might endanger the status quo. The Pharisees, on the other hand, whose leaders were on the whole learned scribes, regarded the interpretation of the Torah as an ongoing activity, and its understanding by the masses of the people a priority. Their influence especially among the lower ranks of the priesthood and working people of all kinds and classes was considerable, and predominated among the communities throughout the diaspora.

Both Josephus and Philo attest to there being four thousand Essenes at the time they were writing. They are also mentioned by the Roman writer Pliny 'the Elder' (23–79 CE) in his *Natural History*. It has been postulated that the members of this ascetic sect may have been successors of the Hasidim of Maccabaean times. There is, however, no clear reference to Essenes in the Bible or in the Talmudic writings, which possibly is the reason why they have not directly influenced the development of Judaism. From the other sources, however, it appears that they lived in communities away from cities, and that membership was restricted to those who had served a probationary period. Their possessions were held in common, and travellers from one community to another did not bother with baggage. They frequently washed their garments, which were usually white, but these and their shoes were worn until they fell to pieces. They seem to have been celibate, or in some cases to have had wives strictly for the purpose of procreation. Their watchwords were cleanliness and godliness, and they worshipped and studied the scriptures in their own synagogues. Their observance of the Sabbath was so strict that, according to Josephus (*The Jewish*

War II. 8. ix), not only did they not handle any tool or utensil, but they refrained from defecating, since this involved the use of the implement with which they would normally dig a hole in the ground.

The ascetic community, part of whose library was discovered by a goatherd in a cave at Qumran in 1947 and comprises the Dead Sea Scrolls, had close affinities with what is known about the Essenes. Subsequent excavations of the ruins on the plain below the cave have established, with the help of coins found on the site, that the settlement was built during the latter half of the second century BCE, but was not fully occupied until the beginning of the following century. It was, in effect, a community village, amply supplied with water by an aqueduct from the hills, and incorporating a place of assembly, a pottery, a scriptorium, and a communal kitchen and laundry. It was largely abandoned after an earthquake in the region in 31 BCE, but restored in about 5 BCE, after which it was fully occupied again until it was destroyed during an attack by the Romans in 68 CE.

The scrolls themselves, the earliest of which date from the third century BCE, are made chiefly from sheep and goat skins, inscribed in a black, black-brown, or occasionally red ink – the black ink of those times was usually made of a mixture of soot and gum. They are written largely in Hebrew, but also in Aramaic and Greek, and comprise a variety of documents, including the oldest known, by a thousand years, Hebrew versions and fragments of books of the Old Testament, and parts of the Apocrypha in Hebrew and Aramaic which previously had been known only in Greek. There are also Biblical commentaries, a philosophical exposition of the military strategy to be directed against the Romans, hymns of thanksgiving for personal blessings, and rules of conduct. From these, various conclusions can tentatively be drawn about the community and its religious convictions.

Its members constituted a monastic society with strict rules of entry and a hierarchical structure; their leader is known only as the Teacher of Righteousness. They claim to have established a new covenant with God, and to be the faithful Remnant of the Israelites for their own and all time. Their doctrine of the messianic age is distinctive in that the Messiah would be the nation's High Priest, who would perform the sacred offices during the conflict, and would ultimately reveal the secrets of the holy scriptures and fully interpret the Law for the present and future ages. The conflict itself is seen as a tremendous battle between the forces of good and those of evil, led by a Satan figure who is clearly the Prince of Darkness himself. This differs from Jewish tradition, in which the Messiah is of the line of David and will lead his people to victory over the Gentiles and initiate the Kingdom of

God, while being answerable to the priests in matters of doctrine and subordinate to them in terms of precedence, and in which Satan means simply 'adversary', and is largely a creature of folklore and superstition.

The Qumran community rejected the authority of the Temple at Jerusalem, since its priests did not follow the prescribed rules, and referred to the High Priest as the 'Wicked Priest'. They disregarded the Jewish lunar calendar of 354 days in favour of one based on the sun, whereby the year was divided into fifty-two weeks exactly, in four seasons each of thirteen weeks. Thus the year began, and every festival fell, on precisely the same day of the week on each occasion, and the community did not necessarily celebrate the special days at the same time as their fellow Jews. This led to a memorable ruction, referred to in the *Commentary on Habbakuk* XI, when the Wicked Priest, in order to embarrass the Teacher of Righteousness, caused a disturbance within the community on what was to them the Day of Atonement.

The identities of the Teacher of Righteousness and the Wicked Priest have been the subject of much scholarly discussion and dissent. According to one view, the events referred to in the Dead Sea Scrolls happened during the time that Antiochus IV was harassing Judaea, that is between about 175 and 164 BCE. A second view is that they occurred a little later, in about the years 152–135 BCE. This has the advantage of identifying the Wicked Priest as either Jonathan 'Maccabaeus' or his brother Simon, neither of whom were qualified for, or particularly interested in exercising, the office of High Priest. Another school of opinion places the events during roughly the following ninety years, with a bias towards the reign of Alexander Jannaeus (103–76 BCE), who, it will be recalled, was appointed High Priest through the influence of his wife and then claimed also the title of king, or during the terms of office as High Priest of his son, Hyrcanus II. A more recent minority hypothesis identifies the Teacher of Righteousness as James, 'the Just', brother of Jesus of Nazareth.

Whatever the answers, the community of Qumran was certainly active during the years in which Christianity emerged from its Jewish roots, and though the Dead Sea Scrolls have more to offer to Jewish scholarship than to the study of the development of Judaism, they contain strong traces of elements which recur in early Christian writings.

In the meantime, however, traditional Judaism had been developing in fresh directions.

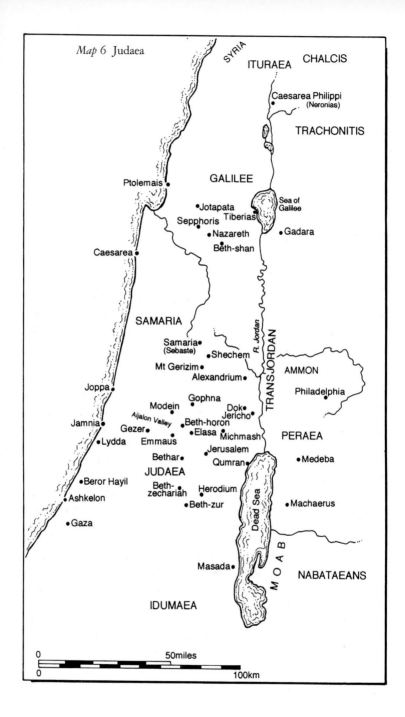

Map 6 Judaea

SYRIA

ITURAEA   CHALCIS

Caesarea Philippi
(Neronias)

TRACHONITIS

Ptolemais

GALILEE

Jotapata
Sepphoris   Tiberias   Sea of
Galilee
Nazareth
Beth-shan   Gadara

Caesarea

SAMARIA

Samaria
(Sebaste)
Shechem
Mt Gerizim
Alexandrium

R. Jordan

TRANSJORDAN

AMMON

Philadelphia

Joppa

Modein   Gophna
Aijalon Valley   Dok
Jamnia   Beth-horon   Jericho
Gezer   Elasa
Lydda   Emmaus   Michmash
Jerusalem
Bethar   Qumran

PERAEA

Medeba

JUDAEA

Beror Hayil
Beth-
zechariah   Herodium
Ashkelon   Beth-zur

Dead Sea

Machaerus

Gaza

M
O
A
B

Masada

NABATAEANS

IDUMAEA

0   50miles
0   100km

164

8

THE JEWS AND THE ROMAN WORLD 63 BCE–135 CE

An entry, written in the middle of the second century BCE, in the Sibylline Books, the treasury of arcane knowledge to which the Roman senate had recourse at times of national stress, refers to the Jews as already filling 'every land and every sea' (III. 271). A letter from the senate delivered in 138 BCE to King Ptolemy VIII of Egypt (145–116 BCE) asked for protection for the Jews in his realm. It was copied to the kings of Syria, Pergamum, Cappadocia, Parthia, and Emesa, and to the rulers of Sparta, all territories in which it may thus be inferred that there were significant Jewish communities. The same message was sent to other places in the eastern Mediterranean region: 'Delos, Myndos, Sicyon, Caria, Samos, Pamphylia, Lycia, Halicarnassus, Rhodes, Phaselis, Cos, Sidé, Aradus, Gortyna, Cnidus, Cyprus, and Cyrene' (NEB 1 Macc. 15:23). Delos, Samos, Rhodes, and Cos are islands in the Aegean sea. Myndos, Halicarnassus, Phaselis, Sidé, and Cnidus were towns along the south coast of Asia Minor. Sicyon was on the Greek mainland, Aradus in Syria, Gortyna in Cyprus, and Cyrene on the north coast of Africa.

The causes of the diaspora were manifold. Wholesale transportations of population removed the ten tribes of Israel to Assyria, and later the tribes of Judah and Benjamin to Babylonia. Ptolemy I and Pompey conducted enforced emigrations of prisoners-of-war to Egypt and Rome. Further movements took place as the result of periodic expulsions, as happened in Rome in 139 BCE, and again in 19 and 49 CE, or of persecution, such as broke out in Egypt in 145 and 38 BCE. Trade and incentives to potential colonisers encouraged emigration of a less involuntary nature. Administrative, agricultural, forensic, medical, military, and other professional skills could be employed advantageously elsewhere. The tiny territory of Judaea was in any case unable to support a growing population. Ritual cleanliness, inbred dietary concern, and a total aversion to exposing unwanted babies, such as was practised for example by the Greeks, contributed to a comparatively high survival rate among the children of Judaea and of the Jewish diaspora. Away from Judaea, it was by nature of their faith that Jews were more likely to absorb into their numbers peoples of pagan religions or of no religion at all, than to be themselves absorbed. And as Jesus observed of the Pharisees, 'You travel over sea and land to make one convert' (NEB Matt. 23:15).

The Jews of the diaspora formed themselves into self-regulating social groupings within the general community in which they settled, whose culture might be predominantly Greek or predominantly Roman, overlaid upon Celtic, African, Egyptian, or Asian traditions, as the case might be. Contact with Jerusalem was maintained by means of an annual Temple tax of half a shekel, paid by all Jews over twenty. In Parthia, for instance, the sums were collected together at Nehardea and Nisibis, and transported under guard to Judaea. Once the caravan was in Roman territory, safe passage was guaranteed by the Roman authorities. One of the charges brought in Rome against Flaccus, the former Roman governor of Asia Minor, in 59 BCE was that he had appropriated large sums of money which had been collected at the island of Cos from various cities for onward transit to Jerusalem. His defence counsel, the famous advocate and politician Marcus Tullius Cicero (106–43 BCE), tried to make out that the court was being intimidated by the crowds of Jews who flocked to the hearing.

In 44 BCE there was another demonstration by the Jews of Rome, of a very different kind. The historian Suetonius (c. 70–c. 140 CE) specifically mentions the fact that numerous Jews came to the forum several nights in succession to pay their respects to the memory of Julius Caesar after his assassination by a band of discontented officials, former soldiers, and members of the senate. After the Roman occupation of Judaea, the government of the Roman empire had effectively been hijacked by a triumvirate consisting of Pompey, Marcus Licinius Crassus (d. 53 BCE), and Gaius Julius Caesar (102–44 BCE). Crassus, having denuded the Temple in Jerusalem of its wealth, died fighting the Parthians. Caesar, needing to rule absolutely if he was not to be prosecuted for past irregularities, had himself appointed dictator and provoked a civil war against Pompey and supporters, whom he pushed out of Italy and defeated in Greece in 48 BCE. Pompey was assassinated the same year in Egypt, where Caesar got himself embroiled in a dispute between the joint rulers, Ptolemy XII (51–47 BCE) and his sister Cleopatra VII (51–30 BCE). Caesar, having taken the side of Cleopatra, who was his mistress, found himself and about three thousand men boxed in at Alexandria by hostile Egyptian troops, who managed also to prevent a relief force reaching him across the southern border of Judaea. He was extricated from this embarrassment by Antipater and Hyrcanus II, who entered Egypt by way of Ashkelon with a Jewish army which was also instrumental in the occupation of the vital frontier fortress of Pelusium.

As a reward for their assistance, Hyrcanus seems now to have become 'Ethnarch of the Jews', implying some nominal responsibility for those also in the diaspora, while Antipater was appointed procurator (administrator) of Judaea, in which capacity he placed two of his sons in influential positions: he made Phasael governor of Jerusalem, and Phasael's 25-year-old younger brother Herod, later Herod 'the Great', governor of Galilee. Caesar also passed measures to protect the interests of Jewish communities outside Judaea, who were to be allowed freedom of worship, to remit contributions to the Temple in Jerusalem, to answer to their own legal system, and to be exempt from conscription into military service. It was Roman policy that, provided there were no breaches of the peace, other cultures within the empire should be free to maintain their own traditions while being assisted to become Romanised. It was in the main in Hellenised cities that opposition to the Jews festered. Conflicts of culture emerged, however, once the Romans began deifying their emperors.

The most serious, and indeed effectively the only, charge brought against the Jews in Roman times was that they were *different*. In an addition to the book of Esther, a Jewish writer encapsulates an extreme Gentile view, which he puts into the mouth of Artaxerxes:

> [Haman] represented to us that scattered among all the races of the empire is a disaffected people, opposed in its laws to every nation, and continually ignoring the royal ordinances, so that our irreproachable plans for the unified administration of the empire cannot be made effective. We understand that this nation stands alone in its continual opposition to all men, that it evades the laws by its strange manner of life, and in disloyalty to our government commits grievous offences, thus undermining the security of our empire.
>
> (NEB Apocrypha, Esther 13:4–5)

Religion had such a bearing on everyday life, that it was impossible for practising Jews to participate with their fellow citizens in festivals and the games. Though they were at times specifically exempted from worshipping the emperor, instead offering sacrifices and prayers merely for his health and well-being, even this could be interpreted as disloyalty. Jews could not eat with their neighbours, nor would Jewish soldiers fight on the Sabbath – there would come an occasion under the Byzantine empire when so many soldiers on both sides were Jewish that a battle had to be postponed. It was not only Jews, however, who observed the Sabbath, it was also their servants. Roman citizens had many days off, but slaves were expected to carry on working regardless: this, and the injunction to let agricultural land in Judaea lie fallow every seventh year, to give it 'a complete rest' (Lev. 25:4), gained for the Jews in some circles an undeserved reputation for idleness.

The Jewish captives brought to Rome as slaves by Pompey reappear a generation later as a significant part of the Jewish population of Rome, where they had settled 'on the other side of the Tiber. . . .

> Having been transported to Italy as prisoners-of-war, they were freed by their owners, and were not pressurised to abandon any of their ancestral traditions. [The emperor Augustus (27 BCE–14 CE)] was aware that they had houses of prayer where they met, especially on the Sabbath, to receive group instruction in their national philosophy. He knew too that they made contributions for religious purposes from the first-fruits of their labours, which they remitted to Jerusalem through those who would conduct the ritual sacrifices on their behalf. Yet he neither expelled them from Rome, nor deprived them of Roman citizenship on the excuse that they assiduously retained their Jewishness, nor vandalised their houses of prayer, nor prevented them meeting for instruction in the law, nor opposed their donating their first-fruits. And what is more, when the monthly dole of corn or cash was handed out in Rome, he never penalised the Jews: if the distribution was to take place on the Sabbath . . . he instructed his agents to hold back the contributions due to the Jewish population until the next day.
>
> (Philo of Alexandria, *The Embassy to Gaius*, 155–157)

That things later began to unwind was sometimes due to the popularity of Judaism rather than to the unpopularity of the Jews. Monotheism in the form of various eastern religions had begun to to infect the cultures of Greece and Rome in the fourth century BCE, so much so that from the second century BCE onwards Egyptian cults were frequently but unsuccessfully banned by the Roman senate or suffered temporary suppression – the all-embracing edict of 139 BCE expelled from Rome all Jewish immigrants as well as eastern astrologers. Judaism offered a concept of a single all-powerful Lord and Creator, who rewards each person according to their moral conduct. The sheer invisibility of God enabled him more easily to be conceived as ruling heaven and earth, and to be exalted beyond the limitations of sense and experience. While most religions offered guidelines for the conduct of daily life, in Judaism these were more specific and comprehensive. The very readiness of the Greeks and Romans to embrace new forms of worship, and the expectation offered by these of a happy afterlife, the possibility of which in some form Jews by no means dismiss, made Judaism a tempting prospect for potential converts.

What was especially attractive was the principle, reflected in the medieval commentary Exodus Rabbah, that 'the gates are open at all times, and whoever wishes to enter may enter' (19:4). To subscribe to the tenets of Judaism it was not necessary, any more than it is today, fully to observe all the ritual requirements. 'As for the foreigners / Who attach themselves to the Lord . . . / All who keep the sabbath and do not profane it, / And who hold fast to My covenant – / I will bring them to My sacred mount / And let them rejoice in My house of prayer' (Isa. 56:6–7). So, the apostle Paul of Tarsus 'argued in the synagogue with the Jews and gentile worshippers' (NEB Acts 17:17), and can state, 'Do you suppose God is the God of the Jews alone? Is he not the God of Gentiles also? Certainly, of Gentiles also, if it be true that God is one' (NEB Rom. 3:29).

There seems to have been a category of Jewish worshippers known as 'God-fearers', who attended synagogue services and might send contributions to the Temple in Jerusalem, without being full proselytes. The term is applied by Josephus (*Antiquities* XX. 9. xi) even to Poppaea Sabina, mistress and later the second wife of the emperor Nero (54–68 CE), on the occasion of her intervening with him in favour of a deputation of priests from Jerusalem – there is also a suggestion that when Nero, after the great fire of Rome in 64 CE, invented scapegoats in the form of Jews and Christians, she persuaded him to settle just for the Christians. The satirist Juvenal (*c.* 55–*c.* 140 CE) gives a biting cameo (XIV. 96–106) of a God-fearing, Sabbath-observing Roman citizen whose son becomes a full convert and subscribes to Jewish rather than to Roman law. A more ambivalent attitude to the Jews than had been exercised by Augustus surfaced under his successor Tiberius (14–37 CE), who was the person responsible in 19 CE for an expulsion order against adherents to all non-Roman cults, especially Jewish and Egyptian. In addition, apparently as a result of a complaint against certain Jews by the husband of a noble lady who had converted to Judaism, four thousand Jewish freedmen were impressed into the army and sent to the most insalubrious area of Sardinia.

The Gaius Caesar to whom Philo of Alexandria addressed his *Embassy to Gaius* was Tiberius' mad successor Caligula (37–41 CE), the occasion being a deputation to Rome led by Philo to plead the interests of the Jews of Alexandria. Caligula's attempt to have a statue of himself erected in the Temple at Jerusalem was foiled by masterly inactivity on the part of the Roman governor of the region, who realised that to proceed with the operation would be the signal for revolution, and by Caligula's assassination. Caligula was succeeded, under improbable circumstances, by his fifty-year-old uncle, Claudius (41–54 CE).

Claudius, a scholar by inclination and upbringing, is recorded in the New Testament as having 'issued an edict that all Jews should leave Rome' (Acts 18:2). This happened in about 49/50 CE, and is presumably the same occasion referred to by Suetonius, on which Claudius 'expelled the Jews from Rome for constantly causing disturbances instigated by Chrestus' ('Claudius' xxv), which could have been strife between Jews who accepted Christian claims and those who did not. Certainly, when faced immediately after his succession with riots in Alexandria between Jews and non-Jews, each of whom sent a deputation to argue their case, he listened to both sides, and refused to apportion to either the blame for starting the fighting. Then, in a strongly worded letter, he pointed out to the non-Jews that they must be tolerant of practices and customs which Augustus had allowed and he himself approved, and to the Jews that they should not agitate for any further privileges than they had had in the past. Never again, he added, would he receive two separate deputations from the same city, as though they lived in places worlds apart.

This letter, written in Greek on papyrus, is preserved in the British Museum. It confirms the report in Josephus (*Antiquities* XIX. 5. ii) of Claudius' actions in defusing the situation in Alexandria. Claudius also detached Judaea and Samaria from the Roman province of Syria, and added them to the client kingdom under the rule of (Herod) Agrippa I (born 10 BCE), the King Herod in Acts 12:1–23. Agrippa was the grandson of Herod the Great (born 73 BCE), who is the Herod of the gospel story in Matthew 2. Agrippa's son, (Herod) Agrippa II (born 28 CE), ruler of the region to the north-east of the Sea of Galilee, is the King Agrippa of Acts 25:13–32, who, on a courtesy visit to Caesarea with his sister Berenice, gives Paul a sympathetic hearing at a meeting which took place in about 60 CE. The Herod of Matthew 14:1–12 and Mark 6:17–28, who has John the Baptist's head

Hasmonaean and Herodian dynasties

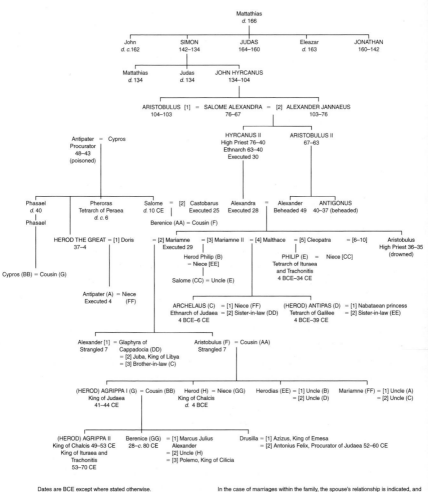

Dates are BCE except where stated otherwise.

In the case of marriages within the family, the spouse's relationship is indicated, and the name is keyed with the appropriate letter or letters, e.g. (A), (AA).

handed on a dish to his stepdaughter Salome, was (Herod) Antipas (20 BCE–39 CE), tetrarch of Galilee, a son of Herod the Great.

The term 'the Great' seems to have been associated by Josephus with the original Herod to distinguish him from those of his descendants who also held offices of state. The judgement of history is that it was justified in that everything he did was on a grand scale; he was

171

also, however, unprincipled, tyrannous, and cruel, not least when dealing with members of his own family.

HEROD THE GREAT

Herod the Great was ambitious by nature, jealous by disposition, Idumaean by birth, Jewish insofar as his people had been forcibly converted by Hyrcanus I, Hellenistic by upbringing and inclination, Hasmonaean by marriage, and, when it suited his interests, a fervent supporter of Rome. He had ten wives, the second of whom, and her mother, he had executed: the other nine ended up arguing with him and among themselves about domestic precedence. He had numerous offspring, some of whom he also executed: he organised dynastic marriages between his children and other members of his family in violation of Jewish law, and between members of his family and the families of other client kings, though his insistence on Syllaeus, chief executive to the king of Nabataea, being circumcised as a condition of becoming the third husband of Herod's sister Salome, caused the betrothal to be called off. His great-granddaughter Berenice (28–after 79 CE), the daughter of (Herod) Agrippa I and Agrippa's first cousin Cypros, was married at 13 to the son of the head of the Jewish community in Alexandria, and after his death to her uncle Herod, king of Chalcis, who died in 48 CE. She then became so closely attached to her brother (Herod) Agrippa II, that in order to allay suspicions of incest she prevailed upon Polemo, king of Cilicia, chiefly on account of her wealth, to undergo circumcision and marry her. She soon left him, however, and set up house again with her brother in Jerusalem, being associated with him in supporting the Roman cause in the rebellion which came to a head in 66 CE. In the Roman camp while Jerusalem was sacked in 70 CE, she induced the emperor's son and heir, Titus, twelve years her junior, to succumb to her charms, and accompanied him to Rome. She lived openly with him, and he reputedly promised marriage, but in 75 CE he bowed to public pressure and sent her back to Judaea.

The Agrippa connection was originally through Marcus Vipsanius Agrippa (63–12 BCE), the emperor Augustus' right-hand man. Josephus claims that at one time Herod ranked first after Agrippa in the emperor's esteem, and first after the emperor in Agrippa's (*Antiquities* XV. 10. iii): even if Augustus is reported elsewhere as having commented, in the context of Herod's family affairs, 'I would rather be Herod's swine than his son.' Herod sent two of his elder sons,

Figure 13 Bronze coin of Herod the Great, carrying an anchor, with the abbreviated inscription in Greek from the right downwards, 'King Herod'. The reverse has two cornucopiae joined together at their lower ends. Between them is a Roman symbol, the staff of office of a herald, indicating a peaceful mission, which was also carried by Mercury, as messenger of the gods. This either indicates insensitivity on the part of Herod, or is further evidence of his ambivalent political nature. (× 2)

Alexander and Aristobulus, to be educated in Rome, as were three younger sons, Archelaus, Antipas, and Philip, who were later to govern his kingdom, and Aristobulus' son, Agrippa I, who from the age of six was brought up as a member of the imperial family.

In 47 BCE Herod had demonstrated his ability to take drastic action by using what the Sanhedrin, the supreme secular council in Jerusalem of seventy-one members, regarded as unnecessary brutality in dealing with opposition to him in Galilee. As a result he took temporary refuge in Syria. In the turmoil following the assassination of Julius Caesar in 44 BCE, Antigonus, son of the former Hasmonaean king Aristobulus II, invaded Judaea with Parthian support. Herod returned, beat off the threat, and was rewarded by a grateful High Priest and ethnarch, Hyrcanus, with the hand of his desirable grand-daughter Mariamne, for whom Herod divorced his first wife, Doris, an Idumaean of Jewish birth. Mariamne was doubly a Hasmonaean; her mother was Hyrcanus' daughter, and her father was the son of Aristobulus II's elder son, Alexander (*d.* 49 BCE).

Herod also showed a greater talent for survival than his father Antipater, who was poisoned in 43 BCE. The defeat at Philippi in Macedonia in 42 BCE of the chief conspirators in the plot against Julius Caesar strengthened the hands of the ruling triumvirate in Rome: Caesar's nineteen-year-old nephew, and adopted son and heir, Octavian (later the emperor Augustus), and Caesar's former chief assistants, Marcus Aemilius Lepidus (*d.* 13 BCE) and Mark Antony (*c.* 83–30 BCE). Antony assumed control of the east, where the borders of his territory were beset by the Parthians and his susceptibility to female charm exercised by Caesar's former mistress, Cleopatra, now sole ruler of Egypt. It was no contest. Antony followed Cleopatra home. In 40 BCE the Parthians invaded Syria and then moved into Judaea, while Antigonus, with a separate Parthian force, entered Jerusalem and occupied the Temple, in spite of the combined efforts of Herod and Phasael to stop him. Phasael and Hyrcanus were duped into entering the Parthian camp, where they were taken prisoner. Herod immediately put into practice his emergency measures: he escaped with his immediate family, whom he settled in the hilltop fortress of Masada, before making his way by a roundabout route to Rome to consult with Antony, who had also repaired there. In the meantime Phasael had committed suicide in captivity, Hyrcanus' ears had been chopped off (Josephus suggests Antigonus bit them off) to disqualify him from continuing in the office of High Priest (see Leviticus 21:16–21), and Antigonus, with Parthian backing, had nominated himself king of Judaea *and* High Priest.

In 37 BCE Herod, with Roman help and largely Roman troops, completed his campaign to secure the crown for himself by besieging Jerusalem and storming the Temple. Antigonus was taken to Antioch on the orders of Antony and beheaded. This was the bloody end to the brief reinstatement of the Hasmonaean dynasty. Herod took over the reins of government as an 'associate' king, answerable to the senate in Rome, which effectively meant whoever was in charge of the Roman empire. That he retained his role for so long was due to his diplomatic relations with Rome, to the magnificence and effectiveness of his civic and military building programmes, to his concern for certain sections of the community, such as he exercised by stripping his palace of personal ornaments to buy provisions and clothing from Egypt for a populace devastated by the famine in 25 BCE, to his penchant for decisive, sometimes drastic, action (particularly in reversing potentially disastrous decisions), and to his ruthless personality. To the people of Judaea, he was an Idumaean; for all his Hellenistic ways and generosity to Hellenistic cities, to the many Greeks in the region he was still a Jew; to the Jews he was only half Jewish, which to be fair was how he acted when away from his kingdom.

He began by confiscating large amounts of gold and silver from the wealthy, out of which he sent rich gifts to Antony and Antony's henchmen. He also executed forty-five of the chief supporters of Antigonus and appropriated their belongings – there is some suggestion that they, or many of them, were members of the Saducean-dominated Sanhedrin. Where for form's sake he required recourse to an advisory

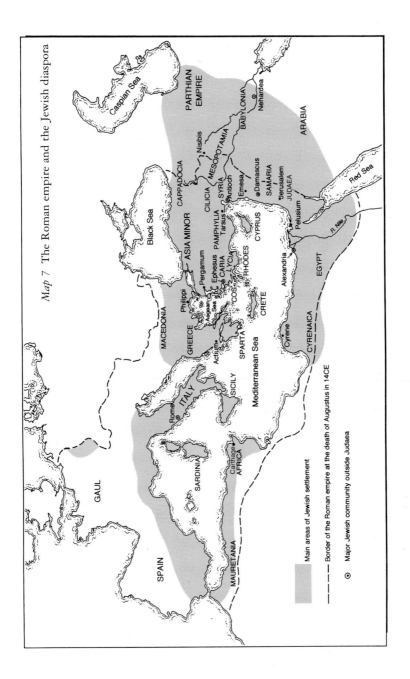

Map 7 The Roman empire and the Jewish diaspora

Main areas of Jewish settlement

Border of the Roman empire at the death of Augustus in 14CE

⊙ Major Jewish community outside Judaea

council, he established a new secular body on Hellenistic lines, which conducted its deliberations in Greek. In place of the mutilated Hyrcanus, he appointed as High Priest Ananelus, an obscure Babylonian cleric who claimed to be a member of the original line of High Priests descended from Zadok. This outwardly diplomatic appointment misfired. The natural successor to Hyrcanus was his sixteen-year-old grandson, Aristobulus, whose sister (Herod's wife Mariamne) and mother (Herod's mother-in-law Alexandra) were especially affronted. Ananelus was replaced by Aristobulus, whose appearance in 35 BCE at the Feast of Tabernacles so impressed the general public that murmurings were heard about a return to the Hasmonaean monarchy. Afterwards, at a reception in Jericho, Aristobulus was encouraged in the heat of the day to go bathing with a party of Herod's young associates, who held him under water until he drowned. Over the next thirty years Herod hired and fired numerous High Priests, thus reducing the status of the sacred hereditary office to that of a mere employee.

While the thunder clouds generated by the disgraceful love affair between Antony and Cleopatra gathered over the commonwealth of Rome, Herod survived several local crises. The most serious nationally was the earthquake in 31 BCE, the most devastating in Judaea in ancient times. While he was away on the orders of Antony collecting tribute for Cleopatra from the Nabataeans, who had decided that in the light of the general situation they could withhold it, the earthquake destroyed homes and cattle, accounted for some ten thousand lives, and caused the community at Qumran to abandon their settlement. Herod also dealt summarily with Hyrcanus, whose daughter Alexandra, in revenge for the death of Aristobulus, put him up to expressing privately a willingness to consider reassuming the rightful trappings of monarchy of which he had been deprived by his brother thirty-seven years earlier, by having the lugless septuagenarian executed on a charge of treason. The open conflict which had now broken out between Octavian and Antony presented Herod with a personal crisis of a different kind. Having sent members of his immediate family to safe places, and given instructions, which were leaked to Mariamne, that if anything happened to him she should be killed to prevent her becoming anyone else's wife, he collected together a sizeable bribe and went to the island of Rhodes to throw in his lot with the man whom he now saw as the new, and sole, ruler of the known world.

Octavian accepted Herod's bribe and assurances of loyalty. After the battle of Actium in 31 BCE and the suicides of the doomed lovers the following year, Octavian transferred to Herod territories which had been leased to Cleopatra. Herod's original kingdom had comprised Judaea, Idumaea, Peraea, and Galilee, with the port of Joppa; he now also had under his control the whole of Samaria and additional territories to the east of the river Jordan, though the Samaritans continued to be fiercely independent of Judaea. It was a kingdom which included in its $2\frac{1}{2}$ million or so inhabitants Greeks, and Arabs of Semitic stock, as well as Jews. The Jews in their ancient kingdom were now far outnumbered by the Jews of the diaspora. It has been estimated that at around this time there were a million Jews in the Parthian-held region of Babylonia, outside the Roman empire. The remainder constituted between 6 and 10 per cent of the population of the empire and its associated kingdoms – for comparison, the number of Jews in the USA in 1975–80 has been estimated at under 3 per cent of the population. The Jews of the Roman empire included a million in Egypt (215,000 of them in Alexandria), a million in Asia Minor, 750,000 in Syria, and 100,000 in Cyrenaica. Of the 100,000 Jews in Italy, about 40,000 may have lived in Rome itself, at a time when the total population of the city was about a million, of whom one-third were slaves. And to the Jews of the diaspora, Herod was their king.

When Herod returned from Rhodes, however, it was straight into family mayhem. Mariamne would not let him forget that he had ordered her death if he should not come back. Herod's mother and his sister Salome accused Mariamne of adultery with the man who had told her about the order, and of planning to poison Herod. Herod had the informant and Mariamne executed, a decision which haunted him for the rest of his life. The next to go was Mariamne's mother, Alexandra, who had instigated one too many plots against him. Salome now betrayed her own husband, Castobarus, for hiding 'two sons of Babas' (*Antiquities* XV. 7. x), who had once professed support for Antigonus; Herod had all three of them executed. Four years after Mariamne's death he married another Mariamne, 'the most beautiful woman of the age' (*Antiquities* IX. 15. iii); since her father, a priest called Simon, was not of sufficient station to be the king's father-in-law, Herod sacked the incumbent High Priest and appointed Simon in his place. Mariamne II was the mother of Herod Philip, who was disinherited towards the end of Herod's life because of the plot in which she was involved, as a result of which she was divorced and her father lost his job. Of Herod's next five wives (he subsequently also married two of his nieces), two are of significance because of their sons. With the Samaritan Malthace Herod had Antipas and Archelaus, and with Cleopatra of Jerusalem he had Philip. These three, but only after

much catastrophic internal intrigue, were ultimately destined to succeed him.

The messiness of Herod's private life belies the magnificence of his building programmes, and the apparent peace and prosperity, albeit sometimes controversially achieved, with which he endowed his kingdom. Though there are echoes of ostentation and sycophancy in much of what he built, there was a shrewd practical brain behind it all; one of his projects was to establish a new irrigation scheme in the valley of the Jordan, while Jerusalem not only benefited from fine new buildings, but also from a new layout, with paved streets and drainage systems. The coastal town of Strato's Tower, predominantly Greek with a Jewish community, became the great city of Caesarea (in honour of his Roman mentor, the emperor Caesar Augustus), with an underground sewage system cleaned out by the tides, and harbour structures supported underwater by piles made of concrete, a Roman invention. It was both an administrative centre and a major port designed to attract to Judaea the trade with and from the Mediterranean. Equally impressive was the rebuilding of Samaria, renamed Sebaste, the Greek form of Augustus. Herod's foresight in reconstructing his fortified hilltop retreat at Masada, 400 metres above the shore of the Dead Sea, into a fortress incorporating two palaces (one of them partly suspended from the rock face), with elaborate food storage and water supplies, paid off eighty years after his death. Its considerable remains are celebrated today as the state of Israel's most significant national symbol of resistance against oppression.

Modern archaeology has confirmed, and complements, much of Josephus' elaborate descriptions of Herod's architectural achievements, of which the rebuilding and refortifying of Jerusalem was the most impressive – the famous Wailing Wall, since the middle of the second century CE the focus of Jewish pilgrimage and prayer, was merely part of the western outer wall round the vast and lavish Temple

Figure 14 (*opposite*) View from the south-east of the model of Herod's Temple, Jerusalem. Bottom right is the outer wall of the precinct, enclosing the court of the Gentiles, with colonnades all round. Within the court of the Gentiles is the wall of the Temple itself; through the gate at the south end is the court of the women. The top of the bronze gate into the court of the Israelites can be seen centre. Between the gate and the entrance to the sanctuary, whose roof towers above the wall, is the great stone altar. Beyond the Temple, at the north-west corner of the precinct, is the Antonia fortress. (Richard Stoneman)

complex. So determined was he that his Temple would recapture, and outshine, the glories of Solomon's, and so elaborate were the plans which he publicly promulgated beforehand, that, according to Josephus (*Antiquities* XV. 11. ii), there was understandable popular concern that after he had pulled down the existing edifice he would be unable to carry out his promises for the new one. He managed somewhat to allay these apprehensions by loading up in advance a thousand wagons with stones for the new building, and by taking on ten thousand skilled builders. As a sweetener he bought a thousand new garments for the priests, and also had some of them taught the crafts of stonemasonry and carpentry, so that the holy places should not be defiled by the presence of unauthorised workers.

The main work in Jerusalem had begun with the construction of a new fortress at the north-west corner of the Temple complex, which he called Antonia, after his one-time Roman patron. Next, starting in 23 BCE, was a new palace on the western side of the city, dominated by three towers, named after Mariamne I, Hippicus (a friend), and his brother Phasael, of which the lower courses of the latter still exist at the base of what is known as the Tower of David. The Temple itself was begun in 20 BCE, and was finished in eighteen months, though work on the outer courts and porticoes went on for many more years. Chronically incapable of leaving well alone, however, he fell foul of those whom he most wanted to impress, by erecting a hugely expensive Roman eagle in gold over the main Temple gate. The Jewish populace bided their time. During Herod's last illness, two students, probably members of the Pharisaic group, with the encouragement of two of their religious teachers, abseiled down from the roof over the gate at midday, with the courts milling with people, and began to hack at the statue with axes, cheered on by the crowd below. Forty men were arrested. The two students, with their teachers, were burned alive: the onlookers who had been charged were executed by more normal means. Herod also dismissed the High Priest as being partly to blame, and appointed the man's brother-in-law in his place.

All this nationwide reconstruction, the games and other entertainments he sponsored, and the personal gifts and bribes he made to his Roman masters, in return for which his subjects had peace in his time, had to be paid for. Herod had his own income from his estates and from those which he confiscated from his political enemies. Augustus made over to him half the revenue from the copper mines of Cyprus, the other half of the business to be administered by Herod. Swingeing taxes were imposed on inhabitants of Herod's kingdom, some of which went as tribute to Rome, but these Herod cunningly reduced from time to time, to give the impression of being a caring monarch. He also on at least one occasion was not averse to a bit of sacrilege. Being aware that John Hyrcanus had robbed the tomb of David to pay for his troops, he secretly broke into the place in case there was any more cash to be found. There was no money, but a considerable store of furniture made of gold and other valuable artifacts, all of which he appropriated. According to Josephus (*Antiquities* XVI. 7. i), he then decided to search farther into the tomb, where the bodies lay of David and Solomon, only for two of his guards to be consumed in a spontaneous eruption of flame.

Augustus, who had assumed his more dignified name in 27 BCE at the same time as effectively becoming emperor, granted Herod the unusual (in the case of a client king), but on this occasion fateful, privilege of nominating his own successor, subject to Augustus' approval. The players in the ensuing unseemly and bloody conflict, which divided both family and court, were not simply Herod's male issue and their wives and mothers, but also Herod's siblings, his brother Pheroras, whom he had persuaded Augustus to appoint governor of Peraea, and his sister Salome, who were past masters at stirring up trouble. The original front-runners were Herod's personable sons with Mariamne I, Alexander and Aristobulus, who in 17 BCE returned from five years completing their education in Rome, spent at the home of Asinius Pollio (76 BCE–4 CE), ex-consul, senator, literary patron (he is also credited with establishing the first public library), and a sympathiser with Judaism. For Alexander, Herod arranged a match with the daughter of the king of Cappadocia. Aristobulus was married to his first cousin Berenice, which made his aunt, the formidable Salome, also his mother-in-law. This did not prevent Salome and Pheroras making slanderous accusations against the brothers, which were supported by other palace incumbents concerned that if Alexander and Aristobulus came to power, they would take revenge on those who had been involved in the death of their mother.

Herod, probably also jealous of his sons' polished ways and popularity with the people, had what obviously seemed to him at the time a good idea: he called back his divorced first wife, Doris, and their son Antipater, to give the brothers some competition. Antipater, who was the equal even of his aunt Salome when it came to intrigue, fuelled the controversy with such cunning that Herod haled Alexander and Aristobulus off to Rome, where in the presence of Augustus and Antipater he accused them of plotting his assassination. Augustus was

not impressed. He merely reprimanded the two brothers for not showing sufficient respect to their father, and sent the family home, where
Herod further muddied the waters by proclaiming Antipater his
principal heir, before Alexander and Aristobulus.

The palace troublemakers were soon back in business. Pheroras,
who had incensed Herod by preferring a slave-girl wife to the royal
daughter of Herod that was on offer, told Alexander that Herod had a
passion for Alexander's wife, Glaphyra. Alexander went to Herod to
complain in person, naming Pheroras as his source. Herod, for whom
it was a new experience to be accused of a sexual peccadillo of which
he was innocent, sent for his brother and vented his anger on him,
whereupon Pheroras pointed the finger of blame at Salome.

Antipater now accused Alexander of attempting to suborn the three
eunuchs who attended to Herod's personal needs, and of sodomy with
them. Herod put the eunuchs on the rack; when, on the instructions
of Antipater, the wheel was turned as far as it would go, they confessed
that Alexander was plotting to seize the throne. Herod went berserk.
The torturers worked overtime. Heads rolled, those of informers as
well as of those they informed against. Even some of Alexander's clos-
est friends were tortured, and died without having said anything to
incriminate him. Amid a welter of accusations and counter-accusa-
tions, forged evidence, and tactical confessions, Archelaus, king of
Cappadocia and Alexander's father-in-law, turned up in Jerusalem to
represent the interests of his daughter. Surprisingly, he managed for
the time being to calm things down.

Nothing daunted, Antipater produced a new witness, of impeccable
qualifications, to testify against the brothers. They were arrested.
Herod wrote to Augustus, setting out the evidence against them.
Augustus, conscious that he had recently offended Herod by reacting
too quickly to an exaggerated complaint against him brought by
Syllaeus, Salome's disappointed lover, advised Herod to convene a
court on Roman soil, under the presidency of the Roman governor of
Syria, to hear the evidence. Herod himself presented the case for the
prosecution. There was no defence, nor did the accused appear in
court. The verdict of guilty was inevitable, but the sentence of death
was not unanimous; the president of the court and several others
among the 150 assessors voted for leniency.

Herod, however, had got the verdict he wanted. Three hundred
army officers and men, and their spokesman, who protested against the
sentence, were arraigned by Herod before an ad hoc assembly and
stoned to death by the mob. Alexander and Aristobulus were transported to Sebaste and strangled. Their bodies were transferred by

night to Alexandrium, and buried beside their uncle, Aristobulus the young High Priest, and other ancestors on their mother's side.

Herod next turned his suspicions on his brother Pheroras, who willingly accepted the suggestion that he should return to his post in Peraea, because, as he publicly announced, he never wanted to see Herod again. He died shortly afterwards in suspicious circumstances. This time, there really *was* a plot to kill Herod. Behind it, needless to say, was the subtly scheming Antipater, who, now in his mid-forties, had decided that time was running out for him. Also implicated were Doris (Antipater's mother), Mariamne II, and Pheroras' widow, and her mother and sister. Antipater, feeling also that his reputation with Herod for being whiter than white would not stand up to much further scrutiny, himself arranged that friends in Rome should advise Herod that Antipater should come and pay his respects to Augustus.

Antipater returned after being away for seven months. He suspected nothing until he reached Cilicia. He pressed on, however, but at Jerusalem his entourage was excluded from the palace. He entered alone, where his father, in the presence of Quintilius Varus, the new Roman governor of Syria, outlined the case against him. He was formally arraigned before a court the next day, and denied all the charges. Varus, who was president of the court, called for the vial of alleged poison which had been mentioned in evidence. He handed it to a prisoner who had been sentenced to death, and ordered him to drink it. The man died instantaneously. Antipater was incarcerated in jail. Varus and Herod retired to compose a report of the proceedings, which was forwarded to Augustus, who confirmed the sentence of death.

By this time Herod, who was in his early seventies, was seriously ill. He died in 4 BCE a few days after the execution of Antipater, having made a final will dividing his kingdom between his two sons with Malthace and his son with Cleopatra. Archelaus was to be ethnarch of Judaea (including Idumaea and Samaria), his brother Antipas tetrarch of Galilee and Transjordan, and Philip tetrarch of the territories to the north and north-east of Galilee, including Ituraea and Trachonitis – a tetrarch (Greek, 'one of four rulers') was a less senior position than ethnarch.

TETRARCHS, PROCURATORS, AND KINGS

First, the arrangements had to be ratified by Augustus. Archelaus, as principal heir, gave his father a suitable funeral and burial, and provided

Figure 15 Bronze coin of Judaea under the procuratorship of Pontius Pilate, depicting the crooked staff which was the badge of office of an augur, a Roman religious symbol which was bound to cause offence to the Jews. The inscription in Greek, from the left upwards, reads 'Tiberius Caesar'. The reverse carries a laurel wreath and a date which equates to 32 CE. (× 2)

the statutory public feast on a lavish scale. He then made the first blunder of his term of office by sending in troops to use force to control an angry crowd who were demonstrating in the Temple courtyard against Herod's treatment of the perpetrators of the destruction of the eagle over the gate. Three thousand members of the public were killed, a foretaste of the volatile situation in Judaea which would end with its destruction. Archelaus then travelled to Rome, accompanied by his younger brother Antipas, his aunt Salome, and sundry other members of the family, all of whose secret purpose was to challenge his rights. They were joined in Rome, with the permission of Varus, by a deputation of fifty leading citizens of Judaea, supported by eight thousand Jews of Rome, who wanted a return to autonomy with a properly recognised High Priest, under overall Roman supervision.

While Augustus was considering the position, news came of an armed uprising in Judaea which had turned into a full-scale revolt, requiring three legions to suppress it. Augustus' decision was to confirm the conditions of Herod's will, promising Archelaus the title of king in due course if he should prove that he had earned it. This was not to be.

Archelaus was removed from office in 6 CE, when Augustus, having listened to the complaints of a joint deputation from Judaea and Samaria, ran out of patience and banished him to Gaul, where he died in about 16 CE. His territory was incorporated into the Roman province of Syria. The duties of the procurator in charge of Judaea apparently included the appointment of the High Priest, whose vestments were kept locked up under Roman control and only released when the next festival came round. Herod and Archelaus at least appreciated

Figure 16 Bronze coin of Herod Antipas, carrying a palm branch and the Greek inscription, from the left upwards, 'Herod the Tetrarch'. At either side of the stem of the branch are the Greek numerals representing 33, that is the thirty-third year of the rule of Antipas = 29 CE. On the reverse, the name of the new capital he founded, Tiberias, is framed by a plant which has been variously identified as laurel, palm, or the reed common to the area of Tiberias. (× 2)

Jewish, if not necessarily Samaritan, sensibilities. A succession of procurators committed blunder after blunder in this respect, making Judaea the most inflammable of all Roman territories, and Jerusalem, to which pilgrims of the area and of the diaspora flocked at times of the great festivals, a particular hotbed of revolt. The most notorious of these procurators was Pontius Pilate (26–36 CE). It was at the time of one such festival during his term of office (probably in 30 CE) that on the eve of Passover, after a sort of trial, an itinerant revivalist preacher called Jehoshua (Greek, Jesus), whose supporters claimed he was the Messiah, was executed under Roman law by the standard Roman method of execution for crimes against the state. He was one of numerous leaders, or alleged leaders, of sections of the Jewish population to whom an edgy administration meted out the same fate.

Antipas was like his father in that he was a builder, in which capacity he created the new Hellenistic city of Tiberias (after the emperor Tiberius), using the hot springs from the southern end of the Sea of Galilee to serve the baths which were a feature of the site. In other respects he was a poor imitation of Herod. His marriage to Herodias, the wife of his half-brother Herod Philip, scandalised his subjects and earned the open hostility of John the Baptist, whose main stamping-ground was Peraea, which fell within Antipas' territory. It was also one of the causes of his own political downfall in that in order to marry Herodias he had to divorce his first wife, daughter of his Arabian

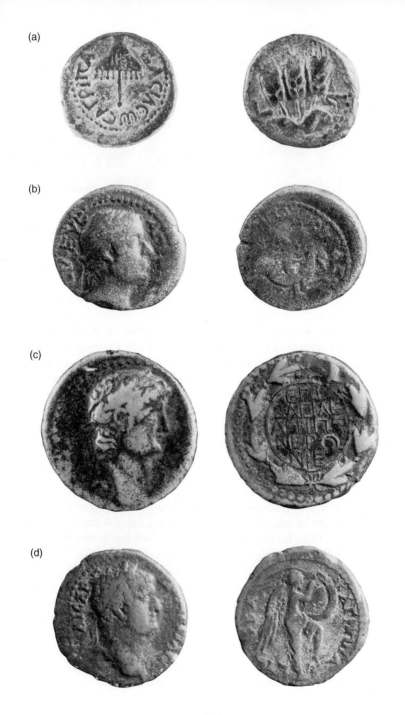

neighbour, the Nabataean king Aretas IV (*c.* 9 BCE–40 CE). Aretas first made trouble along his frontiers and then inflicted on him a serious military defeat, which, according to a passage in Josephus (*Antiquities* XVIII. 5. ii), some Jews regarded as retribution for his execution of John the Baptist. Antipas was finally dismissed in 39 CE by Tiberius' successor, Caligula, and banished to Lyons in Gaul.

Philip proved a successful and constructive tetrarch, though his marriage to the voluptuous Salome was childless. On his death in 34 CE his territories were temporarily incorporated into the province of Syria.

(Herod) Agrippa I was born in 10 BCE to Herod's son Aristobulus and his first cousin Berenice, the daughter of his aunt Salome. Having been sent at the age of six with his mother to Rome, where he was brought up in the household of the celebrated Antonia, daughter of Mark Antony and grandmother of Caligula, he became something of an international playboy. Debt-ridden, he returned to Rome, where Tiberius imprisoned him for being over-enthusiastic in expressing his interests in a subsequent administration which might relieve him from his financial commitments. When Tiberius died in 37 CE, Caligula duly obliged by appointing him king of his uncle Philip's former territory: in 39 CE, on the dismissal of his uncle Antipas, he became king also of Galilee and Peraea. In 41 CE Caligula's successor Claudius appointed Agrippa to the plum position of king also of Judaea, Samaria, and Idumaea, which now ceased to be subject to the authority of the governor of Syria. When at home Agrippa observed

Figure 17 (*opposite*) Bronze coins of (Herod) Agrippa I and (Herod) Agrippa II, of varying weights and values. (a) Agrippa I. Tasselled canopy, with legend in Greek reading from the right downwards, 'King Agrippa'. On the reverse, three ears of corn, with the date, 'Year 6 [of his rule]' (= 42/3 CE). (b) Head of Agrippa I, with legend in Greek reading from left upwards, 'King Agrippa'. On the reverse is the figure of a youth on horseback, which the inscription identifies as his son, the future Agrippa II. (c) Coin of Agrippa II, with the head of the emperor Nero. The Greek inscription on the reverse, within a wreath, refers to 'King Agrippa' and celebrates his enlargement in about 61 CE of the city of Caesarea Philippi, founded by his great-uncle Philip, which he renamed Neronias (where the coin was struck), in honour of Nero. (d) Coin of Agrippa II, bearing the head of Domitian, Vespasian's second son, who became emperor in 81 CE on the sudden, and unexplained, death of Titus. The reverse shows the winged figure of Nike writing on a shield. The Greek inscription, from the left upwards, reads 'Year 6 [of the rule of Vespasian = 74/75 CE] King Agrippa'. (All × 2)

the rituals and performed the duties that Jewish law required with rather more diligence than his grandfather Herod had done, and was respected by the Jews. Away from Judaea, however, he demonstrated his gratitude to his Roman benefactors and his theatrical nature by expansive building programmes and expensive games in the Roman manner. He died suddenly in 44 CE. Claudius, unwilling to entrust the kingdom to Agrippa's seventeen-year-old son, also called (Herod) Agrippa, restored direct rule from Rome, once more under a procurator.

Agrippa II (*b.* 28 CE, *d.* 92 CE) became a Jewish king, in some respects king of the Jews, but never king of Judaea. Claudius initially appointed him king of Chalcis, the tiny principality to the north of Ituraea whose ruler Herod, Agrippa II's uncle and brother-in-law, had recently died. He was also given the role, which he exercised diligently if sometimes controversially, of supervising the Temple in Jerusalem and nominating the High Priest. In 53 CE, Claudius transferred him to the territories formerly governed by the tetrarch Philip, Agrippa's great-uncle, to which Claudius' successor Nero added several cities in Galilee, including Tiberias, and in Peraea. In a continually explosive situation, Agrippa seems to have tried to take a conciliatory line, which hardly endeared him to militant nationalists and religionists. His ambiguous relationship with his sister Berenice did not help matters; nor did the fact that his sister Drusilla had divorced the king of Emesa to marry Antonius Felix, procurator of Judaea. Even the first-century CE Roman historian Tacitus, who was notoriously unsympathetic to the Jews, has nothing good to say about Felix who, having got the job through his brother Pallas, an influential freedman who was Claudius' imperial accountant, proved a disastrous administrator and was recalled by Nero in 60 CE after eight years in office.

That the ferment was so significant was due not only to the understandably nationalistic motives of those who saw no reason why they should be oppressed by Rome or be part of the Roman empire, or still less to pay taxes to Rome, but also to the stark religious differences between Roman and Jewish culture. Throughout this troubled period, Jews continued to struggle to come to terms with the exercise of their faith under the prevailing conditions.

MEN OF GOD

In one respect the situation actually improved under direct Roman rule. The Sanhedrin came back into its own as the central body for interpreting and administering traditional Jewish law, and for making rulings on secular as well as religious matters. It also had some political influence. Under the presidency of the High Priest, it comprised senior priests, who were Sadducees, and scribes, elders, and teachers of the Law, who tended to be Pharisees. These scribes were scholars whose function was to study and expound the words of God. Not all of them were Pharisees: as a class they constituted a group on their own. It was through the scribes and Pharisees that religious observance and an understanding of its implications became no longer prerogatives of the Temple priests, and extended into the community. From about 70 CE those authorised to teach the Law and the scriptures were addressed as 'Rabbi', meaning 'my master'. The Sadducees, who drew their members also from the wealthy and influential classes, controlled the Temple worship and finances, which effectively meant that they were in charge of the national budget.

At the beginning of the first century CE a new group, the Zealots (the Hebrew equivalent means those with zeal for the honour and glory of God), appears alongside the Sadducees, Pharisees, and Essenes. Said to have been founded in 6 CE by Judas the Galilean and a Pharisaic priest called Zadok as a movement to oppose the Roman census of people and property referred to in the second chapter of Luke's Gospel, it became the militant anti-Roman movement while developing a religious philosophy based on the conviction that God is the sole ruler and king of the Jewish nation. The Sicarii, 'men armed with a *sica* [Latin, dagger]', are understood to have been an extreme, terrorist, wing of the Zealots.

Opinion is divided as to whether at the same time or at different times there were two Sanhedrins. Certainly in about 30 BCE the members of the Sanhedrin elected Hillel (*c.* 70 BCE–*c.* 10 CE), a Babylonian scholar of humble origins, to the office of *nasi*, meaning prince or patriarch, who presided over the Sanhedrin. The followers of him and his Judaean-born Sanhedrin colleague Shammai (50 BCE–*c.* 30 CE) formed themselves into two philosophical schools, Beth Hillel (the House of Hillel) and Beth Shammai (the House of Shammai). The Talmud and the Mishnah, the exegesis of the Oral Law compiled by Rabbi Judah-ha-Nasi (*d. c.* 217 CE), contain many accounts of the great debates between the two houses. It is even said that they argued for three years as to whether in principle the Law as a whole should be interpreted in accordance with the dictates of the one house or the other, and that the issue was only settled by a Bat Kol, a communication from Heaven, which appeared to give the vote to Beth Hillel. Traditionally the rulings of Hillel are taken to be more liberal than those of Shammai, and he is credited with the exposition of the 'golden rule', when challenged by a trouble-maker to teach him the whole of the Torah while standing on one leg. Hillel, whose patience was matched by his humility, replied: 'What is hateful to you, do not do to your fellow men. That is the whole of the Law. The rest is explanation.' This injunction in Leviticus 19:18 is reflected also in the words of Jesus: 'Always treat others as you would like them to treat you: that is the Law and the prophets' (NEB Matt. 7:12).

Hillel, Shammai, and Jesus of Nazareth all commented on various significant aspects of Jewish life, such as wealth and poverty, Sabbath observance, cleanliness, marriage and divorce, and one's attitude to enemies. In spite of the fact that some of Jesus' teaching was held to be radical, there was probably nothing in it which contradicted Pharisaic Judaism. Jesus was brought up in Galilee, where he preached to the people of the imminence of the kingdom of God, and gathered around him an inner circle of twelve disciples. Galilee had only been back in the Jewish fold since 103 BCE, when its inhabitants were forcibly converted; compared with Judaea, its ordinary populace may well have been fairly described as 'heathen Galilee' (NEB Matt. 4:15), while sharing with the Jews of Judaea the determination to be free from Roman domination, and Judaism as the focus of their campaign.

The manner of Jesus' entry into Jerusalem was significant or provocative, depending on one's particular sympathies or apprehensions. 'This was to fulfil the prophecy which says, "Tell the daughter of Sion: Here is your king, who comes to you in gentleness, riding on an ass, riding on the foal of a beast of burden"' (NEB Matt. 21:4–5); the prophecy is, 'Rejoice greatly, Fair Zion; / Raise a shout, Fair Jerusalem! / Lo, your king is coming to you. / He is victorious, triumphant, / Yet humble, riding on an ass, / On a donkey foaled by a she-ass' (Zech. 9:9). Jesus was executed in either 30 or 33 CE. If he had not died, he might have been forgotten, for it is central to Christian belief that he came back to life.

THE JEWISH WARS

It was only a matter of time before Jewish reaction to malpractices and insensitivity on the part of successive Roman administrations, fomented by social and economic hardship, erupted first into violence and then into open warfare. During the procuratorship of Cuspius Fadus (44–46 CE), a certain Theudas, who called himself a prophet, had taken a crowd of people to the banks of the river Jordan, where he said he would re-enact the dividing of the waters. A troop of Roman horsemen set off in pursuit and massacred them. Theudas was taken alive, and then had his head cut off. In the time of Ventidius Cumanus (48–52 CE), there was a disturbance in the Temple courtyard when one of the Roman legionaries standing guard in the cloister during the festival of Passover exposed himself to the crowd of worshippers, who reacted with fury. Cumanus ordered the rest of his troops in the city to mobilise at the fortress Antonia. The crowd panicked and tried to escape through the narrow passageways. In the resulting crush, according to Josephus (*Antiquities* XX. 5. iii) twenty thousand died.

Cumanus finally lost his job after failing to deal properly and honestly with an act of armed thuggery perpetrated against a group of Galilean Jews passing through Samaria on their way to worship in Jerusalem, which flared up into a conflict between Zealots and Samaritans. Guerrilla warfare began with Zealots inciting the populace to stand up and fight the Romans; those who refused to do so had their homes burned and plundered. At the same time the Sicarii, their curved daggers hidden under their cloaks, took to mingling with crowds and silently stabbing to death those who were suspected of collaborating with the Roman administration.

In Caesarea the uneasy situation spilled over into incessant hostilities between Jews and Gentiles who were of Greek origin, which came to a head when the Greeks deliberately built a factory to deny proper access to a synagogue. The Jews even offered Gessius Florus, procurator 64–66 CE, eight talents of silver to settle the dispute. He took the money and himself off to Sebaste, from where he organised the hijack of seventeen further talents from the Temple in Jerusalem on the pretext that it was on the emperor's orders. The people gathered in the Temple courtyard to protest, the jokers among them handing round a basket and begging for pennies 'for poor old Florus'! Florus reacted by sending in a troop of cavalry to disperse the crowd, and the next day paraded in front of the palace the senior priests and leaders of the community, demanding that they hand over the culprits. When he received instead only apologies, he ordered his soldiers to sack an area of the upper city, kill as many people as they liked, and bring the rest to him. The survivors, who included Jews who were also Roman citizens of high rank, were flogged and then crucified. Agrippa II was out of town, but his sister Berenice appeared barefoot before Florus to beg him to stop. He took no notice, except to send to Caesarea for a further thousand troops.

The city was divided between those who advocated a policy of nonviolence and those for whom Florus' brutality and insensitivity were the last straw. There were further riots. Berenice and the city magistrates appealed in writing to Cestius Gallus, governor of Syria (*c.* 63–66 CE). Florus also submitted a report. Cestius sent a tribune to investigate the situation, who on the way met up with Agrippa, returning to Jerusalem from a diplomatic mission to Alexandria. The tribune was given a tour of the city and of the devastation, after which he complimented the people on their loyalty to Rome, paid his respects in the outer court of the Temple to the God of the Jews, and returned to Cestius. Agrippa, having placed his sister on the palace roof in full sight of the crowd, made a public appeal, at the end of which he broke down in tears, expounding the futility of armed opposition to Rome. His speech, extensively quoted by Josephus (*Jewish War* II. 16. iv), who was probably in the audience, had only temporary effect in averting war. The rebellious elements soon prevailed, and Agrippa was igno-miniously banished from his own city.

The revolt began in 66 CE peaceably enough, with all offerings to the Temple by or for Gentiles being banned, which meant that the daily sacrifice for the health of the emperor was discontinued, an ingenious and blatant act of disloyalty to Rome. After fighting in Jerusalem between extremists and moderates, and considerable bloodshed and damage to property, the Roman garrison there was forced to give in; survivors, promised safe conduct if they laid down their arms, were then massacred. This was the signal for the revolt to spread, though often its effect was counter-productive: Jews and Gentiles made it an excuse to slaughter each other. Cestius Gallus, with an army of thirty thousand, marched on Jerusalem, but withdrew when he realised that the inhabitants were preparing for a long siege which, with winter coming on, he could not sustain. At the pass of Beth-horon, where Judas Maccabaeus had destroyed the army of Antiochus IV, his troops and baggage train were ambushed and thrown into disarray by the Jewish forces.

Even the moderates in Jerusalem now realised that the revolt had become all-out war. The Sanhedrin was reconstituted as an executive body, a popular assembly was established, which met in the courts of the Temple, and a military commander was appointed to each of the six regions into which the territory was now divided. As commander of the Roman forces, Nero appointed Titus Flavius Sabinus Vespasianus (9–79 CE), a vastly experienced general who had served with distinction in Thrace, Crete, Cyrene, Germany, Britain, and Africa. Vespasian sent his son Titus (40–81 CE) to Egypt to fetch the Fifteenth Legion, while he went to Syria for the Fifth and Tenth Legions, which he led down the sea coast to Ptolemais, to wait for Titus. With the three legions, and auxiliary forces supplied by, among

Figure 18 Roman brass *sestertius* (71 CE) with the head of the emperor Vespasian, the real victor of the first Jewish War. The reverse depicts a captive Jew and a mourning Jewish woman under a palm tree, with the legend in Latin, 'IVDAEA CAPTA' (Judaea subjugated); the letters underneath stand for S[enatus] C[onsulto] (by decree of the senate). (Actual size)

others, Agrippa II and the Nabataean king, Vespasian had about fifty thousand fully trained men under his command, together with artillery and siege weapons.

Now, he advanced into Galilee, whose young commander, Joseph ben Mattathias (37–*c*. 100 CE), a former priest who had spent time in Rome on a diplomatic mission, had mobilised sixty thousand infantry and 250 cavalry, of whom, however, only five thousand were professional soldiers. Sepphoris fell, and then Gadara. Now it was the turn of the main military base in the area, Jotapata, which held out for forty-seven days. Joseph escaped the carnage that followed, and took refuge in a cave with forty leading citizens of the town. When discovered by the Romans, they all drew lots as to the order in which they would commit suicide. Joseph and one other man somehow remained unscathed. They surrendered and were taken prisoner. Joseph was released and defected to the Roman side after, according to his own account, prophesying that Vespasian would become emperor.

Nero died by his own hand in June 68 CE. By a series of great circular marches, tactical strikes, and selective displays of brutality, Vespasian had virtually completed his military assignment by the summer of 69 CE, having deliberately left until last the subjection of Jerusalem, which was rent by opposing Zealot factions and was threatening to destroy itself. On 1 July he learned that the Roman armies in the eastern Mediterranean had sworn their allegiance to him as supreme commander, rather than to Aulus Vitellius (15–69 CE), the third since Nero's death to assume the imperial throne in Rome. Vespasian immediately departed for Rome, leaving Titus to conduct

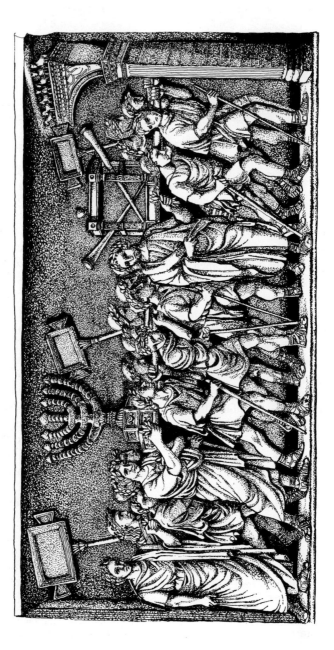

the siege of Jerusalem, which began in April 70 CE. The city held out altogether for five months, and had to be taken in stages. The Antonia was captured and destroyed at the end of July. The Temple fell and was plundered and utterly destroyed in August, traditionally on Tisha b'Av, the ninth day of the month of Av, the same day of the Jewish year on which Nebuchadnezzar had demolished its predecessor, the Temple of Solomon. The upper city was not taken for another month, whereupon the whole of Jerusalem, with the exception of part of the western wall and the three towers of Herod's palace, was flattened.

The horrors were unspeakable. Those who had survived starvation and butchery were rounded up, many of them to die of lack of food while they were being sorted into prisoner categories. The aged and the sick were then slaughtered, and militants, terrorists, and informers executed. Seven hundred of the most handsome youths were transported to Rome to march in the statutory triumphal procession: their ultimate fate is not recorded. The rest of the seventeen-year-olds and over were either put in irons and sent to do hard labour in Egypt or distributed to arenas in different parts of the empire to die in combat

Figure 19 *(opposite)* Conjectural reconstruction by Jennifer Campell of a panel (3.8 m × 2.04 m) from the Arch of Titus in Rome (built about 81/82 CE), following a sketch by Pietro Santo Bartoli (1635–1700) which reveals that it originally contained twenty figures three ranks deep. The panel shows the spoils from the Temple being carried along in the triumphal procession in Rome celebrating the victory over the Jews in 70 CE. In front is the table for the laying out of the shewbread (Exod. 25:23), which Philo describes as being covered with gold and on the Sabbath set with gold plates, dishes, and bowls. According to Josephus it weighed 'many talents' (*The Jewish War* VII. 5. v) – one talent was the equivalent of 36 kg or 80 lb. Balanced between the supports of the table are two sacred silver trumpets (Num. 10:2). Behind is the *menorah*, the holy seven-branched candlestick; there is some suggestion either that the one carried in the procession was not the original candlestick from the Temple, or that the version that survives in the relief is not an accurate representation of it. Josephus says that the spoils displayed in the procession also included the scrolls of the Law. Placards such as those shown were a feature of triumphal processions. They carried inscriptions, for the benefit of the spectators, listing cities captured in the campaign, or depictions of forts, mountains, rivers, lakes, even seas that had been taken. It is likely that in the actual procession which this panel commemorates, the notices indicated that the items were from the Temple in Jerusalem.

or be torn to pieces by wild animals. Those under seventeen were sold into slavery.

Rome gained its victory, Vespasian his imperial throne, and Titus his military glory. Joseph ben Mattathias, whose behaviour had been at least questionable, achieved immortality as the historian Flavius Josephus – the Flavius was in honour of his Roman patrons. After the fall of Jerusalem, which Josephus witnessed from the Roman side, Titus gave him a free hand to take anything he wanted from the loot. According to his own account (*Life of Flavius Josephus* 75), he accepted personally from Titus some copies of the scriptures, but took nothing else. Instead he asked for the lives of his brother and fifty friends to be spared; he also secured the release of nearly two hundred women and children of his acquaintance who were lined up in the Temple court-yard awaiting transportation. Though he was given an estate outside Jerusalem, Josephus prudently decided to accompany Titus to Rome, where he was granted an apartment in the house in which Vespasian had lived before becoming emperor, Roman citizenship, and a pension for life.

Though Jerusalem had fallen, Vespasian and Titus (and the popu-lace of Rome) had enjoyed the victory procession, and Josephus had embarked on his history, *The Jewish War*, the war itself was not quite over: three fortresses, Herodium, Machaerus, and Masada, had not capitulated. Archaeological evidence confirms that Herodium and Machaerus were destroyed before the end of 72 CE by the new governor of Judaea, Sextus Lucilius Bassus, who died shortly afterwards. Masada, Herod's refuge, built on a flat-topped rock higher than the Empire State Building in New York, constituted a different problem alto-gether. It had been taken from the Romans in a commando raid at the beginning of the war, and was now occupied by 960 men, women, and children whom Josephus identifies as Sicarii. They could not be starved out, for thanks to Herod's installations they had ample supplies of food and water. The Romans, about nine thousand fighting men plus several thousand Jewish prisoners-of-war as extra labour, had to carry across the desert everything they needed for the siege, including food and water.

Bassus' successor, Flavius Silva (73–81 CE), first built a wall right round the base of the rock to prevent escape. Then from a position on the western side, 125 metres below the summit, he constructed a sloping ramp of timber, rocks, and crushed stones, up to a point just below the fortress wall. It took seven months to build, while all the time the defenders rained down rocks, fired arrows, and launched from mechanical catapults stones the size of grapefruit. On a stone platform at the head of the ramp, the Romans erected a 30-metre-high iron-plated tower, from inside which they attacked the wall with a battering ram. With defeat staring at them, the defenders committed mass suicide; according to Josephus (*The Jewish War* VII. 9. i) two women and five children survived to tell the tale. Two recently discovered inscriptions suggest that Masada fell not in 73 CE, as had previously been thought, but in 74.

Josephus' original account of the war was written in Aramaic for the benefit of Jews of the diaspora living under Parthian rule and in Babylonia, southern Arabia, and Mesopotamia. Having then translated it into Greek, the lingua franca of the eastern Mediterranean, for inhabitants of the Roman empire, a task which he completed in or soon after 75 CE, he embarked on his massive *Antiquities of the Jews*, a social and historical study from the Creation to the procuratorship of Florus, which he finished in 93 CE.

With the destruction of the Second Temple, the Jewish people had lost the focal point of their nationalistic aspirations and the symbolic centre of their religious life, to which they thronged at times of festivals and where the statutory sacrifices were performed. The traditional Temple tax levied on Jews by Jews was replaced by the *fiscus Judaicus*, levied on all Jews by the Romans, and paid to the temple of Jupiter Capitolinus in Rome. Judaea was now occupied territory, an independent province (incorporating Samaria, Idumaea, Galilee, and Peraea) whose governor had under his personal command a full legion, based in Jerusalem, comprising about five thousand men plus auxiliary troops. Thus the political, social, and economic effects of the war on Judaea were considerable. The consequences to Judaism, however, were nothing like so grave.

The example of the Qumran community is evidence that there were those who questioned the efficacy of the Temple and its cult, among whom also were the Jewish Christians, whose community had been centred on Jerusalem. Christianity was now no longer a sect of Judaism, but was a separate movement which, largely due to the missionary zeal of Paul of Tarsus (*c.* 10–*c.* 67 CE), was gaining support from Gentiles in the Hellenistic world. The Zealot movement was destroyed in the war, and the loss of the Temple meant the end of the Sadducees, for whom it was central to their philosophy and their political existence. The Essenes also disappear from the record at about this time. Pharisaic synagogues of the diaspora had already been providing an alternative form of worship to the Temple observances. Throughout the diaspora too each local community organised its own finances and social and educational services, and worked out its own compromises

(a)

(b)

Figure 20 (a) Jewish bronze *semis* (one-eighth of a Roman *sestertius*) issued during the first Jewish War, depicting a chalice, with the legend in the Early Hebrew alphabet, from the right up: 'For the redemption of Zion'. The reverse carries the date 'Year 4 [of the revolt, that is 69/70 CE]', and depicts items connected with the Feast of Tabernacles: the bunch of twigs tied together (*lulab*) with, on either side, a citron (*ethrog*).
(b) Jewish silver shekel of the second Jewish War, depicting the façade of the Temple sanctuary, with the inscription, in the Early Hebrew alphabet, from the right up, 'Jerusalem'. On the reverse is a *lulab* and *ethrog*, and the legend 'Year 2 for the freedom of Jerusalem [that is 133/134 CE]'. Other coins of this design issued in the same year have the name of 'Simon [bar Kochba]' in place of 'Jerusalem' on the obverse.
(Both × 2)

between the observation of Torah law and local cultural and social conditions. Babylon and Alexandria in particular were in addition centres of excellence for the development of scholarship.

At some point during the Roman campaign in Judaea, Johanan ben Zakkai, former protégé of Hillel and now the leading Jewish intellectual in Jerusalem, had obtained permission to establish a Pharisaic religious academy at Jamnia. According to tradition, he escaped from the city by feigning death, and was then carried through the Roman guard posts in a coffin. Once outside, he engineered an audience with Vespasian, whom he addressed as 'Caesar' (that is, emperor) just before Vespasian received the news that troops around the empire had proclaimed him their new leader. At the centre of the religious community at Jamnia was a reconstituted and democratic Sanhedrin, whose members were rabbis from all walks of life. Their first priority was to assure the Jews of Judaea and the diaspora that the Temple and its rituals and sacrifices were not fundamental to the observance of Judaism; in which connection Johanan is famously recorded as having consoled a colleague, who was gloomily regarding the smoking ruins of the Temple, with the verse: 'For I desire goodness, not sacrifice; / Obedience to God, rather than burnt offerings' (Hosea 6:6). They codified the legal teachings of Hillel and Shammai, giving preference to the more humane, flexible approach of the former, and in about 100 CE finalised the third section of the Hebrew Bible, *Ketuvim*, the Hagiographa or Writings. They also drew up forms of daily service, and adapted certain Temple rituals for observance in synagogues. In particular, the Day of Atonement, formerly the occasion when the High Priest made his solemn entry into the Holy of Holies to offer atonement for his people, now became an occasion for personal atonement and repentance for all.

Whereas before, scholars who were expert in Jewish law had performed their duty to expound it to disciples largely in the colonnades around the Temple courtyard, now rabbinic schools came into being at various centres. After handing over the leadership at Jamnia to Gamaliel II, a direct descendant of Hillel, in about 85 CE, Johanan founded one at Beror Hayil. There was another at Lydda, whose star pupil was Rabbi Akiba ben Joseph (53–135 CE), a man whose legendary status is confirmed by the extent of the legends about him. These often concern his modesty, such as is illustrated in the saying attributed to him: 'Take your place a few seats below your rank until you are bidden to go higher. It is better that people should say to you, "Go higher," than that they should suggest that you do not deserve to be where you are.'

Akiba's main contribution to scholarship was to rationalise the arrangement of the Oral Law on its way to being expressed in the form of the Mishnah. In his humane attitude and concern for the poor, he was a direct follower of Hillel, but though he echoed Hillel in declaring that the basis of the Torah was the injunction to 'love thy neighbour as thyself', this did not extend to Romans who tried to prevent

Jews from observing the rules by which they subsisted. To those who advocated submission to anti-Jewish legislation, he offered the parable of the fish, who when asked by a fox to join him on dry land and thus avoid the attentions of the fisherman, replied: 'If we are afraid when we are in the element in which we live, how much more frightened should we be when we leave that element, for then we are certain to die.' Akiba explained: 'Our element is the Law. If we abandon it, we destroy ourselves.'

While the political situation in Judaea remained overtly peaceable, in about 114 CE a series of revolts exploded in the diaspora. These had a variety of causes, of which messianic zeal and violent clashes between Greeks and Jews were the most frequent. The emperor Trajan (98–117 CE) had these put down with such force that the Jewish communities in Alexandria, north Africa, and Cyprus, were virtually wiped out. The policies of his successor Hadrian (117–138 CE), an enlightened and liberal-minded man except apparently when dealing with the Jews, were of positive influence in that in redefining the boundaries of the Roman empire he excluded Trajan's conquests in Parthia, thus ensuring that the considerable Jewish community in Babylonia was able under its Persian kings to develop further as a crucial centre of Jewish learning.

In the course of his tireless inspection not only of every province in the empire but also of most of their outer frontiers, Hadrian visited Judaea in about 130 CE. Whatever the exact causes of the second war between Judaea and Rome, which broke out in 132 CE, and near-contemporary Roman sources suggest both a prohibition on circumcision and an imperial proposal to build a Hellenistic city on the site of Jerusalem, Rabbi Akiba, now in his eighties, was a fervent supporter of its instigators, and of the Jewish leader, Simon bar Kosiba.

Simon, a giant of a man, was called by his followers 'Bar Kochba', 'Son of a Star', following the saying, 'A star rises from Jacob, / A scepter comes forth from Israel; / It smashes the brow of Moab' (Num. 24:17), and according to tradition Rabbi Akiba acknowledged him as the appointed deliverer of Israel. Bar Kochba called himself 'Prince of Israel'. He was more than a military leader. Letters and other documents found since the 1950s in desert caves about 18 kilometres south of Qumran reveal that his influence extended also to social and economic matters, including property deals, and to religious observance.

It is said that half a million men flocked to Bar Kochba, and that Rabbi Akiba himself journeyed round encouraging recruits to enlist. Victory, earned mainly through guerrilla tactics, followed victory;

fortress after fortress fell. When the time came to march on Jerusalem, the Romans were in such confusion that the governor of the area ordered the evacuation from the city of the Tenth Legion, the same that had sixty years earlier so spectacularly captured Masada.

Things could not last. Hadrian transferred one of his most experienced generals, Sextus Julius Severus, from Britain, where he had only been for about a year, to the Judaean front. Systematically, with the aid of troops drafted in from other regions, he annihilated the opposition. According to the historian Dio Cassius (*c.* 155–235 CE), fifty fortresses in Jewish hands and 985 villages were destroyed, and 580,000 men killed. Bar Kochba and his remaining followers were penned into the fortress of Bethar. In the summer of 135 CE the Romans broke in and massacred all the defenders. Families who had taken refuge in caves were starved to death. Of those who survived, men, women, and children, so many were taken to be sold as slaves that there was a glut on the international slave market and prices slumped. Rabbi Akiba, who refused the imperial edict to cease studying the Law and teaching the word of God, was tortured and then executed at Caesarea. He died reciting the Shema.

Hadrian ordered that the remains of Jerusalem should be ploughed into the ground. He then had a new city built on the site, Aelia Capitolina, which Jews were forbidden to enter on pain of death. Judaea ceased to exist. The Roman province, with its capital now at Caesarea, was renamed Syria Palaestina, or Palestine . . . .

9

LEGACIES OF THE ISRAELITES

The ancient Greeks bequeathed to western society their philosophy and their artistic and literary standards, and the Romans their conception of law, their alphabet, and the basis of many modern languages. The contributions of the Israelites include their religion and its ethics, and the basic rules of conduct known as the Noahide laws, given to Noah after the Flood and applicable to all humankind, whatever their faith; these laws forbid idolatry, blasphemy, adultery and incest, murder, theft, and causing unnecessary suffering to animals, while demanding the maintenance of proper judicial systems.

Initially through Jesus and Paul, a Pharisaic Jew of the diaspora, from Tarsus, the religious thought of the Israelites, centred on the principle of one God, was introduced, in a modified but basically identical form, to what now constitutes the Christian world. Six centuries later, in 622 CE, Muhammad established the faith of Islam, naming as its true founders Abraham and Ishmael. Ishmael, traditionally the progenitor of the Arab peoples, was Abraham's son with Hagar, Sarah's Egyptian maid. As in the case of Judaism, the religion and law of Islam are largely inseparable. Many Jewish principles are reflected in the Koran, which also refers to other Biblical personalities such as Noah, Joseph, Moses, Aaron, the Queen of Sheba, and Jonah, as well as to historical incidents in and stories from Israelite tradition.

The Hebrew Bible, much of it deriving from oral tradition, and comprising thirty-nine 'books' selected from written sources of the period between about 1000 BCE and 150 BCE, was finalised in three stages: first the Torah (Pentateuch), then the Prophets, and then the Writings (or Hagiographa, 'Holy Writings'). It is known collectively as *Tanakh*, an acronym of Torah, *Nevi'im* (Prophets), and *Ketuvim* (Writings). Apart from the Pentateuch, the Christian Bible has a different arrangement of books. The Roman Catholic Church also includes in its canon the Apocrypha, the collection of Jewish writings compiled during the period of the Second Temple. The Pentateuch was first translated into English (from the Hebrew) by William Tyndale (*c.* 1495–1536), and printed on the Continent in Marburg in 1530, followed by the book of Jonah in 1531. The first complete English Bible, also printed in Marburg, was that of Miles Coverdale (1488–1568), dated 1535. The Geneva Bible (1560) was probably the translation which influenced Shakespeare; it is also called the Breeches Bible, from 'They sewed fig leaves together, and made themselves breeches' (Gen. 3:7). The great King James Bible, or Authorised Version, came about accidentally as the only tangible outcome of a conference called by James I (James VI of Scotland) in 1604, soon after his accession to the throne of England, to discuss religious changes demanded by disaffected members of the Church of England. Only superseded as a translation in the twentieth century, and never bettered as religious prose, its teachings, now expressed in the vernacular, on the monarchy, and on government founded on an agreement between God, the ruler, and the people, were the heart of the philosophy of the supporters of the commonwealth of Oliver Cromwell, which lasted from 1651 to 1660. They became the basis of the general conception of rule on the return of the monarchy in England, and in due course also of the founding precepts of the American Revolution. English Protestants found in the words of God more inspiration than was offered by the Roman Catholic Church.

Considerable portions of the Hebrew Bible were written down before the works of Homer were composed. Within its grand scheme it contains, in addition to genealogies, chronologies, and legal codes, an astonishing variety of literary forms and styles such as in modern literature are practised by the poet, short-story writer, novelist, biographer, and historiographer. The Biblical tradition, or Biblical parallels, or the language of the Authorised Version are especially reflected in the works for example of John Bunyan, John Milton (who was also a Hebrew scholar), John Dryden, Lord Byron, William Wordsworth, Thomas Carlyle, George Eliot, Alfred Tennyson, Walt Whitman, Rudyard Kipling, T. S. Eliot, John Berryman, and Robert Lowell.

The original language of the Old Testament is known as Biblical Hebrew. Primarily a literary language, it continued to be used for some five hundred years after the Babylonian exile, though from 539 to 331 BCE Aramaic was the official language of the region and was spoken by many Jews. In about 200 BCE a new form of spoken Hebrew emerged, developed not from Biblical Hebrew but from some local dialect; it is known as Mishnaic Hebrew, because it is the language of the Talmudic rabbis of the first two centuries CE, in which the Mishnah is written. Biblical Hebrew made a comeback in the Middle Ages and again in the age of the Haskalah, the Jewish Enlightenment in Europe, which began in Germany in the middle of the eighteenth century. Modern Hebrew is an amalgam of words and usages from earlier versions of Hebrew, with accretions of loan words and new forms where these are needed to express contemporary terms. It is written, and printed, in the square script which came into use at the end of the first millennium BCE. Hebrew terms survive in English and American common usage: amen, bar mitzvah (for girls, bat mitzvah), chutzpah, golem, goy, Hanukkah, Kabbalah, kosher, matzo, mazel tov, oy (as in the interjection 'oy vey!'), Pesach, pitta bread, rabbi, Rosh Hashanah, shalom, Sukkot, Yom Kippur. Yiddish, spoken by the Ashkenazi Jews of northern Europe, was once widely used by immigrant Jews in the USA, by whom English terms were introduced into a language that derived predominantly from German, with some Hebrew, Slavic, French, and Italian usages or derivations.

The vast movements of Jewish humanity within the diaspora from the eleventh century CE onwards were the result primarily of oppression and persecution. Anti-Semitism (the term was coined in about 1875) existed before the crucifixion of Jesus as a response to Jewish religious principles which did not allow Jews to eat with outsiders, to marry them, to worship with them, or to acknowledge the existence of other gods. Christian anti-Semitism was originally based on the conviction that Christians were the rightful inheritors of the faith of the Israelites. Matthew, writing about forty years after the crucifixion, described the events leading up to it in such a way that the Jews collectively were subsequently accused of being implicated in the death of Jesus. After Muhammad's initial failure to convert to Islam Jewish communities within his orbit, Muslim rulers tended to show greater sympathy towards Jews than they received in Christian Europe. As the influence of Islam grew in the east, in north Africa, and then in Spain, so its peoples became divided into separate states. The Jews among them were still, as were Christians in Muslim lands, second-class citizens, and, compelled by land taxes to seek alternative livings to farming, many of them became traders and international merchants, which in former times Jews had never been. In Christian Europe, Jews were forced into the business of money-lending because there was no other trade open to them, and the Church forbade its members from indulging in it. From these beginnings, and the fact that money-lending was a necessity in a society which was changing from a subsistence economy to one based on coin, the term 'money-lender' became, in the thirteenth century, almost synonymous with

'Jew'. With Jews also widely accused of desecrating the Host (the consecrated elements of the Mass), of killing Christian children for their blood, and of poisoning wells, there followed multiple massacres and mass expulsions, which in Russia continued into the twentieth century.

Between 1881 and 1930 almost three million Jews emigrated to the USA from Europe, 1,750,000 of them from Russia. Collective responsibility is a fundamental principle of Judaism. One of the aphorisms of Hillel recorded in the Talmud is the often-quoted, 'If I am not for myself, who will be for me? But if I am only for myself, what am I? And if not now, when?' (*Avot* 1:14). Thus, 'all Israel is responsible, the one for the other' (*Shevuot* 39a). So the communities in the diaspora contributed to the upkeep of the Temple in Jerusalem, and have continued to help Jews to emigrate or to settle as immigrants. It is this collective social awareness which has largely enabled the culture and religion of the Israelites to survive, against all odds.

In spite of the obliteration of Jerusalem by Hadrian, it remained a symbol of Jewish inspiration: 'Next year in Jerusalem' became a ritual saying, and many worshippers turn to the east while intoning the *Shemoneh Esreh* (Eighteen Benedictions), which includes the prayer for God to dwell in the rebuilt Jerusalem. While the term Zionist was coined only in the 1890s, the longing for Zion was central to the thoughts and prayers of Jews throughout the diaspora. To those who pressed for the establishment of a Jewish state rather than for a greater measure of assimilation into the communities in which Jews lived, direct access to Jerusalem was an essential condition. Thus an initial British proposal in 1903 for territory to be utilised for a Jewish state in Uganda, though favoured as an interim measure by moderate Zionists, was thrown out. In the meantime the number of Jewish immigrants into Palestine, where initially they established agricultural settlements and in the early years lived in comparative harmony with their Arab neighbours, grew from 65,000 between 1882 and 1914 to 339,000 between 1919 and 1939, despite riots, acts of terrorism (on both sides), and latterly restrictions on entry.

The Holocaust and the final establishment of the independent state of Israel on 14 May 1948 completely altered the balance in Europe between Jews and those of other faiths. In 1939 there were approximately 9.2 million Jews in Europe, of whom an estimated six million were killed by the Nazis; in 1994 there were less than two million. European immigrants into the state of Israel have totalled about 1.5 million, of whom 540,000 have come from USSR/Russia, 200,000 of them in 1989 alone, following measures to ease emigration. In 1991 the total population of Israel was about 5 million, of whom 4.1 million were Jews.

That the faith of the Israelites survives still in the diaspora would seem to be borne out by the fact that, according to an article in the New York journal *Commentary* (January 1996), of the 5.8 million people in the USA who are classified as Jewish, 24 per cent are 'actively engaged' and a further 20 per cent 'moderately engaged' in Jewish activities, by attendance at synagogue, ritual observances in the home, membership of Jewish organisations, contributions to Jewish charities, subscriptions to Jewish periodicals, and visits to Israel. The tiny state of Israel, once the kingdom of the Israelites, has emerged as a formidable power in world politics; the continued heritage of the Israelites themselves is in the hands of those who still believe in the providence of their God.

APPENDICES

APPENDIX 1

THE JEWISH CALENDAR

1 Nisan (March–April)
30 days

    15–21 (or 22) Pesach

2 Iyyar (April–May)
29 days

3 Sivan (May–June)
30 days

    6–7 Shavuot

4 Tammuz (June–July)
29 days

5 Av (July–August)
30 days

    9 Tisha b'Av

6 Elul (August–September)
29 days

7 Tishri (September–October)
30 days

    1–2 Rosh Hashanah
(New Year)
10 Yom Kippur
15–21 Sukkot

8 Heshvan (October–November)
29 or 30 days

9 Kislev (November–December)
29 or 30 days

    25–29/30 Hanukkah
(8 days)
1–3/2 Hanukkah

10 Tevet (December–January)
29 days

11 Shevat (January–February)
30 days

12 Adar (February–March)
29 days

Adar Rishon
30 Days
13 *Adar Sheni*
29 days

The calendar basically follows the phases of the moon, but is adjusted to the solar calendar by the insertion of an extra month in the third, sixth, eighth, seventeenth, and nineteenth years of each nineteen-year cycle. In these years the twelfth month is called Adar Rishon (First Adar) and the extra month Adar Sheni (Second Adar). Though the New Year falls in the seventh month, traditionally (Exod. 12: 2) Nisan is the first month in the calendar

APPENDIX 2

WEIGHTS AND MEASURES

Linear measures were based on the parts of the arm and hand, a cubit being the distance between the point of the elbow to the tip of the middle finger, and varying from about 45 cm to 52 cm.

4 fingers	=	1 palm
3 palms	=	1 span
2 spans	=	1 cubit

Liquids were measured in baths: one bath was the equivalent of about 23 litres.

6 hins	=	1 bath
10 baths	=	1 homer

The equivalent measure for dry-goods was the ephah.

10 omers	=	1 ephah
10 ephas	=	1 kor

The basic unit of weight was the shekel, equivalent to about 12 gm.

50 shekels	=	1 mina
60 minas	=	1 talent

In Old Testament times payment was by barter or by a measured quantity of silver, though mention is made, in the post-exilic period, of Persian gold coins. The earliest local coins, inscribed 'Yehud' (Judaea), were struck by Persian governors of the territory in the fourth century BCE. A Hasmonaean currency appears to have originated with John Hyrcanus I, in the form of bronze coins of low denominations, based on a unit called the *peruta*. Since Herod the Great and his descendants were only allowed by Rome to produce coins in bronze, the currency favoured by the Temple authorities in Jerusalem was the Tyrian silver shekel or half-shekel. Silver shekels, half-shekels, and quarter-shekels, as well as bronze coins, were struck in Jerusalem by the rebels during the wars against Rome in 66–74 and 132–135 CE.

APPENDIX 3

TABLE OF DATES

This table should be read in conjunction with the charts of the kingdoms of Israel and Judah, (page 80) and of the Hasmonaean and Herodian dynasties (page 171).

Many of the dates are approximate.

BCE

3000 to 2000	Early Bronze Age in Canaan to 2200	Minoan civilisation in Crete 3000–1400
		Skara Brae settlement, Orkney, occupied 3000–2500
		Sumerian/Akkadian empires in Babylonia 2850–2180
		Eblaite empire flourished in Syria 2500
	Middle Bronze Age in Canaan 2200 to 1500	Great Pyramids and Sphinx built in Egypt 2500
	Amorite incursions into Canaan 2000–1800	Stonehenge in Britain, first phase 2000

2000 to 1000	Abraham 1800	Fall of Ur 1950
	Joseph in Egypt 1600	Hyksos rule in Egypt 1720–1550
		Ugaritic texts 1500–1200
		Mycenaean civilisation in Greece 1400–1200
	Exodus 1280	*Amarna letters* 1400–1300
	Israelite movements into Canaan from 1250	Sea Peoples' invasions 1400–1175
	Philistines settle in Canaan 1170	Destruction of Troy 1220
	Period of Judges 1150–1050	*Merneptah inscription* 1219
	Phoenician civilisation flourishes 1100–750	End of Hittite empire 1100
	Samuel and Saul 1050–1005	
	David 1005–965	

1000 to 500	Solomon 965–925, and the First Temple		
	KINGDOM OF JUDAH	KINGDOM OF ISRAEL	Fluctuating Assyrian dominance 900–605
		Omri dynasty 876–842	*Moabite Stone* 850
		Elijah, Elisha 860–800	*Black Obelisk of Shalmaneser III* 841
	Uzziah 783–742	Jehu dynasty 842–745	
		Amos 770	*Works of Homer, 'Iliad' and 'Odyssey'* 750
	Isaiah I 742–700	Hosea 740	Traditional date of founding of Rome 735
	Ahaz 738–715	Fall of Israel 721	Fall of Syria 732

Micah 720–700
Hezekiah 718–686
Siloam inscription 703
Sennacherib's campaign
   703–701   *Lachish frieze and cylinder of Sennacherib* 700
Zephaniah 625–620
Josiah's reforms 632   Babylonian empire 605–539
Jeremiah 625–587
First deportation 597
Lachish letters 588
Fall of Judah and
   destruction of
   Temple 586

Ezekiel, Isaiah II 593–538   Rise of Persia 550
Babylonian exile 586–538   Persian empire 539–336
Building of Second Temple 537–515   *Cylinder of Cyrus* 538
Haggai, Zechariah 520   Egypt conquered by Persia 525
                                   Republic of Rome 509–27

500
to
CE

Ezra, Nehemiah 458–433   Persian wars against Greeks 490, 480–79
                                   Classsical age of Greek literature and
                                     philosophy 476–330
                                   Elephantine documents 450–399
                                   Fluctuating dominance of Greek world by
                                   Athens, Sparta, and Thebes 403–338
Alexander takes Judaea 332   *Samaritan papyri* 332
                                   Empire of Alexander the Great 336–323
Judaea under permanent Ptolomaic rule   Rule of Ptolomaic and Seleucid dynasties begins
   301–198   323
                                   Parthians secede from Seleucid empire 247
Judaea under Seleucid rule 198–142   *Dead Sea Scrolls* 200–68 CE
Maccabaean revolt 167–160   Final destruction of Carthage by Rome 146
Rule of Hasmonaean dynasty 142–63   Expansion of Roman empire into Asia begins
                                   133
Pompey takes Jerusalem 63   Roman conquest of Syria (end of Seleucid rule)
                                   63
Judaea a client kingdom 63–6 CE   Assassination of Julius Caesar 44
Herod the Great 37–4   Roman annexation of Egypt (end of Ptolomaic
                                   rule) 30

CE

Judaea a province of Rome 6–41, and from 44   Death of Augustus 14, followed as emperor by
                                   Tiberius (14–37), Caligula (37–41), Claudius
First Jewish War with Rome 66–74   (41–54), and Nero (54–68)
Destruction of Second Temple 70   Flavian emperors, Vespasian (69–79),
                                   Titus (79–81), Domitian (81–96)
Second Jewish War with Rome 132–135   Hadrian, emperor 117–138

BIBLIOGRAPHY

ATLASES

Barnavi, Eli (ed.), *A Historical Atlas of the Jewish People: From the Time of the Patriarchs to the Present*, 3rd edn, Kuperard, London, 1998

Cohn-Sherbok, Dan, *Atlas of Jewish History*, Routledge, London and New York, 1994

May, Herbert G., *Oxford Bible Atlas*, 3rd edn rev. John Day, Oxford University Press, Oxford, 1984

Negenman, Jan H. (ed. Harold H. Rowley), *New Atlas of the Bible*, Collins, London, 1969

REFERENCE WORKS

Comay, Joan, *Who's Who in Jewish History: After the Period of the Old Testament*, new edn rev. Lavinia Cohn-Sherbok, Routledge, London, and Oxford University Press, New York, 1995

Encyclopaedia Judaica, 16 vols, Ketter, Jerusalem, 1971–72

Jacobs, Louis, *The Jewish Religion: A Companion*, Oxford University Press, New York and Oxford, 1995

Jordan, Michael, *The Encyclopaedia of Gods*, new edn, Kyle Cathie, London, 1994

Roth, Cecil, and Wigoder, Geoffrey, *The New Standard Jewish Encyclopaedia*, 5th edn, Doubleday, New York, 1978

Unterman, Alan, *Dictionary of Jewish Lore and Legend*, new edn, Thames and Hudson, London, 1997

Woude, A. S. van der (ed.), *The World of the Bible*, Eerdmans, Grand Rapids, 1986

GENERAL, HISTORICAL, AND ARCHAEOLOGICAL STUDIES

Ackroyd, Peter R., *Israel under Babylon and Persia*, Oxford University Press, Oxford, 1970

Aharoni, Yohanan, *The Archaeology of the Land of Israel: From the Prehistoric Beginnings to the End of the First Temple Period*, tr. Anson S. Rainey, SCM, London, 1982

Aharoni, Yohanan, *The Land of the Bible: A Historical Geography*, tr. Anson S. Rainey, rev. edn, SCM, London, and Westminster Press, Philadelphia, 1979, 1980

Anderson, Bernhard W., *The Living World of the Old Testament*, 4th edn, Longman, Harlow, 1988; in USA as *Understanding the Old Testament*, 4th edn, Prentice-Hall, New York, 1986

Anderson, G. W., *The History and Religion of Israel*, Oxford University Press, Oxford, 1966

Brettler, Marc Zvi, *The Creation of History in Ancient Israel*, Routledge, London and New York, 1995

Bright, John, *A History of Israel*, 3rd edn, Westminster Press, Philadelphia, and SCM, London, 1980, 1981

Cantor, Norman, *The Sacred Chain: A History of the Jews*, HarperCollins, New York and London, 1994, 1995

Davies, W. D., and Finkelstein, Louis (eds), *The Cambridge History of Judaism, vol. I: Introduction; The Persian Period*, Cambridge University Press, Cambridge and New York, 1984

De Vaux, Roland, *Ancient Israel: Its Life and Institutions*, tr. John McHugh, new edn, Darton, Longman and Todd, London, 1973

De Vaux, Roland, *The Early History of Israel*, tr. David Smith, 2 vols, Darton, Longman and Todd, London, and Westminster Press, Philadelphia, 1978

Frank, Harry Thomas, *An Archaeological Companion to the Bible*, Abingdon Press, Nashville, and SCM, London, 1971, 1972

Freedman, David Noel, and Graf, David Frank (eds), *Palestine in Transition: The Emergence of Ancient Israel*, Almond Press, Sheffield, 1983

Goldberg, David J., and Rayner, John, *The Jewish People: Their History and Their Religion*, Viking, London and New York, 1987

Grant, Michael, *The History of Ancient Israel*, new edn, Weidenfeld, London, 1996

Hall, H. R., *The Ancient History of the Near East*, 10th edn, Methuen, London, 1947

Hayes, John H., and Miller, J. Maxwell (eds), *Israelite and Judaean History*, SCM, London, and Westminster Press, Philadelphia, 1977

Heaton, Eric W., *The Hebrew Kingdoms*, Oxford University Press, Oxford, 1968

Hoffmeier, James K., *Israel in Egypt: The Evidence for the Authenticity of the Exodus Tradition*, Oxford University Press, New York and Oxford, 1997

Isserlin, B. S. J., *The Israelites*, Thames and Hudson, London, 1998

Jagersma, H., *A History of Israel from Alexander the Great to Bar Kochba*, tr. John Bowden, SCM, London, 1985

Kenyon, Kathleen M., *Digging Up Jerusalem*, Benn, London, 1974

Mauchline, Revd Professor John, *God's People Israel*, Church of Scotland, Edinburgh, n.d.

Miller, J. Maxwell, and Hayes, John H., *A History of Ancient Israel and Judah*, SCM, London, and Westminster Press, Philadelphia, 1986

Noth, Martin, *The History of Israel*, new edn, SCM, London, 1996

Parkes, James, *A History of the Jewish People*, rev. edn, Penguin, London and New York, 1964

Pritchard, James B. (ed.), *The Ancient Near East*, vol. I: *An Anthology of Texts and Pictures*; vol. II: *A New Anthology of Texts and Pictures*, Princeton University Press, 1958, 1975

Roth, Cecil, *A Short History of the Jewish People*, rev. edn, Phaidon, Oxford, 1943

Russell, D. S., *The Jews from Alexander to Herod*, Oxford University Press, Oxford, 1967

Schoville, Keith N., *Biblical Archaeology in Focus*, Baker, Grand Rapids, 1978

Schürer, E., *A History of the Jewish People in the Age of Jesus Christ*, 2 vols, rev. edns ed. G. Vermes et al., 1973, 1979

Welch, Adam C., *Kings and Prophets of Israel*, Lutterworth, London, 1952

Wiseman, D. J. (ed.) *Peoples of Old Testament Times*, Oxford University Press, London and New York, 1973

INDIVIDUAL BACKGROUND STUDIES

The complete works of Josephus (9 vols, ed. H. St J. Thackeray et al., 1926–65) and of Philo (12 vols, ed. F. H. Colson et al., 1929–53) with English translations are in the Loeb Classical Library, Harvard University Press.

Adler, E. N. (ed.), *Jewish Travellers*, Routledge, London, 1930 (includes the travels of Eldad the Danite)

Bentwich, Norman, *The Jews in Our Time*, Penguin, London and Baltimore, 1960

Bermant, Chaim, *What's the Joke: A Study of Jewish Humour through the Ages*, Weidenfeld, London, 1986

Bevan, Edwyn R., and Singer, Charles, *The Legacy of Israel*, Oxford University Press, London, 1927

Boardman, John, Griffin, Jasper, and Murray, Oswyn (eds), *The Oxford History of the Classical World*, Oxford University Press, Oxford and New York, 1991

Bulliet, Richard, *The Camel and the Wheel*, Harvard University Press, Cambridge, MA, 1975

Carcopino, Jerome, *Daily Life in Ancient Rome*, tr. E. O. Lorimer, new edn, Penguin, London, 1956; Yale University Press, New Haven, 1977

Carpenter, Humphrey, *Jesus*, Oxford University Press, Oxford and New York, 1980

Cary, Max, and Scullard, H. H., *History of Rome: Down to the Age of Constantine*, rev. edn, Macmillan, London, 1980; new edn, St Martin's Press, New York, 1982

Connolly, Peter, *The Jews in the Time of Jesus*, new edn, Oxford University Press, Oxford, 1994

Daniel-Rops, *Daily Life in Palestine at the Time of Christ*, tr. Patrick O'Brian, Weidenfeld, London, 1962

Eisenman, Robert, *The Dead Sea Scrolls and the First Christians: Essays and Translations*, Element, Shaftesbury, Dorset, and Rockport, 1996

Glinert, Lewis, *The Joys of Hebrew*, Oxford University Press, New York and Oxford, 1992

Glover, T. R. *The Ancient World*, new edn, Penguin, London and New York, 1944

Hackett, General Sir John (ed.), *Warfare in the Ancient World*, Sidgwick and Jackson, London, 1989

Hayward, C. T. R., *The Jewish Temple: A Non-Biblical Sourcebook*, Routledge, London and New York, 1996

Heaton, E. W., *Everyday Life in Old Testament Times*, Batsford, London, 1956

Herodotus, *The Histories,* tr. Aubrey de Sélincourt, new edn, Penguin, London and New York, 1996

Herzog, Chaim, and Gichon, Mordechai, *Battles of the Bible*, new edn, Greenhill, London, and Stackpole, Mechanicsburg, 1997

James, Peter, and Thorpe, Nick, *Ancient Inventions*, O'Mara, London, and Ballantine, New York, 1994

James, T. G. H., *Ancient Egypt: The Land and Its Legacy*, British Museum, London, 1988

Josephus, *The Jewish War*, tr. G. A. Williamson, rev. edn, Penguin, London and New York, 1981

Juvenal, *The Sixteen Satires*, tr. Peter Green, rev. edn, Penguin, London and New York, 1974

Kamm, Antony, *The Romans: An Introduction*, Routledge, London and New York, 1995

Kamm, Josephine, *A New Look at the Old Testament*, Gollancz, London, 1965; as *Kings, Prophets and History*, McGraw-Hill, New York, 1965

Kamm, Josephine, *Leaders of the People*, Abelard-Schuman, London and New York, 1959

Keller, Werner, *The Bible as History*, tr. William Neil, rev. edn, Hodder, London, 1963

Laqueur, Walter, *A History of Zionism*, new edn, Schocken, New York, 1989

Matthews, Victor H., and Benjamin, Don C., *Social World of Ancient Israel 1250–587 BCE*, Hendrickson, Peabody, 1993

Niditch, Susan, *Ancient Israelite Religion*, Oxford University Press, New York and Oxford, 1997

Niditch, Susan, *Oral World and Written Word: Ancient Israelite Literature*, Westminster John Knox Press, Louisville, 1996

Pettinato, Giovanni, *Ebla: A New Look at History*, tr. C. Faith Richardson,

Johns Hopkins University Press, Baltimore, 1991

Piggott, Stuart, *Wagon, Chariot and Carriage*, Thames and Hudson, London, 1992

Pritchard, James B. (ed.), *Solomon and Sheba*, Phaidon, London, and Praeger, New York, 1974

Roth, Cecil, *A History of the Jews in England*, new edn of 3rd edn 1964, J. Trotter, London, 1989

Roth, Cecil, *The Jewish Contribution to Civilisation*, new edn, Phaidon, Oxford, 1943

Scrolls from the Dead Sea, Library of Congress, New York, 1993

Shelton, Jo-Ann, *As the Romans Did: A Sourcebook in Roman Social History*, 2nd edn, Oxford University Press, New York and Oxford, 1997

Sowerby, Robin, *The Greeks: An Introduction to Their Culture*, Routledge, London and New York, 1995

Suetonius, *The Twelve Caesars*, tr. Robert Graves, rev. edn, Penguin, London and New York, 1979

Tacitus, *The Histories*, tr. Kenneth Wellesley, rev. edn, Penguin, London and New York, 1975

Taitz, Emily, and Henry, Sondra, *Remarkable Jewish Women*, Jewish Publication Society, Philadelphia, 1996

Tubb, Jonathan N., *Canaanites*, British Museum, London, 1998

Vermes, G., *The Dead Sea Scrolls in English*, 4th edn, Penguin, London and New York, 1995

Vidal-Naquet, Pierre, *The Jews: History, Memory, and the Present*, tr. David Ames Curtis, Columbia University Press, New York, 1996

Vogt, Joseph, *The Decline of Rome*, tr. Janet Sondheimer, new edn, Weidenfeld, London, 1993

Vriezen, Th. C., *The Religion of Ancient Israel*, tr. Hubert Hoskins, Lutterworth, London, and Westminster Press, Philadelphia, 1967

Whitelam, Keith W., *The Invention of Ancient Israel: The Silencing of Palestinian History*, Routledge, London and New York, 1996

Williamson, G. A., *The World of Josephus*, Secker, London, 1964

Woolley, Sir Leonard, *Ur of the Chaldees*, 2nd edn, Benn, London, 1950

Xenophon, *The Persian Expedition*, tr. Rex Warner, new edn, Penguin, London and New York, 1972

Yadin, Yigael, *Masada: Herod's Fortress and the Zealots' Last Stand*, Weidenfeld, London, and Random House, New York, 1966

INDEX

Homer (*fl. c.* 750 BCE), Greek epic
poet 203, 212
horses 7, 10, 16, 30, 43, 64, 65, 99,
118, 148, 187, 191, 193
Hosea, book of 6:6 199; 6:9 6; 7:7
72
Hosea, prophet 72, 73, 80, 90, 98,
212
Hoshea, king of Israel (*c.* 732–*c.*
724) 80, 89
houses 79, 134
Huldah, prophetess 101
Hurrians (map 1) 9, 31, 56
Hyksos (map 1) 8, 12, 13, 31, 212
Hyrcania (map 5) 153
Hyrcanus (*d. c.* 169), son of Joseph
the Tobiad 145
Hyrcanus I *see* John Hyrcanus
Hyrcanus II (*c.* 103–30), High
Priest and ethnarch 155–6, 157,
163, 167, 171, 173, 174, 176

Idumaea (map 6), Idumaeans 149,
153, 154, 171, 173, 174, 177,
183, 187, 197
Ijon (map 3) 87
Immanuel 74
immigration 9, 10, 12, 13, 90, 98,
107, 128–9, 135–6, 165, 169,
205
incense 10, 103, 158, 160
India 93, 136, 143
Ipsus (map 5) 144
iron 45, 53, 57, 78, 99, 114, 119,
141, 197
Iron Age 52
Isaac, son of Abraham 3, 5, 9, 11,
14, 37, 107
Isaiah, book of 52, 72, 74, 84; 1:6
114; 1:8 115; 2:4 141; 6:1 73;
7–8 73; 7:3–4 73; 7:14–16 74;
10:28–32 99; 11:11 128–9;
20:2–3 73; 22:16 75; 28:13 74;
28:15 74; 33:20 21; 36 100;
36:3 75; 37 100; 37:36 74;
40ff. 131; 44:28 73; 45:1 73,
131; 49:6 52; 50–66 131; 52:13
to 53:12 131; 56:4–5 137;
56:6–7 169
Isaiah, prophet 73–5, 76, 80, 85,

87, 97, 98, 100, 112, 212; First
Isaiah 72, 90; Second Isaiah 73,
130, 131, 213
Ishbaal *see* Ishbosheth
Ishbosheth, son of Saul 55–6
Ishmael, son of Abraham 202
Ishmaelites 10
Ishtar, Babylonian goddess 45, 89
Islam 8, 13, 67, 119, 202, 204
Israel, children of 10, 11, 16, 86,
127
Israel, kingdom of (map 3, 5) 29,
69, 70, 71, 72, 73, 74, 76, 80,
81–90, 93, 94, 95, 96, 97–8,
101, 102, 117, 118, 122, 128,
131, 133, 135, 165, 212
Israel, son of Isaac *see* Jacob
Israel, state of 34, 140, 144, 179,
205, 206
Israelites 7, 8, 10, 12–15, 43, 53,
54, 55, 58, 60, 62, 63, 64, 67,
91, 92, 93, 94, 97, 107, 118,
155, 200, 205, 206; convocation
at Shechem 20, 21, 33, 36–7,
101; in the desert 17–23, 115;
Exodus from Egypt 1, 8, 12,
15–17, 18, 36, 37, 38; family
life 1, 12, 13, 15, 18, 41, 46,
68, 72, 73, 74–5, 83, 106–14,
117, 122; homes 79, 82, 106,
111–14; literature 16, 34, 39,
51, 67, 68, 77, 109, 124; and
monarchy 38, 40, 46, 47, 51,
52, 54, 55, 56, 57, 58, 59,
60–1, 64, 67, 68–9, 81, 83, 87,
96, 102, 123–4; music 33, 58,
70, 95, 108, 110, 118, 123–4,
127, 141; origins 1–10, 68, 106,
135; religion 1, 7, 13, 14, 15,
17–21, 22, 23, 26–7, 33, 35,
36–8, 41, 45–6, 47–8, 51–2, 53,
58, 60–1, 67, 68, 70, 71, 72,
73–4, 76, 77, 79, 81, 96, 98,
101–2, 103, 105, 106, 107, 109,
113, 114, 115, 119–23, 127–8,
130, 131, 134, 202, 204, 205,
206; settlement in Canaan 12,
33–6, 37, 55, 56, 212; slavery,
attitude to 35, 58, 64, 105, 107,
109, 116–17; tribes 10, 13, 21,